GLASGOW

Maurice Lindsay is a well-known poet, broad-caster and prolific writer on many aspects of Scottish life and literature. Among his books published by Robert Hale are: *A History of Scottish Literature, The Burns Encyclopedia, Robert Burns: The Man, his Work, the Legend*, the two volumes of *The Lowlands of Scotland*, an entertaining autobio-graphy, *Thank You For Having Me*, and three volumes of verse, *A Net to Catch the Winds, The French Mosquitoes' Woman* and *Requiem for a Sexual Athlete*. He is also the compiler of *A Book of Scottish Verse, Scottish Comic Verse* and *Modern Scotish Poetry*.

Formerly Director of the Scottish Civic Trust, he is now Honorary Secretary-General of Europa Nostra. He was made CBE in 1979, had the honorary degree of Doctor of Letters conferred on him by the University of Glasgow in 1982, and in 1985 became an Honorary Fellow of the Royal Incorporation of Architects in Scotland.

Overleaf: *Langside Memorial (1887) and Langside Hill Church (1856), both by Alexander Skirving. The Memorial commemorates the Battle of Langside, the site from where Mary Queen of Scots fled into England.*

By the same author

POETRY
The Enemies of Love
Hurlygush
At the Wood's Edge
Ode for St. Andrew's Night and Other Poems
The Exiled Heart
Snow Warning
One Later Day
This Business of Living
Comings and Goings
Selected Poems 1912-1942
The Run From Life: More Poems 1942-1972
Walking Without An Overcoat: Poems 1972-76
Collected Poems (1979)
A Net to Catch the Winds
The French Mosquitoes' Woman
Requiem for a Sexual Athlete

PROSE
The Lowlands of Scotland: Glasgow and the North
The Lowlands of Scotland: Edinburgh and the South
The Scottish Renaissance
Robert Burns: The Man: his Work: the Legend
The Burns Encyclopedia
Clyde Waters
By Yon Bonnie Banks
The Discovery of Scotland
Environment: a Basic Human Right
The Eye is Delighted
Portrait of Glasgow
Robin Philipson
History of Scottish Literature
Lowland Scottish Villages
Francis George Scott and the Scottish Renaissance
The Castles of Scotland
Count All Men Mortal: the Story of Scottish Provident
Victorian and Edwardian Glasgow

ANTHOLOGIES
Poetry Scotland 1-4 (4 with Hugh MacDiarmid)
No Scottish Twilight (with Fred Urquhart)
Modern Scottish Poetry: an Anthology of the Scottish Renaissance
John Davidson: Selected Poems: with a preface by T.S. Eliot
    and an introduction by Hugh MacDiarmid
A Book of Scottish Verse
Scottish Poetry 1-6 (with George Bruce and Edwin Morgan)
Scottish Poetry 7-9 (with Alexander Scott and Roderick Watson)
Scotland: An Anthology
As I Remember: Ten Scottish Writers Recall How for Them Writing Began (Ed.)
Scottish Comic Verse

GLASGOW

Maurice Lindsay

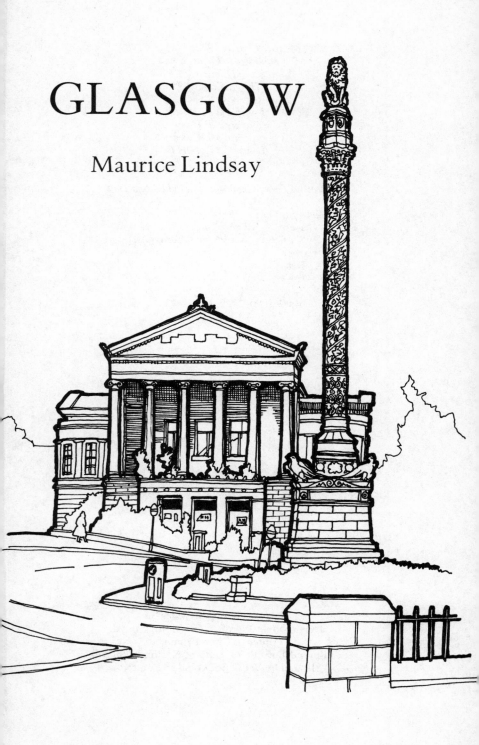

© *Maurice Lindsay 1972, 1981 and 1989*
First published in Great Britain 1972
Second Edition 1981
Third Edition 1989

Robert Hale Limited
Clerkenwell House
Clerkenwell Green
London EC1R 0HT

British Library Cataloguing in Publication Data

Lindsay, Maurice, 1918–
Glasgow – 3rd ed.
1. Scotland. Strathclyde region. Glasgow,
history
I. Title
941.4'43

ISBN 0–7090–3720–1

Photoset in North Wales by
Derek Doyle & Associates, Mold, Clwyd.
Printed in Great Britain by
St Edmundsbury Press, Bury St Edmunds, Suffolk.
Bound by WBC Bookbinders Limited.

Contents

Illustrations

Preface to the Third Edition

Nobody who sets out to re-tell Glasgow's story can do so without the help of those who have previously recorded its details in various forms. To the historians and chroniclers of times past I make grateful acknowledgement.

I am grateful to Mr James Milligan and Dr John Butt, of the University of Strathclyde, who read my original typescript and made valuable suggestions regarding facts and statistics relating to Glasgow's sociological and industrial history; and to my old wartime friend, Mr Douglas McLeman, who advised me upon some legal points. The help I received from the Glasgow Room of the Mitchell Library was considerable and given with unfailing courtesy.

Since this book first appeared in 1972, Glasgow has undergone an astonishing regeneration; indeed, almost a renaissance, sloughing off regret, albeit reluctantly, for her lost heavy industrial past and facing up to a future that includes involvement with high technology, service industries and steadily expanding tourism. I have tried to reflect these changes in relation to Glasgow's long history.

There are those who regret the old couthy Glasgow, with its neighbourly slums: they include business men who have long since taken Johnson's 'noblest prospect which a Scotchman ever sees' and settled in the south-east of England; Marxists who regard advances made by democratic means as somehow a defeat for themselves and their dogma; even celebrated comedians, who purvey their profitable Glasgow humour from a comfortable London base. They are, all of them, talking romantic nonsense from the safety of distance in time or circumstance.

I am grateful to Professor John Leech, the University of Stirling, for his suggestions improving the text of the second

edition, and to helpful comments from the late Mr Arthur
Steward and Mr David Walker, Principal Inspector of
Historic Buildings at the S.D.D. (Scottish Development
Department).

While I regret that the new format ruled out any possibility
of reproducing the photographs from the first two editions, I
welcome the delightful line drawings of Mr Jon Magnusson
and Dr Robert Sproul-Cran that adorn this third edition, for
both the beginning and the ending of which I have written
entirely new chapters.

Conductors

(For Sir Alexander Gibson)

Words and the notes of music – meanings pointing
to distances we can't get to unaided
unless someone conducts us. Dictionaries
define *conduct* as 'manage', 'guide', 'direct',
or 'serve as a channel'. We conduct ourselves
from place to place, and travel situations
we often wonder why we've reached. Conductors
in uniform are there for us to purchase
a piece of distance from, for us to use
with our own good or insufficient reasons.
Tall buildings, brittle in their fixed importance,
conduct unbolted lightning straight to earth
by circumventing their own distances.
But above others most to be revered,
conductors of music; subtle channellers
who give life back itself, mind out of time,
through notes that hint some brief imagined glory
that plays upon our shabby human story.

MAURICE LINDSAY

Introduction

Opinion as to what constitutes a fair portrait has varied from age to age. In pre-photographic days, a detailed reliable physical likeness was generally regarded as being the essential characteristic. Later, the advent of Impressionism and the movements which followed it produced portraits where character, or symbols for it, rather than facial accuracy was aimed for. Later still, portraits were subjected to the theories of Cubism or Abstraction.

Today, the painter of a portrait on canvas is, in one sense, a curiously isolated creature. Abstraction has currently swept all before it, in varying fashionable terms; yet you can rarely practise abstraction on a human face and produce something likely to satisfy the sitter. So the portrait-painter has to find his own individual answer, without the collective reassurance of being part of the mood-movement of his contemporaries. He has, in fact, to find a largely personal solution.

The writer, attached to words, is faced with a somewhat similar problem. One can think of several contemporaries who might paint a poetic word-portrait of Glasgow, abstracting this or that aspect which suited their particular literary purpose or political bent. However fascinating, possibly the result might not be recognizable to those familiar with, or anxious to identify, the sitter.

If a portrait is to have any merit at all, it must surely depict the measure of experience reflected in the features of its subject. In this portrait of Glasgow, I have therefore adopted a highly subjective approach, through which the present reflects the past. Clearly, my Glasgow may not be the same as another man's; but at least my portrait of it sets down my native city as I have come to know it, either through the imaginations or reportings of past observers, or through my own senses. My range of enjoyments is, I hope, sufficiently wide to have allowed me convey to those who do not know Glasgow – and perhaps also to those who, though they may have lived much of their lives within the city's boundaries, know only their own local sub-division of it – something of the life and the physical quality of a city that is, and long has been, unique in Europe.

1

The Subjective City

Thirty years ago, the visitor who arrived in Glasgow would have discovered a grey and grimy city, encased in the sooting of an obsolete coal-burning age. He would have come upon street after street of grim, crumbling nineteenth-century tenements in the poorer suburbs of the last century, weeds and discarded rubbish disfiguring the back courts, almost every defaceable surface carrying the chalked or painted slogans of frustrated and hopeless urban illiteracy. He would have found whole rows of derelict buildings awaiting demolition, and probably been dismayed at the absence of imaginative distinction in many of the new concrete-and-glass structures rearing their way through the tightly knit architectural cohesion of the city centre.

He would naturally have been saddened, if not altogether surprised, to learn that most of the industries on which Glasgow's economic prosperity had been built were extinct, or in serious decline; dismayed, perhaps, to observe that in their desperate withdrawal, they had managed to leave behind an ingrained belief that the world still owed a living to the workers who once built the ships and railway engines for half the world and fashioned the iron and steel for a hundred other vanished uses. He would have been amazed at the sincerely held conviction that some mysterious 'they' in Westminster should be pouring subsidies from a God-provided purse into the lost causes of factories, yards and workshops still struggling to produce over-priced goods that nobody any longer wanted to buy.

If the same visitor were to return today, he would find that an astonishing transformation has taken place, both in the condition of the fabric of the city and the outlook of its

15

inhabitants. An energetic policy of conservation and, where necessary, re-use, has revivified the Victorian heart of Glasgow, now classified as an Outstanding Conservation Area, and the similarly categorized nineteenth-century westward suburbs of the Park Area, Hillhead, Dowanhill and Kelvinside. Even such areas as Shawlands, Langside and Springburn, and the once separate burghs of Partick and Govan, reflect, along with the more imposing neighbour-hoods, this new environmental pride.

More astonishing still is the change in attitude of Glaswegians towards their city. In 1963, the then Lord Provost of Glasgow, Dr Michael Kelly, devised the slogan GLASGOW'S MILES BETTER. Being a good publicity man he no doubt already sensed a growing change of mood. His catchy slogan has certainly focused outside attention on Glasgow's growing list of positive achievements, and in so doing lent the constructive forces behind them increasing strength. There are some who fear that the old spirit of arrogance – it once led Scots to boast: 'Here's tae us. Wha's like us? Damn few, and they're a' deid!' – could again reassert itself in a display of overconfidence; a failure to appreciate that achievement has to be sustained and built upon if its benefits are to prove enduring. I do not think this is likely to happen. Glasgow's history is one of last-minute adaptability and eventual, if sometimes reluctant, willingness to meet recurring challenges with matching new ways.

For that reason, it is impossible to appreciate the Glasgow of the late twentieth century without understanding the forces which enabled it to mould itself from a convenient ford over the Clyde into a medieval centre of piety and learning: then to develop successively into an expanding centre of international trade, a place of rapidly growing manufacturing importance, a powerhouse for international heavy engineering products and a cradle for the construction of a major proportion of the ships that sailed the seven seas throughout most of the nineteenth century and into the early years of the twentieth.

While still the second city of the British Empire, the power first faltered then failed, and Glasgow found herself low in the trough of the depressed years of the late 1920s and 1930s. When she painfully climbed out again, aided by the artificial stimulus of the Second World War, it was to find that in the piping times of peace her once-unique strong craft skills neither commanded demand nor earned prosperity, having been profitably copied by the very countries whose developing needs she had formerly so plentifully met; that her established labour force was unable to adapt to the new skills of a fast-changing technological age; and that her wartime housing conditions were among the most densely overcrowded and dilapidated in Europe.

The extent of the changes reshaping Glasgow in the closing years of the twentieth century are no less dramatic than those which governed the expansionist years of the mid nineteenth century, when rows of honey-coloured or rose-tinted tenements steadily encroached upon the fields and hills that had surrounded the Glasgow Daniel Defoe knew and praised, engulfing many of the surrounding villages. The enormous magnitude of the slump-plus-wartime background of over-crowding, social squalor and economic collapse out of which Glasgow has had to pull herself, undoubtedly resulted in some environmental mistakes. Nevertheless, it has called forth a concentration of energy: different, perhaps, in its composition, application and means of delivery, but no less intense than that which successfully thrust to prosperity her tobacco trade, her cotton industry and the shipyards and heavy engineering workshops of the Victorian age. These earlier periods of greatness were brought about by native Glaswegians with business acumen and fierce Presbyterian energy: and herein lies the modern difference. That tough old breed of Scots entrepreneur has become an extinct species. Much of the city's modern economic regeneration has therefore had to be effected in circumstances where the provision of public money is essential and where private sector commerce and industry have to rely upon international investment and initiative, often in the face of strong foreign competition.

Glasgow is a city with a large admixture of Celtic blood. Its connections with Ireland go back to pre-medieval times. It welcomed with open arms Irishmen and Highlanders to its industrial heart in the hectic expansionist days. Even in these times of numerical decline, it still retains a comparatively large Gaelic-speaking population, probably in the region of 12,000.

Like most other urban areas in the United Kingdom which

developed rapidly during the nineteenth century, Glasgow
produced a stratified society. True, its land-owning
aristocrats soon moved out to cleaner air as the industrialists
moved in, but the cotton-mill owners, the ironmasters and
the kings of heavy engineering and shipbuilding in turn
formed a new élite, from which so much of the drive and the
energy came. They built the churches, endowed the schools
and hospitals and liberally patronized the arts. They were
serviced by an expanding middle class of lawyers,
accountants, and smaller-scale merchants and businessmen,
who came to reflect the interests and tastes of the social
leaders.

It is common Marxist practice to distort the achievements
of these men with the spurious wisdom of hindsight,
applying to their age the very differently orientated criteria of
our own. The Glaswegian entrepreneurs existed at a time
when commercial opportunity offered itself for the taking,
and they took it. Without their determined efforts there
would have been neither job opportunities for Highlanders
forced to leave their crofts because of the Clearances, nor an
escape route for the hordes of starving Irishmen driven to
emigration by the potato famine. However grim to us their
conditions of labour and livelihood in the monstrously
overcrowded medieval core of the city may now seem, the
alternative would have been, at best, malnutrition, at worst,
death by starvation. On the other hand, without this steady
nineteenth-century infusion of cheap Celtic labour, there
could well have been no industrial Glasgow.

The fact that many of the incomers were Catholic,
breeding large families, played some part in altering the
Glasgow stratification. The majority of Glasgow's
population is now what, to use Victorian terminology,
would once have been called 'working-class'.[1] We no longer
use such out-moded, patronizing terminology, but the
stratification still manifests itself in leisure pursuits. Broadly
speaking, football, for example, is primarily a 'working-
class' passion. The arts tend to be supported by those who
consider themselves to be members of the middle-class.
Until television sapped the popular theatre's economic
foundations, pantomimes, light plays and music-hall shows
attracted support from those who felt that they came

Kelvingrove Art Galleries (1892)
by Sir J.W. Simpson and Milner Allen.

somewhat in-between. Nowadays, television, the arch
purveyor of entertainment, mainly trivial, has become, with
sex and death, the third great leveller.

Happily, anti-Semitism and anti-Catholicism, both all too
common among the middle-classes in the twenties and
thirties, have declined. The settlement of citizens of the
former British Empire, mainly Pakistanis, into the now
multi-racial Glasgow community has fostered tolerance;
though it can still become overstrained when a soccer match
between Celtic and Rangers stirs up meaningless outworn
prejudices mainly imported from the impossible province of
Northern Ireland, or when mindless sectarian hatreds are
stirred up by annual ritual marches around 12 July.[2]

Educational opportunities have widened, although nature
remains stubbornly anti-egalitarian: a large section of the
population remains more or less ineducable. Although,
increasingly, some Glaswegians still energetically and
expensively exercise free choice and spend their hard-earned
taxed money on having their children educated at schools in
the private sector, social stratification no longer denies the
opportunity of university or other forms of higher education
to anyone adequately qualified to receive it. There are some
who regret those halcyon days when it was possible for a
future playwright or an aspiring politician to take ten or so
leisurely years over the getting of a degree. Others, though,
with attitudes less dilettante, may now very well view with
increasing alarm the official tendency to equate higher
education with providing a meal ticket in an increasingly
technological and specialist-minded society.

Since television, radio, jet aircraft, rockets, orbiting
satellites and moon-landings have shrunk whatever mystery
was left in distance, most fashion cults sooner or later wash
up on Glasgow. Some, like Bingo, which offered its
vicarious thrills mostly to middle-aged women, presumably
as an escape from domestic drabness, have peaked in
popularity and settled into a minor social phenomenon.
Others, like drinking – of a dark intensity in Glasgow, due to
the practice of following a pint of beer with a 'chaser', as a
measure of neat whisky thus consumed is called in Glasgow –
still retain their escapist popularity. Drug-taking, though in
some areas an equally dangerous menace to the young, does

not have the upper-class social endorsement it sometimes appears to have elsewhere in the United Kingdom.

In this, as in most other forms of extremism, the rainy climate of Glasgow encourages a certain measure of traditional conformity. For similar reasons student protest, endemic in many parts of Europe during the late sixties, was shown to thrive better in hot climates than in cold. At the height of all the Paris-centred furore, a then celebrated youthful revolutionary came to Glasgow to rouse Scottish students to a suitable awareness of the sins of their fathers (many of whom were paying towards the cost of their offspring's education). The inflammatory one, Tariq Ali, found that he had to raise the temperature of mostly empty seats, many students preferring a different kind of rousing with a Scottish National Party folk group.

In a sense, Glasgow has always done its own thing. Naturally, climatic conditions and other related circum-stances have made it a different kind of thing to that of London, Amsterdam or San Francisco. To a Glaswegian, the essential point is that if your thing is anything, it must be intense. Glasgow has always been, and still is, nothing, if not that.

Any overview of Glasgow must ultimately be a subjective one. Apropos the often-expressed view that there is no such thing as objective history, someone, probably a Scot, wisely pointed out that this is not the case. In reality, there is no such thing as an objective historian. My viewpoint is that of an arts-orientated observer with a restless curiosity about practically everything; a Scot who has always felt himself more strongly part of the European cultural scene than of the chauvinistic Anglo-British; an internationally minded nationalist who admires the English, yet regrets Scotland's sell-out of political and economic control; a non-believer in the proposition that what has been thus done can now be undone; one who, in any case, is more concerned with the possibilities of the future than the mistakes of the past. I have tried to keep out too much autobiography when dealing with my own experiences of a small part of Glasgow's existence, but a poet must be allowed a stanza or two by himself and his fellow writers. In attempting to portray vividly, there is no substitute for personal experience.

Notes

1 A meaningless term, since large numbers of the so-called 'working-class'
are unfortunately unemployed, and the middle class works.
2 The anniversary of the Battle of the Boyne in 1688.

2

Religion by the Clyde

Although Stone Age remains have been found on the Clyde, and canoes in crannogs unearthed in St Enoch Square in 1780, Stockwell Street in 1824 and Victoria Dock in 1875, and we know that when the Romans were here the Clyde Valley was peopled by a Druidical tribe, the Damnoni, it is virtually impossible accurately to trace Glasgow's origins further back than the Middle Ages. The present city lies in an area that was just inside the Antonine Wall, built by the Romans as an outpost to contain the fierce northern Caledonians. Presumably the Romans had a fort there. A Roman ford crossed the Clyde near the site of the Old Glasgow Bridge, and another fort was excavated at Balmuildy, on the northern boundary of the modern city, just before the First World War.

When St Ninian arrived in Scotland from Rome early in the fifth century, he is said to have founded a cemetery roughly where Glasgow Cathedral was later to rise.

About A.D. 525, a hundred years or so after Ninian's death, the King of Lothian, who no doubt had ambitious matrimonial plans for his daughter, discovered that she was pregnant. According to legend the culprit was a prince to whom the lady had secretly given herself. The King is thereupon supposed either to have set his erring child adrift in a currach on Aberlady Bay, from where she was blown ashore at Culross and found and cared for by St Serf; or to have tossed her from the top of Traprain Law, where she and her unborn child Kentigern (or Mungo, as he has become popularly known) were miraculously saved from death.

Whichever unfatherly if unverifiable tradition you settle for, the boy grew up in Fife, a holy man credited with a

23

Glasgow Cathedral, from the Necropolis

reputation for achieving miracles. Later, he moved westwards, serving under the venerable Abbot Fergus in Carnoch, Stirlingshire. This Fergus, so the old story goes, had a curious whim. His disciple had to promise Fergus that when he died his body should be put on a cart drawn by two untamed bulls and buried at the spot where they first rested. In due course Mungo found himself called upon to fulfil this unusual promise. After a very long walk, the obliging creatures stopped just outside Ninian's cemetery, by the Molendinar burn; so there Fergus was buried, and there Mungo set up his own religious community, calling it Glaschu, which is thought to mean 'the church within the enclosed space', or 'the Dear Green Place'.

King Rhydderch of Strathclyde gave Mungo whatever was then the equivalent rank of bishop, and Christianity flourished, until counter-action by a pagan king called Morken forced Mungo to flee. He sought safety with St David in Wales, and founded the monastery of St Asaph. In 573 the Strathclyde Christians under King Rhydderch won the Battle of Arderyd and called Mungo back. He apparently spent some time in Dumfriesshire before returning to Glaschu, where he died about the year 590.

Glasgow's armorial bearings, designed by a lawyer, Andrew MacGeorge, in 1866, refer to events in Glasgow's early Christian history. The bird is a pet robin owned by St Serf, but restored to life by Mungo. The tree represents the now fully-grown bough which, when frozen, Mungo blew into a living flame that lit St Serf's monastery lamps. The fish and the ring are reminders of the virtues of fidelity and honesty. Queen Languoreth, forgetting the former, gave a ring she had received from the King to a courtly lover. Coming upon the sleeping man the King noticed the ring, removed it from the man's finger, threw it into the Clyde and ordered the Queen to show it to him. In a panic the Queen went to Mungo for help. The saint told her to cast a line into the Clyde. The salmon she caught had the ring in its mouth, thus enabling the Queen to fulfil her lord's command. The bell represents one brought back by Mungo from Rome, and the mound on which the tree grows was miraculously raised by Mungo for him to stand upon when preaching a sermon on his return from Rome.

'Let Glasgow flourish by the preaching of the Word' was the ancient motto arising out of all this: but by 1866 the good MacGeorge shortened the motto to 'Let Glasgow flourish'.

At that time Glaschu can only have been a village with a holy cemetery and a convenient ford over the Clyde. The old capital of Strathclyde was Dumbarton, further down the river. It was not until Scotland had come together more or less as a single entity under David I that the next step forward was achieved. Anxious to bring Scotland into line with European civilization, with its organization of abbeys and bishoprics, the King by-passed the Archbishop of York and in 1110 persuaded the Pope to appoint the former royal tutor, John Achaius, Bishop of Glasgow. Glasgow thus became an acknowledged centre of religion and learning, a position confirmed in 1188 when Bishop Jocelin got from Rome the Pope's decision that the Scottish bishops were directly dependent on the Holy See, and further confirmed in 1488, when Glasgow became an archbishopric.

Bishop Achaius built the first cathedral, a timber structure, over the tomb of St Mungo. It was consecrated in 1136, but burnt down about 1190. No trace of it has survived. Rebuilding went ahead, and under Bishop Jocelin a new cathedral was re-consecrated in 1197, though it may perhaps have been in an unfinished state at the time of the ceremony. Although there was substantial rebuilding between 1233 and 1258 under Bishop William de Bondington, there are grounds for believing that part of the south-west section of the lower church and some of the lower walls of the nave may well have been put up by Jocelin's masons.[1]

As it has come down to us today, it has been succinctly described by Ronald G. Cant and Ian G. Lindsay in their pamphlet *Old Glasgow* (1947).

> In plan, the building consists of a nave and eight bays, a central tower and transepts, and a choir of five bays with eastern chapels beyond. Under the choir is the lower church, and its north-east angle is the chapter-house. The transepts extend no further than the line of the nave and choir aisles, save on the crypt level, where the Fergus aisle forms a prolongation of the South transept. The centre spire, by far the most ambitious of its kind in medieval Scottish architecture, rises to a height of about 220 feet above the crossing. The style employed throughout

most of the Cathedral is the form of early Gothic known in Scotland as First Pointed.

Though not a big church by European standards, in its hey-day Glasgow Cathedral was the second largest Gothic church in Scotland, with an internal length of 285 feet. Only the Cathedral of St Andrews, destroyed by the Reformers, must certainly have been larger.

Glasgow Cathedral might well have shared the melancholy fate of St Andrews, for towards the close of the sixteenth century the lead was stripped from its roofs, and its altars and statues were destroyed – what Scott's Andrew Fairservice described in *Rob Roy* as 'an old dog shaking itself free of fleas'. Fortunately, someone less barbaric than his fellows persuaded the Trades to halt the damage. The fabric was restored and turned into three Protestant churches made out of nave, chancel and crypt, with added galleries and, later, plaster ceilings which were to be removed in subsequent restorations.

The west front of the nave was once flanked by two towers of different size and character. The Consistory House was destroyed in 1846 on the orders of Her Majesty's First Commissioner of Works, the smaller tower being demolished two years later. Priceless historical documents in the Consistory House were set on fire before the work of destruction was begun, a few being saved from the flames by chance, and later published by a scholar, Gabriel Neill. The Commissioner apparently objected to the fact that the towers were of a later date than the rest of the structure. Between 1833 and 1846, the year of the old towers' removal, various schemes were drawn up to provide the cathedral with suitable new towers. A committee under the then Lord Provost, and with an enthusiastic Glasgow architect and benefactor, Dr Cleland as secretary, drew up admirable proposals, raised a lot of local money and secured a government grant; but by some mischance, the old towers came down and the new did not go up, so that the cathedral has since been left with its present somewhat shorn appearance.

Once the cathedral was established, the next important event was the building of Old Glasgow Bridge, a fine stone

erection of eight arches, which Bishop Rae and Lady
Lochow[2] caused to be put across the Clyde in 1345 at the
Stockwell shallows, on the site of an earlier wooden bridge
mentioned by Blind Harry in his poem 'Wallace' as 'Glasgow
bryg that byggy[3] was of tree.' Old Glasgow Bridge was a toll
bridge. Those who were unwilling to pay still used the
ancient ford. So solidly did the masons put the bridge
together that, with minor alterations of various kinds, it
carried traffic for more than five centuries, being replaced
only in 1847.

Medieval Glasgow, protected from the marauding
Norsemen by its position up-river and the sandy shallows of
the Clyde, developed around the cathedral its criss-cross
pattern of streets. To the south-west, there were buildings
connected with the cathedral: the palace or castle of the
bishops, and later archbishops, with its great hall built by
Bishop John Cameron between 1426 and 1446, added to by
Archbishop James Beaton early in the sixteenth century and
by Gavin Dunbar about 1540; and in the surrounding streets
the prebendary manses of the cathedral canons. Their houses
in Drygate, Rottenrow, Kirk Street and Castle Street all had
orchards and gardens. Only one has survived, Provand's
Lordship, the manse of the prebendary of Barlanark, whose
alternative title was Laird of Provan. Built about 1470, with
wings added or adapted two centuries later, it is Glasgow's
only surviving domestic medieval building. Yet the medieval
city played an important part in Scottish life, some of its
bishops being made Chancellors of their country. But the
development of trade with the Continent gradually gave the
east coast greater political importance. Thus the ecclesiastical
centre moved to St Andrews, where Scotland's first
university was established half a century before Glasgow's,
and Edinburgh eventually became the Scottish capital.

However, the founding of Glasgow University by Bishop
William Turnbull in 1451, on a site in Rottenrow, made it
certain that, whatever temporary set-back in trade the move
to the east might have produced, the city's future importance
was assured. The university later moved to the site south of
the cathedral, where, largely rebuilt during the seventeenth
century, it survived until 1869.

So far as can now be established, medieval Glasgow, with

Provand's Lordship (1471, back portion 1670)

land to spare, did not feel any need to emulate Edinburgh's
cramped-up towering tenements or 'lands'. Many of
Glasgow's houses were single-storeyed thatched cottages;
others had wooden upper storeys, rather like Edinburgh's
Huntly House in the Canongate. After 1450, the bounds of
the city extended. Stretching at that time from the Cathedral
in the north, south to the Blackfriars Monastery, and from
Drygate in the east to what became in Victorian times
Balmano Street on the west, several extensions were made:
one, south from Blackfriars Monastery to the Cross along
the line of High Street; another to the east, over the Gallow
Muir in the line of the Gallowgate; and a third westwards as
far as the Tron, named after the 'trone' or weighing machine

put up towards the end of the fifteenth century. Although the town was not walled, it did have ports at the end of its principal streets.

The older name for the Trongate had been St Thenew's Gate, named after the well and chapel dedicated to Mungo's mother, on what became St Enoch Square (the modern name being a corruption, through the halfway stage at St Tennoch, of Saint Thenew). One of the many other medieval chapels or churches that have disappeared without trace was the Collegiate Church of the Blessed St Mary, on the south side of Trongate (where the Tron Kirk now stands), founded in the 1520s by a sub-dean of Glasgow, James Houston, and destroyed by fire in 1793. A little to the west of it was the Sang Schule, run by one of the prebendaries.

St Nicholas Hospital, founded by Bishop Muirhead in 1460, which survived until 1808, stood on the west side of Castle Street. Glasgow Green, tree-covered, was then the Bishop's Forest. On the other side of the river stood that necessary adjunct to life in the Middle Ages, the Leper Hospital.

Isolated on their knuckle-end of Europe, the Scots have traditionally cared little for their environment. Until the national character began to decline in the twentieth century under such pressures as the speeding-up of means of communication and the consequent tendency for United Kingdom governments to become more firmly centralized in London, Scots energies were convulsed, first, by long-drawn-out differences of religious opinion, and then by the quasi-religious fever and fervour of industrial and commercial expansion. As with some other countries where Reformers carried the day, the sense of environment was all but swept away along with the aesthetic associations of the old Catholic forms of worship. The favoured god became Mammon, euphemistically dubbed Progress, regardless of what course he might eventually lead his worshippers.

The Archbishop's Castle was badly damaged by the Reformers, and, though restored by Archbishop Spottiswoode in 1611 (when he also put lead back on the Cathedral roof), was in ruins by the end of the century. In 1755 the magistrates sanctioned its use as a quarry, and its foundations disappeared to make way for Robert Adam's Royal

Infirmary in 1792. Several disastrous fires, one early in the seventeenth century lasting three days, removed some of the surrounding domestic buildings. Most of what was still left disappeared between 1864 and the late 1880s, when the university moved to Gilmorehill and the City Improvement Trust swept all before it in an enthusiastic sustained wave of zealous social, if architectually misguided, reform.

Within the modern city's boundaries, traces of a few pre-Reformation castles or houses survive: Crookston, standing above the junction of the River Levern and the White Cart; Cathcart Castle, and Provan Hall, now joined to an eighteenth-century house, but once the manor of the Provan Lairds, whose prebendary occupied Provand's Lordship.

Although the physical violence associated with the Reformation erupted mostly in the east of Scotland, such a national holocaust was bound to be felt severely in a place which had for so long been an ecclesiastical centre. The cathedral was badly damaged, but was repaired by voluntary public subscription after 1574. Not only the fabric of Glasgow was affected by the triumph of Protestantism in Scotland in 1560; the whole social orientation of St Mungo's Glasgow was deprived of its purpose.

In times such as these, Glasgow could not entirely escape disturbances to its peace. There was, for instance, the Battle of the Butts in 1544, when during Queen Mary's minority the heir-presumptive, James Hamilton, Earl of Arran, was appointed Regent, an appointment which the Queen's Regent, the Earl of Lennox could not abide. So Lennox garrisoned the Bishop's Palace in Glasgow, and retired to Dumbarton Castle. The Regent besieged the palace with an army equipped with cannon, and after ten days accepted the capitulation of the garrison on honourable terms. No sooner did the besieged men emerge, however, than all but two, who somehow escaped, were massacred.

To avenge this murder, Lennox and the Earl of Glencairn decided to march through Clydesdale and devastate the Hamilton lands. Hamilton got word of their intention, and moved to occupy Glasgow. Glencairn's troops forestalled him. A fierce, if small-scale, battle took place at the Butts, or scene of the holiday of the 'wappenschaw' exercises.

Glencairn's side might well have won the day had not Robert
Boyd of Kilmarnock arrived with a detachment of horse to
aid Hamilton, misleading Glencairn's men into believing that
a whole new army had taken the field against them. As they
fled, the Regent entered Glasgow, his troops plundering so
extensively that, according to one contemporary, they even
removed the doors and window-frames from the houses.

Just over two decades later, there was the affray which
resulted in the urgent flight into France in 1560 of the last
Catholic archbishop, James Beaton, taking with him the
cathedral's treasures and relics and the records of the see from
the earliest times. On that occasion 'James duke of
Chatelherault, erle of Arran, Lord Hamiltoune' had gone
back on his undertaking of 1550 to defend the archbishop, the
cathedral and its possessions against anyone who might
attack them. Indeed, Hamilton went over to the Protestants,
attacked the cathedral and destroyed the altars and relics
therein, and took possession of the palace, from which he
was with some difficulty expelled by a detachment of troops
of the Queen Regent, Mary of Guise. The relics the
archbishop took with him went partly to the Scots College in
Rome and partly to the Charteuse in Paris, from which they
were rescued and returned to Scotland by the patriotic Abbé
Macpherson, a member of the Scots College, when the
French Revolution again threatened them.

There was also the final episode which, in three-quarters of
an hour on 13th May 1568, for ever lost Mary, Queen of
Scots her throne. News was brought to the Regent Moray
that his half-sister had escaped from Lochleven Castle, and
was making with her forces for Dumbarton Castle, then still
a Marian stronghold, where she could perhaps have held out
until events moved again in her favour. Gathering round him
the Earls of Glencairn, Montrose, Mar and Monteith, the
Lords Semple, Home and Lindsay and Kirkcaldy of Grange,
the Regent took up his position at the head of an army of
about four thousand, many of them Glaswegians. He had set
up camp on the Burgh Muir – which ran from Glasgow
Green, through Borrowfield, to the cathedral – when news
reached him that the Queen's forces were moving towards
Renfrew, where they intended to cross the Clyde. The
strategic importance of the hill of Langside then became

considerable. The Regent's troops were able to move to it quickly, before Mary's forces, hampered by the illness of the Earl of Argyll, could get there.

When the Queen's forces reached the top of the hill, they were too exhausted to be able to deal with the Regent's pikesmen. Even so, the fighting was severe, and Sir James Melvil of Halhill, who was present with Mary and who described the battle in his *Memoirs*, tells us that the long pikes were 'so closely crossed and interlaced, that when the soldiers behind discharged their pistols, and threw them or the staves of their shattered weapons in the faces of their enemies, they never reached the ground but remained lying on the spears'.

At the moment when the battle was wavering, Kirkcaldy brought up the Regent's reserves. Under pressure from their attack the Queen's forces gave way and a general flight followed.

Bothwell parted from his wife for a future which was to include his incredibly unlucky capture by a Norwegian sea captain whose daughter he had seduced many years before; imprisonment in Malmo Castle, Sweden; and, when it became clear that he was no longer a political pawn of any value, final degradation and death in chains in a cell of Dragsholm Castle, Denmark.

His wife, the Queen, who had been watching the battle from a hill near Cathcart House, just over a mile to the rear, fled in such terror, it was said, that she never slackened rein till she reached Sanquhar, 60 miles away. She rested at Terregles, Dumfriesshire, before crossing the Solway into England, to throw herself on the mercy of English Elizabeth – mercy that was to mean eighteen years of imprisonment ending with death on the block at Fotheringay.

By this time, the changes to which these various troubles gave rise were beginning to affect the civil governance of Glasgow. When Archbishop Beaton left so hastily for France of his own accord, neither he nor his bishops had been legally divested of their temporalities. There therefore followed the appointment by the King of a series of 'Tulchan' bishops, so called because they represented calves, the milk of their benefices being drawn off not by them but by lay favourites of the court or officers of state.

Some of the 'Tulchans', like the gentle Archbishop

Leighton and the historian Archbishop Spottiswoode – he who, before he was translated to St Andrews, did his best to restore both cathedral and palace – were distinguished men. Others were not. None were viewed with great favour by the citizens. One of them, Robert Montgomery, was appointed Protestant Archbishop of Glasgow in 1581, on the understanding that in his case the milk-pail was to be the Lennox family. This arrangement so annoyed Glaswegians that prior occupation of the cathedral pulpit by a Presbyterian preacher, Robert Howie, was arranged, so that Montgomery's induction could not take place. The Provost of Glasgow, Sir Matthew Stewart of Minto, thereupon forced his way into the cathedral with a band of men, to carry out the royal wishes. During the ensuing struggle, Howie was pulled from the pulpit and lost part of his beard and several teeth. The preacher thereupon brought down a curse upon the head of Sir Matthew and his family. One Victorian historian traced the efficacy of this curse to the eventual impoverished extinction of Sir Matthew's descendants, though doubtless other factors played a part. In any case, Montgomery had to resign – he ended his days as parish minister at Stewarton, in Ayrshire – though another 'Tulchan' was appointed in his place. The system continued until Scots exasperation with episcopacy as a system of Church government finally erupted in 1638.

Direct Church rule over Glasgow had ended in 1450, when the city became a Burgh of Regality, Bishop Turnbull and his successors then holding their authority on behalf of the King. In 1636, Glasgow became a Royal Burgh, responsible directly to King and Parliament. The growing numbers of traders and merchants of the middle classes throughout the seventeenth century brought about a new social balance.

In 1605, the Trades House and the Merchants' House both received recognition. The traders were mostly shopkeepers and craftsmen, there being already a dozen crafts by 1600. The merchants were the wealthier exporters and importers. Those two legal corporations took over the running of the city from the heads of the Church, and for more than two hundred years effectively controlled the town council.

Just before the Cathedral was demoted, it was visited by the future successful Parliamentary general in the English

Civil War, Sir William Brereton. Thirty years old and with the politico-religious problems of the day not yet his concern, he arrived in Glasgow on 1st July 1634. He thought the cathedral 'a brave and ancient place', and commented on the medieval lay-out of the city's streets: 'two streets like a cross, in the middle of which the Cross is placed, which looks four ways into four streets'. The second 'Cross' in Brereton's word-play was the mercat cross, which stood at the junction of Rottenrow, Drygate and High Street, Glasgow's heart. Brereton was still able to admire 'the Archbishop of Glasgow's Palace', and the university's Faculty of Arts, one side of which had been newly built. He was also able to get a good view of the changing city from the top of the nine-year-old Tolbooth. Although he could hardly have known it, he was surveying a Glasgow embarked upon one of the earliest of those massive shifts of energy which were to occur and recur over succeeding centuries.

Notes

1 Anyone who wishes to trace the somewhat confused history of Glasgow Cathedral should see John Honeyman's essay in *The Book of Glasgow Cathedral* (1898), edited by George Eyre-Todd, and *Architecture of Glasgow* (2nd Ed. 1987) by Andor Gomme and David Walker.
2 She bore the cost of one arch.
3 Built.

3

Trade and Merchants

Though the sight which greeted Brereton's gaze from the top of the Tolbooth tower included both medieval ecclesiastical Glasgow, before it was too seriously affected by decay and destruction, and the foundations of the new trading Glasgow, which was to grow from small beginnings throughout most of the seventeenth century and flourish in the eighteenth, the city had not yet experienced the end of its trade-hampering troubles over religion.

While the National Covenant, which defied the King's intention to perpetuate episcopacy in Scotland, was signed on 28th February 1638 in Greyfriars Kirk, Edinburgh, the Assembly held in November of that year gave practical implementation to its proposed reforms. It took place in Glasgow Cathedral.

Laud's liturgy had already provoked a certain amount of trouble when it had been introduced the previous year. On that occasion, the Reverend William Annan, who had preached a sermon defending the liturgy, was set upon in the dark by 'some hundreds of enraged women of all qualities ... with staves and peats'. They beat him sore until 'his cloak ruff and hat were rent'. One or two of 'the meanest' of his attackers were arrested and imprisoned, but it was not possible to deal in this way with so large a body of dissidents. Consequently, there was some anxiety in the official mind as the day for the meeting of the Assembly approached. The magistrates bought a special supply of 'muskets, staffs and bandelieris', to say nothing of powder and pikes, with which they equipped 'ane gaird of men' to preserve the peace while the town was full of strangers come to the Assembly.

The aristocracy was well represented, Rothes, Wemyss,

Balmerino, Lindsay, Yester, Eglinton and Loudon among them. Each of the four Scottish universities sent three representatives. In all, there were present 14 ministers, two professors and ninety-eight elders from presbyteries and burghs.

The elders themselves represented a social cross-section, there being among them seventeen noblemen, nine knights, twenty-five lairds and forty-seven burgesses. But, as one contemporary historian aptly put it, in the midst of this company there were 'ane, twa or thrie of ablest convenanting ministeris with ane twa or thrie reulling elders who sould voice as they voiced'.

To preside over these people, the King had appointed the heir to the Scottish crown through the Stewarts, the Marquis of Hamilton, great-grandson of that James Hamilton, Duke of Chatelherault and Earl of Arran, who had so decisively let down Archbishop Beaton at the time of the Reformation by switching his allegiance to the Reformers. It was the most impressive gathering of its kind that Glasgow had ever witnessed, although the marquis, no doubt aware of the academic quality of so many of them, was distressed to observe that 'not a gown was among them all, but many had swords and daggers about them'.

After some fairly typical Scots quarrelling about procedure, Alexander Henderson, a minister from Leuchars, was appointed Moderator – he who once proclaimed that 'the visible Church only demanded the destruction of the flesh for the saving of the soul', a doctrine, as Cyril Pearl remarked, 'which Torquemada would have recognized'.

It quickly became clear that the intention of the Assembly was to alter the whole system of church government in defiance of the King. On Wednesday 28th March, therefore, after seven sittings, the Marquis of Hamilton formally left the cathedral and, under warrant from the King, declared the Assembly dissolved. In fact the Assembly refused to be dissolved, and, under the Earl of Argyll, who threw in his lot with the Covenanters, declared null and void most of the previous Assemblies of the century on account of kingly interference. It condemned the Prayer Book, the Book of Canons, the Court of High Commission and the Five Articles of Perth, excommunicated the bishops, refused to allow ministers to take any civil office or to sit in Parliament and declared episcopacy to be unlawful.

King Charles raised an army but, confronted with the Covenanting army on the Borders, decided that he could not fight it. The resulting negotiations, though not directly concerned with Glasgow, meant that by 1641, as J.M. Reid puts it in *Kirk and Nation*, the Covenanters had 'all that they had ever hoped for. The Scottish Kirk and states could rule themselves in their own way. Scotland was free to make her own future'.

Having achieved this success, the Scots unfortunately made the mistake of trying to foist their Presbyterian form of Church government on England, which was the real purpose of the Solemn League and Covenant passed by the General Assembly and the Scots Parliament in August, 1643, and by the English Parliament a few weeks later. It soon became apparent that the English and Scottish interpretations of reformation 'according to the Word of God and the example of the best Reformed Churches' differed. The decision of the Presbyterian Scots to fight with the English Parliament against their king produced a rising in Scotland itself, under the Marquis of Montrose, who had some successes against his rival Argyll, now also a marquis.

As every schoolboy knows, Cromwell's New Model Army got hold of Charles. The Scots tried to rescue him, but were defeated at Preston. Cromwell thereupon had the King tried and executed. The Scots could not forget that the King was, after all, a Stewart, and proclaimed his son Charles II. Cromwell thereupon invaded Scotland, and by August 1651 had the country powerless before him.

So it came about that one Sunday in 1650 Cromwell made a formal procession to the cathedral to hear a sermon by the minister of the Barony Church,[1] the Reverend Zachary Boyd. Boyd preached a lengthy sermon, during which he vigorously attacked Cromwell and the English Independents. The Protector listened stolidly, but Thurloe, Cromwell's secretary, whispered to his master, 'Shall I pistol the scoundrel?' 'No, no,' Cromwell replied, 'We will manage him another way.' The Protector thereupon invited Boyd to a supper which ended with a prayer of several hours duration, lasting till three o'clock in the morning.

Boyd, incidentally, left his not inconsiderable fortune to Glasgow University on condition that it should publish a collected edition of his verse. Several of the more banal of the Scottish metrical paraphrases are Boyd's work. His most ambitious effort, 'Zion's Flowers', contains a dialogue in which Potiphar's Wife tempts Joseph, of which this is the dramatic climax:

Potiphar's Wife
Now time is come. My heart it springs for haste,
About his neck my milk-white arms to cast.
I'll hold him, hug him, saying Welcome mine!
Dear mine thou art, and I am also thine!
Here's fair occasion; why desire we thus
To sport in love? None is to hinder us.
While we have time now let us do with speed.
Lovers must dare, and for no dangers dread.
Why burn we daylight? We have time and place –
My dearest Heart, now let me thee embrace!

Joseph
Madam, madam! How fair misled ye are!
Think that ye are the wife of Potiphar,
My noble lord, who doth us all command.
He would not look to get this from your hand.
Sith as ye hear the matters so and so,
Now loose your grips, and quickly let me go.
If from you I this favour cannot find,
I'll rather choose to leave my cloak behind.

Potiphar's Wife
O dule! O dule! Help, help, O dule, O dule!
I am abused by a slave – a fool!

The College took Boyd's money, used part of it to improve the buildings, but put off publishing his verses for so long that in the end it was able to get away with erecting a small bust of him instead.

The ordinary folk of Glasgow had plenty to put up with, apart from Cromwell. There are even grounds for supposing that they did not too much dislike his dour enforced calm. Between the Reformation in 1560 and 1786, when Burns so mercilessly flayed in verse the retreating ministerial tyrants,

the Kirk imposed a joyless regime, sometimes featuring plain
masochistic cruelty. There was scarcely any aspect of life into
which the Church did not peer and pry, punishing with
vicious energy such 'crimes' as absenting oneself from service,
or 'gaming' on the Sabbath. The use of informers was actively
encouraged, not only to seek out parties guilty of 'fornication'
so that they could be humiliated upon the stool of repentance
week after week, according to the supposed enormity of their
crime, but also in less heinous cases. Thus, as late as 1690, the
town council of Glasgow, at the request of the Church,
adjured 'the inhabitants and others residing within this burgh,
that they, nor nane of thame drink in any tavern after ten
o'clock at night on the week days under paine of forty shillings
Scots to be payed by the furnisher of the drink, and twentie
shillings Scots by the drinker'. One half of this was to be used
for the relief of the poor and the other half to pay the informer.
This disagreeable 'nebby' (interferingly curious) aspect of the
Scots character was assiduously developed, surviving in all its
prurient obnoxiousness well into the nineteenth century.

The Kirk's worst penalties were naturally reserved for
sexual offences. St Paul of Tarsus has much to answer for in
having established these guilt complexes associated with sex
which the Calvinists used to torture themselves and those who
fell under their influence. Fear, even hatred of sexual pleasure
succeeded the trials and torture of witches as a favourite
church-approved pastime. It is therefore hardly surprising
that when Glasgow's God-fearing town councillors bought
the Prebendary manse of Cambuslang from the Earl of
Glencairn to be a 'house of correction' for 'dissolute women',
the Kirk Session saw to it that those confined there should be
'whipped every day during pleasure'.

Religious inflictions apart, Glaswegians had also temporal
tribulations to bear. There had been an outbreak of plague in
1647 so serious that the professors and the students from the
university betook themselves off to Irvine. A fire had
destroyed many of Glasgow's thatched-roof houses in 1600.
Over a thousand families were made homeless in June 1652,
when the 'great fire' of Glasgow destroyed one third of the
town's housing-stock. It is therefore not surprising that in
May 1657, Glasgow acquired its first 'ingyne for casting water
on land that is on fyre'.

The restoration of Charles II in 1660 was not greeted in Scotland with as much enthusiasm as it aroused in England, because many Scots feared that before long he would once again try to force episcopacy upon them.

No one has ever satisfactorily explained whether the Scots themselves masochistically created the early excesses of Presbyterianism, or whether the system was foisted upon them by chance historical circumstance and they simply grew used to such absurdities as the alleged existence of a chosen body, 'the Elect', who could do no wrong, and the preordained damnation of the majority, who had no possible means of escaping the torments of hell – 'ten thousand times ten millions of dayes' of it, according to one mathematically inclined seventeenth-century divine, a member of 'the Elect'. Whatever the reason, the defence of the system became a matter of life or death concern for many Scots.

In 1662 the King appointed the Minister of Duns, Andrew Fairfoul, Archbishop of Glasgow, arming him with strong civil powers. Few of the Church's ministers would acknowledge his authority, and so, on 1st November, an edict was pronounced which banished the dissenting clergy from their churches and manses.

The 'killing time' followed, when the Covenanters were a kind of human game. They won a victory at Drumclog and marched to Glasgow, whence Graham of Claverhouse and the royal forces had retired. As a result the Covenanters attack was repulsed. The city narrowly escaped an organized burning[2] after the battle of Bothwell Brig, when the Duke of Monmouth's officers did their best to persuade their leader to destroy Glasgow.

A number of Covenanters were executed in Glasgow in 1666. Others suffered the same fate in 1684, having their heads cut off and publicly exhibited. The Tolbooth was so crowded with prisoners that, according to tradition, they had to sleep in turns.

The citizens thus at first welcomed the arrival of James II and VII to the throne, although when he needed their help in 1688, 1,200 men raised for the purpose refused to obey the magistrates and would not leave the city. By then, the hopes of Glaswegians were centred on William of Orange; hopes that were also to be frustrated, though in a strictly secular manner.

In 1695 the Scottish Parliament passed an Act giving powers to a company trading to Africa and the Indies. On advice from the economist William Paterson, who later became the founder of the Bank of England, the company decided to establish a colony at Darien, in Panama. On 26th July, 1698, the first pioneer ships sailed from Leith, reaching Darien on 4th November with the loss of only fifteen men. Although their fort of New Caledonia was set up successfully, lack of provisions, sickness and some indiscipline amongst the settlers, together with the fever-laden Panama climate (which was later to wreak similar havoc among the workers engaged on the construction of the Panama Canal) decimated the colony, who re-embarked in three ships in June, 1699.

The hostility of the English traders and colonizers who operated from more salubrious bases in the Americas, very much irked the Scots. From the Scots point of view, the Darien Scheme had to succeed. So the second expedition began to sail in the middle of 1699, four frigates leaving Rothesay Bay on 14th September, carrying 1,200 emigrants (including the last of the Stewarts of Minto) and £3,000 sterling invested by the city council on behalf of Glasgow's citizens, to say nothing of much of the fortunes and personal savings of private individuals.

When the final company of this second force arrived, under Captain Alexander Campbell of Forrest, it was to find that a Spanish force of about 1,600 men was encamped nearby at Tubacanti, waiting only the arrival of a Spanish squadron to attack the fort. Campbell decided to attack first, and inflicted a surprise defeat on the soldiers. But the Scots forces could not stand up to the Spanish squadron when it did arrive, and New Caledonia had to capitulate.

Less than fifty emigrants managed to make their way back to Scotland. By then, about the middle of 1700, news of the disaster had reached Glasgow. Whole families were ruined, and when it was learned that the English West India colonists, with the connivance of the English government, had been forbidden to trade with the Scots, there was anger as well as despair in Glasgow hearts. It was beginning to look as if the English design, on both the secular and the religious fronts, was to bring Scotland to her knees.

Throughout this century of religious and economic upheaval, the physical shape of Glasgow had been changing. The increasing population – 4,500 in 1560, about 7,000 by 1600 and 9,994 in 1701[3] – crowded into houses built on the long riggs or gardens of the houses that fronted the main streets. The street plan remained more or less unaltered. New merchants' houses were built or rebuilt (all of them have since disappeared). Some of them, like the mansion of the Campbells of Blythswood in Bridgegait, and Silvercraigs Land, in the Saltmarket, were undoubtedly imposing.

The university consisted of 'two roughly square courts, arranged like those of a Cambridge college, with a tall steeple placed asymmetrically over the range which separated the two. For the inner court (1639) the master mason was John Boyd, For its completion and for the outer court (1654–61), the master mason was John Clerk. Boyd, incidentally, also built the Tolbooth. One court was partly arcaded on the ground floor ...'[4] Except for a gate, transplanted in the nineteenth century to the New University on Gilmorehill, and the largely rebuilt 'lion and unicorn' staircase by John Riddel (1690), also transferred, nothing else survives the sad decision of those city fathers of the 1860s, who, for the best possible sociological reasons, destroyed so much that could have been saved and would have left Glasgow a more gracious physical character than it has since been able to construct for itself.

Three seventeenth-century towers of other public buildings have survived. The square-fronted five-storeyed Tolbooth or Town House, put up in the 1620s, was partly rebuilt and gothicized in 1814 by David Hamilton, but pulled down, except for the elegant seven-storey steeple, in 1921. The steeple, islanded by traffic as it now is, has more than once been threatened by those who think the easy passage of vehicles more important than the visual satisfaction of people. However, perhaps the improved attitude to environmental quality of the late twentieth century means that it will never again be in real danger.

The Merchants' Hall in Bridgegait, built in 1629 by Campbell of Blythswood, a member of one of Glasgow's oldest trading families, was arranged round a courtyard, and included a hospital and guildhall, all of which were pulled

down in 1817, again excepting the steeple, which now surmounts the former Fishmarket. Its attribution to the great Sir William Bruce is no longer thought to be probable.

The third survival has a medieval link, since the Tron Kirk was a rebuilding (1592) of the collegiate church of St Mary and St Anne, the spire being added in the 1630s. The main body of the church was accidentally set on fire by members of the Hell Fire Club, who had taken refuge in it after a debauch, and rebuilt by James Adam in 1794. At one time, the Tron, or weight–beam, was housed in the tower, although it was taken out in 1853 when the present arches were put up. Tower and building survive, once a plumbers' store but now an experimental theatre.

While Hutcheson's Hospital, founded by George and Thomas Hutcheson of Lambhill, survives, only the two statues of the founders are older than 1805, the date of the present building by David Hamilton. The original building of 1641 stood in the Trongate, but was removed so that Hutcheson Street could be connected with the Trongate. Hutcheson's Hospital is now the Glasgow headquarters of the National Trust for Scotland.

Much of the growing trade in the earlier part of the seventeenth century came up the river in small boats, Glasgow's harbour at Newark (later Port Glasgow), intended to meet the needs of expanding foreign trades, not being built until 1688.

When Cromwell had the idea of incorporating Scotland 'into ane Commonwealth with England' in 1652, he appointed Commissioners to go to Scotland and enforce such a union, and at the same time 'by all possible waies and meanes to inform themselves of the state of that countrie, and consider of the readiest and best way for settling and continuing the peace and good government of the same'. On 17th August 1655 Thomas Tucker, Registrar to the Commissionaires for the Excise in England, was instructed to proceed to Scotland to 'give his assistance in settling the excise and customs there'. Thus it came about that we have an impartial record of the kind of foreign trading in which Glasgow was already engaged in the middle of the century.

Of Glasgow, Tucker recorded that all but the students of the College were 'traders and dealers: some from Ireland

Glasgow University (1866-87) by George Gilbert Scott and John Oldrid Scott

with small smiddy coales, in open boats from four to ten tonnes, from whence they bring hoopes, ringes, barrell staves' – all things needed for the craft of coopering – 'meale, oates and butter; some [for] France with pladding, coales and herring, for which they return salt, paper, rosins [raisins] and prunes – some to Norway for timber and every ane theyr neighbours the Highlanders, who come hither from the isles and western parts.'

Tucker, not unnaturally, was a great believer in the beneficent effects of trade. He was impressed by the situation of Glasgow, in spite of the fact that 'no vessels of any burden could come nearer than 14 miles', and by 'the mercantile genius of the people'. He also inspected the ports on the Clyde which came under the Glasgow Collector, and thus saw Newark, not yet reconstructed as Glasgow's official port but already the place 'where all vessels doe ride, unlode, and send theyr goods up river to Glasgow in small boates'; Greenock, where 'small open boats trade in fish with the Western Isles and with Ireland'; Fairlie, Kelburn and Saltcoats, 'from which fish and cattell were carried into Ireland'; Bute, where the inhabitants were all 'countreymen and cowherds, who feede cattell and spinne, and make some woollen clothe which [they carry] to be dyed and dressed at Glasgowe, where they bring … whatever they have occasion of for theyr expence and provision'; and Irvine, then a small port 'clogged and choaked up with sand, which the Western Sea beats into it, soe as it wrestles for life to maintaine a small trade to France, Norway and Ireland, with herring and other goods brought on horseback from Glasgow, for the purchasing [of] timber, wine, and other comodityes to supply theyr occasions with'.

Tucker's fellow Cromwellian, Richard Franck, a trooper in the Protector's army, had found himself in Glasgow on his professional duties about the same period. He recorded his impressions in his *Northern Memoirs* 'writ in the year 1658'. In the matter of trade he was, of course, a layman: even so, he commented on 'the merchants and trades … whose store-houses and ware-houses are stuft with merchandize, as their shops swell big with foreign commodities and returns from France, and other remote parts…. Nor is this all, for the staple of their country consists of linens, friezes, furs, tartans, pelts…. They generally exceed in good French wines, as they naturally superabound with fish and fowl.' Incidentally, Franck also commented on 'the splendour and gaiety of this city of Glasgow, which surpasseth most, if not all the corporations of Scotland'. He admired Glasgow's 'four large fair streets, modell'd, as it were, into a spacious quadrant; in the centre whereof their market-place is fixed: near unto which stands a stately tolbooth, a very sumptuous, regulated, uniform fabrick, large and lofty, most indus- triously and artificially carved from the very foundation to the superstructure … infinitely excelling the model and usual build of town halls … without exception, the paragon of beauty in the west'.

In spite of Glasgow's religious troubles following the Restoration, the physical appearance of the city continued to impress travellers. John Ray, the Essex-born minister naturalist who prepared and published in Cambridge in 1660 the first catalogue of the plants of a district ever to be issued in England, but who was deprived of his minor fellowship at his *alma mater* by the Act of Uniformity, rode into Glasgow in 1662. No doubt he would have sympathies with the independence of mind being shown by this rebellious town. At any rate he thought it 'fair, large, and well built, crosswise, somewhat like unto Oxford, the streets very broad and pleasant'. The college itself struck him as being 'a pretty stone building, and not inferior to Waltham and All Soul's in "Oxon" '. Of the cathedral, he merely noted that 'they call it now the High Kirk', and that they had divided it.

The most lyrical of all the recorded approval of late-seventeenth-century Glasgow, however, comes from the English clergyman John Browne, who saw the city in 1669. 'Tis situated upon the River Glotta, or Cluyd, over which is paved a very fair bridge, supported with eight arches, and for pleasantness of sight, sweetness of air and delightfulness of its gardens and orchards enriched with most delicious fruits, surpasseth all other places in this tract.'

The circumstance which enabled the children of these enterprising citizens of Glasgow, who had produced this prosperous and pleasant place, to take the next step forward was the Act of Union of 1707.

There was opposition to it in Glasgow while it was being

negotiated. Indeed, as a result of a sermon preached in the Tron Kirk by the Reverend James Clark on 7th November 1706, a mob assembled, overthrew the attempts of the magistrates to restore law and order and attacked the council chambers and the home of the Provost of the city, forcing him to flee to Edinburgh. A Jacobite publican by the name of Finlay persuaded some of the rioters to march with him to Edinburgh, with the intention of overthrowing Parliament. When they heard that a body of soldiers was on its way from Edinburgh to put down the riot, Finlay's men returned to Glasgow and separated. He and some others were arrested, but pardoned after the Act had become law.

It is perhaps difficult for us to imagine the feelings of those more educated Scots who saw nothing but advantage in the Union. They had endured a century of religious upheaval in which they were frequently at odds with England, culminating in the defeat, with English connivance, of their economically vital Darien trading venture. With the hindsight of two and a half centuries, it is easier for us to see that the advantages of federal union as recommended by that statesman and patriot Andrew Fletcher of Saltoun, rather than the incorporating union which in fact took place, would probably have been equally beneficial to the growth of the Scottish economy, and might have prevented that sapping of Scottish initiative which, throughout the twentieth century, has robbed Scotland of control of her industries to such an extent that to try to name half a dozen major Scottish-owned firms located in or near Glasgow in 1990 is a difficult task.

However, we cannot take refuge in history. Daniel Defoe, who had spent some time among the Scots as Alexander Goldsmith, an English spy with the task of furthering the Union by all possible means, declared of the Scots just after the 'auld sang' had ended:

> If nothing else were the consequence of the Union, this must be allowed, that they are thereby disarmed from the power of doing themselves right against us, in a parliamentary manner, which strongly implies that they are more particularly in the parliamentary justice that remains, and that we ought to esteem everything that touches the honour of Scotland nationally as equally affecting all Britain. Nay, we should be nicer in an

affront to the nation and nobility of Scotland, by how much the more frankly they have by the Union given themselves, as it were, into our hands.

England has not normally regarded the nations she has swallowed with such open generosity; nor has she always remembered so to regard Scotland.

There were, of course, discouragements to the continuation of such amiability in that, self-interest apart, it was from Scotland that the two Jacobite risings of 1715 and 1745 erupted.

Glasgow was not directly affected by the Earl of Mar's attempts in 1715 on behalf of the Old Pretender, James VII and II's son (incidentally, the year in which Glasgow's first newspaper appeared, the thrice-weekly *Glasgow Courant*, twelve pages at one penny to subscribers). The city raised a force of between five and six hundred volunteers, paid at the rate of 8d. a day, to aid the Government. It was used mainly for guarding Stirling Castle and the approaches to that town while the Duke of Argyll marched to Sheriffmuir. There, in a skirmish rather than a battle, Mar's Highlanders were put to flight. Glasgow's own defences were thus never tested, though the city's patience was, when, in 1710, the magistrates were protesting about having to maintain 353 of the Duke of Argyll's prisoners in the former Bishop's Castle, a guard of 100 being needed, rather surprisingly, to ensure their security. In 1718, however, the Government reimbursed the city just over £735 to meet their expenses.

The Glasgow forces were under Colonel William Maxwell of Cardonald, who, for his loyal pains, and as a mark of the city's gratitude for services rendered, was presented with 'a silver tankard, weighting forty-eight unce, thirteen drop, at 7s. sterling per unce; and a sett of sugar boxes, weighting nineteen unce, fourteen drop, at 8s. per unce; and a server wing, weighting thirty-one unce and twelve drop, at 6s 4d per unce'. The record of such precise particulars is perhaps a minor indication of Glasgow's growing commercial awareness.

Ten years later, Glasgow had to contend with another riot, this time over the imposition of a malt tax, 3d. on every barrel of beer. On 23rd June 1725, the day upon which this tax on beer came into operation, a mob attacked Shawfield (where Glassford Street now is), the home of Daniel Campbell, Glasgow's Member of Parliament, who had voted for the tax. A detachment of soldiers commanded by a Captain Bushnell failed to suppress the rioters. Eventually, under the provocation of a shower of stones, the soldiers fired on the mob, killing two people. Fearful of the consequences of a further clash, Provost Miller ordered Captain Bushnell to withdraw his men. As they made their way to Dumbarton Castle, a further nine citizens were shot and killed.

General Wade then arrived to occupy the city, accompanied by the Lord Advocate, Duncan Forbes of Culloden, who caused nineteen people to be arrested and taken by Captain Bushnell to the Tolbooth in Edinburgh. Forbes, for good measure, also ordered the arrest of the Provost and all the magistrates, including some who had not been in Glasgow when the trouble arose. After a day's imprisonment, the city fathers were freed, and received back by welcoming crowds. Of the others arrested, two were forbidden to return to the city, nine were whipped through the city streets, and eight were given prison sentences. The magistrates thereupon did their best to bring Bushnell to trial for murder, but were prevented from doing so by the Government. Campbell petitioned Parliament for indemnification of his losses, and Glasgow was ordered to pay him over £6,000, which he used to buy land in Islay. Since there were additional mandatory expenses of more than a further £3,000, the Shawfield affair rankled long in the memories of Glaswegians. The deficit was met, ironically enough, by a special tax imposed by the corporation on ale and beer sold in the city.

Twenty years later, there were more serious troubles to occupy their attentions. In September 1745 the magistrates received from Edinburgh a letter which today is preserved in the People's Palace, Glasgow Green. Its author was Prince Charles Edward Stuart, and its contents made the Shawfield losses seem trivial. The sum of £15,000 sterling was demanded by the Prince, together with all arms then in the city and any arrears of taxes due to the Government.

At first the magistrates delayed paying up, having hopes

that the troops of Sir John Cope would come to their assistance. Even before the Battle of Prestonpans put paid to that general's military usefulness, the Highland army's quartermaster, John Hay, an Edinburgh writer to the Signet, backed by members of the Clan MacGregor, turned up in person to collect their levy. Hay was persuaded to accept £5,000 in money and £500 in goods, as interim payment.

The volunteers raised by Glasgow to oppose the Jacobites took part in the Battle of Falkirk on 17th January, 1746, the final Jacobite 'victory', if such it could be called, in which General Hawley was defeated and soon after which Linlithgow Palace was accidently set on fire by his shivering soldiers. Dugald Graham, a chapman versifier who later became bellman of Glasgow, was out with the Jacobite forces. In his usual atrocious verse he commemorated the Highland attitude to the Glasgow soldiers:

> The south side being fairly won,
> They faced north as had been done,
> Where next stood to bide the brush
> The Volunteers, who zealous
> Kept firing close till near surrounded,
> And by the flying horse confounded
> They suffered sair into this place;
> No Highlander pity'd their case:
> 'Ye curs'd milita' they did swear,
> 'What a devil did bring you here?'

On the way north from Derby, the Prince and his army again entered Glasgow on 26th December 1745. Angry that the Glasgow Volunteers should have fought against him, the Prince this time demanded – and quickly got – 6,000 coats, 12,000 linen shirts, 6,000 pairs of hose, a similar quantity of shoes and 6,000 blue bonnets. The Prince himself occupied Shawfield House, at the foot of Glassford Street, still the most elegant mansion in the city and then owned by John Glassford.

To instil some heart into his tired troops, the Prince held a review on Glasgow Green, on the Fleshers' Haugh. Robert Reid, who wrote *Glasgow Past and Present* under the pseudonym of 'Senex', no doubt heard from his own father that the Prince's 'newly-clad ragamuffins ... marched to the

Green by way of Saltmarket in splendid military array, with
colours flying, drums beating, and the skirling notes of the
Highland piobaireachd[5] resounding from the pipes of every
clan'.

Another commentator recorded that the inhabitants of
Glasgow 'looked coldly' on the review, and indeed closed
most of their shops by way of protest. The Prince felt so
bitter about his treatment while in Glasgow that he is
supposed to have contemplated sacking the city before his
troops evacuated it on 3rd January 1746, but was persuaded
from such violent action by Cameron of Lochiel. Even so,
Bailies Cameron and Coats made an enforced journey north
as hostages for the balance of the goods demanded by the
prince's quartermaster.

After the victory of the Duke of Cumberland at Culloden,
Whiggish Glasgow hearts rejoiced, and Provost Andrew
Cochrane (1693–1777), a merchant from Ayr who had settled
in Glasgow in 1722 and prospered, set about trying to
recover from the Government the £14,000 exacted from the
city by the Jacobites. The 'hostage' bailies each received £13
15s. 8d. 'expenses' to cover the cost of their own enforced
stay with the Prince. In 1749 Parliament made a grant of
£10,000 in part indemnification, and with that the Provost
and his magistrates had to be content.

During the uncertain years after the Union, Scotland was
still finding that English merchants from Bristol, Liverpool
and Whitehaven were doing their best to obstruct their
Glasgow counterparts through lawsuits charging them with,
among other things, evading the duty on their importations
of tobacco. However, in 1735, the wars of the French had the
effect of closing many of the Atlantic ports of the south-west,
and the trade came north. Sugar from the West Indies and
tobacco from America came in in ever increasing quantities,
and were then exported to England, France and the Low
Countries. By 1775, more than half the tobacco imported to
these islands was coming in through Glasgow.

In his later years Andrew Cochrane – himself a pioneer of
the tobacco trade, a shipowner and a partner of the Glasgow
Arms Bank – expressed the view that the spectacular rise of
Glasgow was due to the business acumen of four men:
Alexander Spiers of Elderslie, James Ritchie of Busby,

William Cunninghame of Lainshaw, and John Glassford of Dougalston – who had started out in business without £10,000 between them.

Alexander Spiers (1714–82) was the biggest importer, owning a seventh of all that came into the Clyde, and a twelfth of what Europe imported. He used his immense fortune to buy Elderslie, the Renfrewshire lands associated with the memory of Sir William Wallace. In his lifetime a prudent speculator, after his death his fortune continued to help Glasgow, for his wife and daughter were generous in giving money for charities to be administered by the Merchants' House, where Spiers's portrait hangs today.

Ritchie somehow managed to combine a dour business mien with a more relaxed *alter ego* when attending the meetings of the Hodge-Podge Club.

John Glassford (1715–83), Prince Charlie's unwilling host, though at one time owner of the largest number of ships and the second most important tobacco owner – according to Tobias Smollett in *Humphrey Clinker* (1771) he was known to have had 'five-and-twenty ships with their cargoes his own property, and to have traded for above half-a-million sterling a year' – proved to be deficient in Glaswegian canniness, in that his speculations turned out in the end to be unsound. He was also such an enthusiastic gambler that he had a private gaming house built on his estate. He must nevertheless have been an interesting character. When the American War of Independence broke out, unlike his colleagues in the trade, he supported the revolutionaries.

The only one of the four tobacco 'lords' to live through the crash which followed the American upheaval was William Cunninghame (d. 1789), and he turned it to advantage by buying up all the existing stocks of tobacco on which he could lay his hands. With the fortune thus made through the profitable sale of what quickly became a very scarce commodity, he was able to buy his estate of Lainshaw, in Ayrshire.

All four men are remembered in Glasgow, and the mansion of one of them, Cunninghame's house, still stands in what is now Royal Exchange Square. Built in 1788, it was enlarged between 1827 and 1832 by David Hamilton, when it became Glasgow's Royal Exchange. Indeed, it was held in so much affection that when there was a proposal to pull it down in the 1940s to join Ingram Street and Gordon Street, public outcry forced the planners to think again. It was further added to by David Thomson in 1880, and, with its Corinthian columns to remind us of its second life, it now enjoys a third usefulness as Stirling's Library.

The Shawfield Mansion was demolished in 1795, but Glassford Street, which runs through what were its grounds, commemorates its most famous former owner.

There are a few humbler survivals of those years when the 'tobacco lords' walked the crown of the road dressed in scarlet cloaks and cocked hats and carrying gold-mounted canes, lesser persons making way for them as they swept past. The east side of Candleriggs, with its plain four-storey commercial buildings on top of warehouses, gives some idea of the sort of buildings in which tobacco fortunes were made. In spite of their names, Virginia Street and the Tobacco Exchange (later, Crown Arcade) both date from the second decade of the next century. In the Trongate itself, the last of these survivors of the tobacco days was number 182, formerly Spreull's Land, unfortunately demolished in 1978. The street as a whole has suffered a sorry decline from the grace and dignity it must once have possessed. Daniel Defoe, who knew Glasgow both as 'Alexander Goldsmith', a spy amongst us sending back secret reports to Queen Anne's Minister, Robert Harley, and later, when he came openly on four short journeys made between 1724 and 1726 to enable him revise impressions for his *Travels Through Great Britain*, recorded that it made a vigorous impression on him.

He found the university, 'a very spacious building, contains two large squares or courts, and the lodgings for the scholars and for the professors' which he pronounced 'very handsome', adding 'the whole building is of stone, very high and very august'. Of the city itself, he wrote: 'The four principal streets are the fairest for breadth and the finest built that I have ever seen in one city together. The houses are all of stone and generally equal and uniform in height, as well as in front; the lower story generally stands on vast square Dorrick columns, not round pillars and arches, which gives passage to the shops, adding to the strength as well as the beauty of the building. In a word, 'tis the cleanest and beautifullest and best built city in Britain, London excepted.'

The most famous and probably the most distinguished building in eighteenth-century Glasgow was the town hall, put up eleven years after the third edition of Defoe's book had appeared. It was erected by Allan Dreghorn between 1737 and 1748, its style influenced by the piazzas of Covent Garden, designed by Inigo Jones and Isaac de Caux after 1630. Added to at the end of the 1750s, its real fame, however, only came to it after 1780, when it was bought by the Tontine Society, whose chairman was Pat Colquhoun, a future provost of Glasgow. It was then remodelled inside by William Hamilton to include a coffee room, well stocked with newspaper and periodicals and 'universally allowed to be the most elegant of its kind in Britain, perhaps in Europe', and renamed the Tontine Hotel. The breadth and spaciousness of the street it dignified has, fortunately, been preserved for us in a picture painted by John Knox early in the nineteenth century, just before the long decline towards slumdom had begun.

Dreghorn, who was primarily an iron and lead merchant, is also credited with the beautiful St Andrew's Church – he probably depended heavily upon his technical advisers – which went up in 1739 to form the eventual centre-piece of St Andrew's Square, laid out in 1768 but from which the original houses have now all gone or been so drastically altered as to be unrecognizable. Incidentally, Dreghorn is said to have had his own workmen build for him in 1752 the first four-wheeled carriage to be seen on Glasgow streets.

St Enoch Square, begun in 1782, has now none of its original buildings left. The former North British Hotel, presently the Cophorne Hotel, though with an added storey, an extension to the west and a glass-enclosed extended front lounge, is now the sole reminder of the graciousness of the original George Square, laid out in 1787. Loomed over by an ugly twentieth-century tower, it has become the far from homogeneous administrative centre of the city.

By the time the American War of Independence ended in 1783, the residents of these new squares, and of the more prosperous older parts of the city, had other forms of financial support than the revenues from the sale of tobacco on which to rely. Once ships began regularly to arrive with cargoes of tobacco, it was not long before Glaswegians realized that these same ships could carry on their outward journey articles manufactured in the city which would meet the growing day-to-day needs of those who, until the outbreak of war in 1775, were colonists.

John Gibson, whose *History of Glasgow* was published in 1777, listed the industries which had grown up in his own lifetime as including the manufacture of hardware, nails, shovels, threads and tapes, leathercraft, glass-making and – most important of them all – cotton textiles.

The 1780s marked the real impact of the Industrial Revolution on Glasgow. From 1780, the pace of change quickened, and the old Scots way of life altered, both in the country and in the town. Before we allow ourselves to move forward with these changes, let us take a look at the social customs and enjoyments of those who lived in this still countrified city.

Alexander ('Jupiter') Carlyle, later Minister of Inveresk, and the man who successfully defied the Kirk's post-Reformation ban on theatre-going by attending a performance in Edinburgh of the verse tragedy of *Douglas* by his friend and neighbour, the Reverend John Home of Athelstaneford, recalled in his *Autobiography* his student days in the Glasgow of the 1740s. He considered that learning was then thought to be 'an object of more importance' in Glasgow than in Edinburgh, but that Edinburgh had the advantage when it came to 'manner of living, and in those accomplishments, and that taste that belong to people of opulence and persons of education'. Glasgow had few 'gentry', and, according to Carlyle, the manner of living was 'coarse and vulgar'. In contrast with Edinburgh, less than half a dozen families had manservants, some of whom were kept by professors who took in boarders.

What was a typical middle-class day like in the tobacco era?

The merchants would have been up early to collect their mail, after which they returned home for a porridge and herring or egg breakfast, washed down by beer of their own brewing. Morning was the time for commercial bargaining. There followed a long lunch hour as afterwards the shops stayed open until eight. Then there was, perhaps, a final tavern hour, before supper was taken at home, followed by family prayers and a ten o'clock bedtime.

Some, however, varied this order of things, for Carlyle goes on: 'The principal merchants took an early dinner with their families, and then resorted to the coffee-house or tavern to read the newspapers, which they generally did in companies of four or five in separate rooms, over a bottle of claret or a bowl of punch'. Carlyle thought that the young ladies of his youth had ungainly manners (which he attributed in practical terms to the absence of a teacher of French or music in the city) and little otherwise to commend them but 'good looks and fine clothes'. Carlyle also tells us that living was cheap, it being possible to dine on roast beef, potatoes – turnips and potatoes had been introduced into Scotland in 1723 – and small beer for 4d.

Captain Thomas Hamilton, the son of Professor Hamilton, who occupied the Chair of Anatomy and Botany from 1781 to 1790, had been brought up in the Glasgow of the tobacco lords, along with his brother Sir William Hamilton, the philosopher. After fighting through the Peninsular Campaign, in which he was wounded, Captain Hamilton 'commenced author' (to use Burns's phrase) by producing a novel, *The Youth and Manhood of Cyril Thornton*, which Blackwood published in 1827. It is a racy tale in the Galtian manner, much of it set in Glasgow, where young Cyril Thornton comes to be educated, and where his uncle was David Spreull, whose 'country-house in the Trongate formed part of a large tenement which he had originally built, and which, from this circumstance, was generally known by the patronymic of "Spreull's Land" '.[6]

Because of his important family connection, young Cyril found himself invited to dinner at the home of the Provost of Glasgow. The description, if perhaps less than fair to the ways of the tobacco lords, nevertheless was doubtless inspired by Hamilton's own early recollections of Glasgow society: 'The dinner, if not elegant, was plentiful. Corned beef and greens at the top; roast sirloin at the bottom; ham and boiled mutton, *vis-à-vis*, at the sides; the goose and turkey at the opposing corners.'

After ten minutes silent food-stuffing, and then some animated conversation, when the jaws of the guests were occupied in a manner less concentrated, the ladies rose from the table and withdrew from the company.

The ladies were no sooner gone than Bell Geordie made his appearance bearing a bowl of extraordinary dimensions, which he deposited on the table. Lemons, sugar, limes, rum from Jamaica and the Leeward Islands soon followed, and expectation sat on every brow. It was not a matter of easy arrangement by whom the ingredients were to be mingled. The Lord Provost called on Mr Walkinshaw, but Mr Walkinshaw could not think of officiating in the presence of so superior an artist as Mr Mucklewham. Mr Mucklewham modestly yielded the palm to Major Macguffin: Mr Macguffin begged to decline the honour in favour of Mr Pollock; Mr Pollock in favour of Dr Struthers; and Dr Struthers once more pushed the bowl to Mr Mucklewham, who after many bashful excuses, was at lengths prevailed on to 'handle the china'.

I have already noticed the solemnity and entire absorption of mind with which this portion of the Bacchanalian rites is uniformly celebrated in Glasgow, but it was now for the first time that I became witness of the fact. When the beverage had been duly concocted, at least half an hour passed, during which the merits of the punch formed the sole topic of conversation in the party. On this subject, even the most taciturn and obtuse members of the company waxed eloquent. Whether the liquor was too strong or too sweet, whether it would be improved by another 'squeeze of yellow', or an additional lump of sugar, became topics of animated and interesting debate, in which all but myself took part.

Every improvement which human ingenuity could devise with regard to punch, having been at length suggested, the business of drinking commenced in good earnest, each replenishing of the glasses being prefaced by a loyal or patriotic toast by the Lord Provost. 'The King, the Queen, the Prince of Wales', 'the Trade of Clyde' having been drunk in bumpers, the current of conversation was gradually diverted into other channels. They were channels, however, in which the lack of any understanding was little calculated to swim. The state of the markets, the demand for ginghams, brown sugar, cotton, logwood and tobacco, were matters on which my interest was precisely equal to my knowledge.

There were jokes, it is true, and, judging from their effect, good ones; but they were so entirely local, and bore a reference so exclusive to people of whom I knew nothing, and manners of which I really desired to know nothing more, that I found some difficulty in contributing the expected quota of laughter to the general chorus of my more hilarious companions.

Standards of living varied according to where one had one's home. Since virtually everything had to be transported by sea, people living near seaports had an easier life than those who lived out of range of the delicacies and up-to-date household goods imported from London. As the century went on, food began to be served on pottery, sometimes even on china dishes, rather than on pewter plates or on still older wooden platters. Sunday observance was strict. On the Sabbath day, some people 'did not sweep or dust the house, nor make the beds, nor allow any food to be cooked or dressed', while others 'opened only as much of the shutters of their windows as would serve to enable the inmates to move up and down, or an individual to sit at the opening to read'.

The first self-contained house, as opposed to a flat entered from a common stair, went up, Carlyle tells us, in 1735. Spinets and harpsichords could be found in the homes of the wealthy, and, after 1780 pianos, some of them manufactured by John Broadwood, a Scots carpenter who had gone to London and who played a leading part in the founding of the piano-making industry there. The attempts by Robert Foulis to found an academy of arts in 1754 unfortunately foundered in 1775 because of lack of public support, but the press[7] which he ran with his brother, Andrew, made Glasgow-printed books widely 'esteemed on the Continent no less than at home'.

Furniture was mostly made by local craftsmen. Wealthier people who wanted upholstered mahogany furniture had to send to London for it until 1760 when an upholsterer found it worth his while to set up shop in Edinburgh. Water had to be fetched by carriers from wells. Hygiene was non-existent, all refuse being left on the street in stinking heaps. Those who could not afford wax candles had to make do with the smelly, flickering light of a cruse. Coal was available in Glasgow and in coastal towns. Club life developed. Among the more famous were the Hodge-podge, a literary club which met fortnightly in Cruickshank's Tavern and had Dr John Moore for a member; the Anderston, which met on Saturday afternoons in John Sharpe's inn at Anderston with Professor Robert Simson, the mathematician, as its leading light; and the Morning and Evening Club, which met twice daily at Currie's Close, on the east side of the High Street, for discussions over punch. The Merchants' Hall, rebuilt in 1659, was the scene of the winter assemblies of Glasgow society. For humbler folk, there were inns and taverns, like the 'Saracens Head', opened in 1755 by the brewer Robert Tennent, and the 'Black Boy', both in the Gallowgate; Jane Hunter's in Trongate; Lamont's at the head of the Stockwell Street; and Mrs McAlpine's oyster shop on the north side of Trongate.

In good weather, golf could be played on Glasgow Green. A student attending the university in 1721, left us an amusing account of the game, couched in exalted heroic couplets:

> In Winter, too, when hoary frosts o'erspread
> The verdant turf, and naked lay the mead,
> The vig'rous youth commence the sportive war,
> And, arm'd with lead, their jointed clubs prepare;
> The timber curve to leathern orbs apply,
> Compact, elastic, to pervade the sky;
> These to the distant hole direct they drive;
> They claim the stakes who hither first arrive.
>
> Intent his ball the eager gamester eyes,
> His muscles strains, and various postures tries
> Th'impelling blow to strike with greater force,
> And shape the motive orb's projective course.
> If with due strength the weighty engine fall,
> Discharged obliquely, and impinge the ball,
> It winding mounts alofts, and sings in air;
> And wondering crowds the gamester's skill declare.
>
> But when some luckless wayward stroke descends,
> Whose force the ball in running quickly spends,
> The foes triumph, the club is cursed in vain;
> Spectators scoff, and e'en allies complain.
>
> Thus still success is followed with applause;
> But ah! how few espouse a vanquished cause.

Golf has always been regarded by its Scottish devotees as an adjunct to good health. Provided one retained one's health – and woe betide the eighteenth-century Glaswegian unlucky enough to fall into the hands of doctor or surgeon! – then Glasgow must have offered its better-off citizens a life of cheerful bustle, countryside diversions and the steadily expanding promise of developing opportunity. For many generations to come, Glasgow was to produce plenty of men who knew how to turn opportunity to good purpose, both for themselves and for their city.

Notes

1 At this time the Barony Church was housed in the lower choir of the Cathedral, the separate church being built in 1798.
2 Accidental burnings had done great damage in 1652, and again in 1677.
3 The peak population of Glasgow in the seventeenth century was reached in 1660, when the figure was 14,678.
4 *Architecture of Glasgow*.
5 Reid senior's knowledge of pipe-music must have been weak. While the Jacobites had doubtless much to lament, the pibroch is neither used for marching nor for collective performance.
6 I visited 'Spreull's Land' shortly before its demolition in 1978. Though largely sub-divided into seamstresses' rooms, it was still a moving final echo of Glasgow's lost eighteenth-century graciousness.
7 The first printer to settle in Glasgow, George Anderson, had to be bribed with £100 Scots to move from Edinburgh with his goods and chattels in 1638. On Anderson's death, his son received a similar 'subsidy' to take over his father's business. Robert Sanders succeeded Anderson junior in 1661. In 1713 Thomas Harvie became printer to the university. In 1718 James Duncan introduced type-making in his Saltmarket shop. Robert Urie set up as a printer in the Gallowgate in 1740, printed the first issue of the *Glasgow Journal* in 1741, and was responsible for several of Robert Foulis's fine books.

4

King Cotton

In 1777, John Gibson had proclaimed: 'Let but a spirit for manufacturing be diffused among the people, and we will never want manufacturers; for, should a change of fashion, which operates powerfully upon manufacturers, banish at once any particular branch, the people possessed of his spirit will immediately turn their attention to others.'

In 1765, the population of Glasgow was 28,000. By 1780, it had jumped to 43,000, by 1791 to around 67,000, and by 1830 to 200,000. This rise in population reflects the growing employment opportunities which the city was able to offer. The growth of industry and commerce is well illustrated by David Macpherson, writing in 1805, in his *Annals of Commerce*.

> Before America became independent of Great Britain, the foreign commerce of Glasgow was chiefly with that country; and consequently it was deranged by that event. But the enterprising spirit of the merchants has found new channels of commerce, sufficient to employ their capitals and industry. They have also turned their attention more than formerly to manufactures, whereby the city has become the centre and fostering parent of a prodigious number of manufacturing establishments. There are thirty printfields within the influence of this hive of industry. The towns and villages in a circuit of many miles around, and some at considerable distances, are filled with spinners, weavers, and many other classes of work-people, depending upon the fabrics of the loom and the stocking frame; and there are in the neighbourhood several ironworks for making cannon and all other articles of cast iron, which, taken collectively, are perhaps scarcely inferior to the Carron Works.[1] The works for window glass, bottle glass, and

ornamental glass are extensive and thriving. Sugar baking, malting and brewing are all established concerns. But it would be almost as difficult to particularise all the manufactures of Glasgow as those of London, and it may suffice to say that manufactures of almost every kind are carried on with spirit and activity, and generally in joint stocks by companies, or, as they generally are called here, *concerns*, under the management of one or more of the partners; and that the manufactures requiring fire have the vast advantage of coals close to the city.

The machinery which ran the mid-eighteenth-century factories had to be imported from England, Holland or France. The man who was to make it possible for Scotland to manufacture the machines she needed, and to export to others, was James Watt (1736-1819), the son of a Greenock ship chandler.

As a young man, Watt got a job as an instrument-maker in the physics department of Glasgow University. In 1764, while repairing a model of a Newcomen steam engine owned by the university, he realized that if the steam was condensed in a separate vessel which could be kept cold, the efficiency of the engine would be greatly increased and fuel consumption reduced. His own laconic description of how the idea came to him is worth quoting, if only for its splendidly Scots matter-of-factness:

I had gone to take a walk on a fine Sabbath afternoon. I had entered the Green by the gate at the foot of Charlotte Street, and had passed the old washing-house. I was thinking upon the engine at the time, and had gone as far as the herd's house, when the idea came into my mind that as steam was an elastic body, it would rush into a vacuum, and if a communication were made between the cylinder and an exhausted vessel, it would rush into it, and might there be condensed without cooling the cylinder.... I had not walked further than the golf-house when the whole thing was arranged in my mind.

Thus, while he did not invent the atmospheric steam engine – Thomas Newcomen did that in 1712, though the steam engine goes back at least to Hero of Alexandria – Watt produced the first expansion steam engine, which he later made double-acting, fitting it with a centrifugal governor.

Because his engines worked under what was termed technically 'low pressure', they were also safer than their uneconomic predecessors. In 1769 and 1773, he took out with Matthew Boulton of Birmingham patents which incorporated the basic features of the steam engine which was to dominate Victorian transportation and industrial life.

Their first engines were used to pump water out of the tin and copper mines of Cornwall, and elsewhere. Before long, cotton mills using water-power had converted themselves to steam. The first Watt steam engine is said to have been put into a Scottish cotton mill at Springfield, on the Clyde, in 1792. Lancashire mills had Watt engines earlier and Newcomen engines were functioning at Leadhills and elsewhere well before 1792.

Cloth-making, of course, had been carried on in Glasgow, at least domestically, since medieval times, though the quantities produced must have been small. The plaids which Thomas Tucker saw worn both in Edinburgh and Glasgow represented an advance for the industries. Defoe described the material of which they were made as 'a stuff crossed-striped with yellow, red and other mixtures'. He also tells us that at the time of his visit, muslins were manufactured and 'sent into England and to the British plantations, where they sell at a good price'.

In 1727 Parliament appointed a commission, later known as the Board of Trustees for Manufacturers, to administer a fund for the encouragement of industry, particularly the linen industry. (The board became the corner stone of the future British Linen Bank.) This gave encouragement to housewives to grow lint (flax) and hemp, and led to the development of linen-making, particularly in the east.

Linen seems to have been introduced to Glasgow in 1725, as a result of the enlistment of a certain William Wilson of East Kilbride to the Scots Guards. When he returned to Glasgow from service on the Continent in 1700, he brought back from Germany a blue and white chequered handkerchief, and proceeded to experiment in copying it, eventually with success. Wilson himself had not the capital to exploit his discovery, and died in poverty, his last contribution to society being his occupancy of the post of town drummer. But others profited. The first Cambric and Printfield was erected in Pollokshaws in 1742, and soon legislation against the importation of French cambrics provided encouragement for the expansion of the linen industry. Furthermore, a Glaswegian named Harvey in 1732 managed to import from Holland not only two inkle looms but also a skilled Dutch workman, thus breaking the Dutch monopoly in the making of tapes.

The invention by Hargreaves of the spinning jenny, and by Arkwright of the spinning frame, further stimulated production of cotton yarn. An English firm set up the first cotton mill at Rothesay in 1778. In 1780, James Monteith, a Glasgow linen-weaver who had been experimenting in the mixing of a fine hard-spun cotton yarn with linen yarn in the making of cheap fabrics at his Anderston factory, discovered how to weave an imitation Indian muslin entirely out of cotton. So successful was he, in fact, that he caused a dress of it to be woven and embroidered with jewels for presentation to Queen Charlotte. Such success provoked imitations. By 1787, many new mills were set up beside Scottish rivers. His own six sons all became cotton manufacturers. In the west, cotton began to oust linen. By the end of the century, Glasgow had gone over wholeheartedly to cotton-making, leaving Forfarshire and Fife the centres of Scotland's linen industry.

One of James's six sons, also James, an ambitious man, is often referred to by early historians of Glasgow as the father of the Glasgow cotton industry, principally because during the troubles of the 1790s, when many Glasgow banks failed, causing a trade paralysis, he opened an auction room in London which enabled him to make a profit of £80,000 in a very few years, and thus keep the industry he led prosperous. But another son, Henry (1765–1848), who took over his father's factory in Anderston, was the more prominent citizen. He triumphantly defied the tobacco lords' privilege of exclusively attending the more select assemblies and twice became Provost of Glasgow – in 1814 for a year, and again in 1818 – a position to which no weaver's son would have dared to aspire in his father's hey-day. He represented Lanark district of burghs in Parliament in 1821.

Another pioneering contemporary of James Monteith senior was David Dale (1739–1806). Dale was the son of an

Ayrshire shopkeeper and the prototype of Sir Walter Scott's
Bailie Nicol Jarvie in *Rob Roy* (at whose hands, incidentally
James Monteith's ancestors, who came from Aberfoyle, had
suffered, thus driving them to Glasgow to earn a living).
Dale began as an importer of Dutch and French linen yarns,
but soon came to realize that there was more profit to be
made in the manufacturing side. Along with James Monteith
and some others, David Dale invited Arkwright to visit
Glasgow in 1783. Dale showed Arkwright a site by the Falls
of Clyde at Lanark, and persuaded the inventor to enter what
proved to be a short-lived partnership in a cotton-spinning
mill set up at the town of New Lanark which Dale founded.
Not all Arkwright's English friends were pleased at the help
thus briefly given to the Scot, and Arkwright, who had
begun life as a barber, was frequently teased for having 'put a
razor in the hands of a Scotsman who would one day shave
us all'.

By 1793 Dale had the largest mill of its kind in the United
Kingdom, employing some thirteen hundred men and
women, many of whom had formerly been destitute. Dale
fed, clothed and housed these workers, ruling them with a
kind of benevolent paternalism.

Three years after Dale's death, the Poet Laureate, Robert
Southey, in company with the great Scots civil engineer,
Thomas Telford, visited New Lanark, and commented on
the establishment. He thought the mills

> perfect of their kind, according to the present state of mechanical
> science, and that they appeared to be under admirable
> management; they are thoroughly clean and so carefully
> ventilated, that there was no unpleasant smell in any of the
> apartments. Everything required for the machinery is made
> upon the spot, and the expence of wear and tear is estimated at
> 800£ annually. There are stores also from which the people are
> supplied with all the necessaries of life. They have a credit there
> to the amount of sixteen shillings a week each, but may
> elsewhere deal if they chuse. The expences of what he calls the
> moral part of the establishment, he stated at 700£ a year. But a
> large building is just completed, with ball and concert and
> lecture rooms, all for 'the formation of character', and this must
> have required a considerable sum, which I think must surely be
> down to Owen's private account, rather than to the cost of the
> concern.

Owen's stores were, in fact, the first stirrings of the Cooperative Movement in Scotland.

Southey, however, had doubts about the long-term practicability of this Utopia by the Clyde. By this time, it was being run by Dale's son-in-law, Robert Owen, who took over new Lanark by purchase in 1799, and came to manage it on 1st January 1800. Southey went on:

> Owen in reality deceives himself. He is part-owner and sole Director of a large establishment, differing more in accidents than in essence from a plantation; the persons under him happen to be white, and are at liberty by law to quit his service, but while they remain in it they are as much under his absolute management, as so many negro-slaves. His humour, his vanity, his kindliness of nature (all these have their share) lead him to make these *human machines* as he calls them (and too literally believes them to be) as happy as he can, and to make a display of their happiness. And he jumps at once to the monstrous conclusion that because he can do this with 2210 persons who are totally dependent on him – all mankind might be governed with the same facility…. He keeps out of sight from others, and perhaps from himself, that his system, instead of aiming at perfect freedom, can only be kept in play by absolute power. Indeed, he never looks beyond one of his own ideal square villages, to the rules and proportions of which he would squeeze the whole human race. The formation of character! Why, the end of his institutions would be, as far as possible, the destruction of all character. They tend directly to destroy individuality of character and domesticity – in the one of which the strength of man consists, and in the other his happiness. The power of human society and the grace, would both be annihilated.

Whatever may have been the situation at New Lanark, it is doubtful if, in 1819, the year of Southey's visit, much grace was to be found in Glasgow's 'eighteen steam weaving factories, containing 2,800 looms, and producing 8,400 pieces of cloth weekly'; doubtful, too, if those who laboured long hours in the city's fifty-two cotton mills, with their 511,200 spindles, weaving over a million yards valued at £5 million, found much time or opportunity to develop their character.

In 1804 James Graham (1765–1811), the son of a Glasgow lawyer and himself an advocate, produced anonymously a

poem called 'The Sabbath', which, in spite of being savaged
both by the *Edinburgh Review* and later by Lord Byron,
achieved a broad measure of popularity; so much so that
Graham's wife, reading the poem in ignorance of the identity
of the author, is said to have remarked to her husband, 'Ah,
James, if you could only write like this!' While today we
would hardly share Mrs Graham's literary enthusiasm, the
social comment her husband's lines contain is probably a
more knowledgeable reflection than Southey's.

> With dovelike wings peace o'er yon village[2] broods
> The dizzying millwheel rests; the anvil's din
> Hath ceased; all, all around is quietness.
> Less fearful on this day, the limping hare
> Stops and looks back, and stops, and looks on man,
> Her deadliest foe. The toil-worn horse, set free,
> Unheedful of the pasture, roams at large,
> And, as his stiff, unwielding bulk he rolls,
> His iron-armed hoofs gleam in the morning ray.
>
> But chiefly man the day of rest enjoys.
> Hail, Sabbath! thee I hail the poor man's day!
> On other days the man of toil is doomed
> To eat his joyless bread, lonely, the ground
> Both seat and board, screened from the winter's cold
> And summer's heat by neighbouring hedge or tree.
> But on this day, embosomed in his home,
> He shares the frugal meal with those he loves …
>
> Hail, Sabbath! thee I hail, the poor man's day!
> The pale mechanic now has leave to breathe
> The morning air pure from the city's smoke,
> While wandering slowly up the riverside
> He meditates on Him whose power he marks
> In each green tree.…

The wretchedness of these 'pale mechanics' – to say
nothing of their children labouring twelve or thirteen hours a
day – who toiled for six weekdays at looms and in factories,
was aggravated by a number of outside factors. There was a
failure of the harvest in 1799, when it was the poorest and
largest section of the community that starved. On 15th
February 1800 – the year in which the first Glasgow police

force came into being, an earlier attempt by the magistrates to appoint one of their own number 'Intendant of Police' having been defeated in Parliament in 1788 – bread riots occurred. There was another, equally basic cause of unrest: growing unemployment, chiefly among the hand-loom weavers.

The earliest power-mills in Glasgow had spun cotton yarn for the hand-loom weavers to make into cloth. When, in the early decades of the nineteenth century, the factories began manufacturing their own cloth, the economic pressures on the hand-loom weavers operating from their own cottages became considerable. There had been the Calton weavers' riot in 1787, as a result of their employers' refusal to grant a wage increase. The 56th regiment arrived from Ayr to assist the 39th regiment in preserving the peace, though in the doing of this three weavers had been shot. Providence, it seems, was on the side of the law and order on this occasion, for on a September night 'the Captain of patrole' ordered a roll of his men to be called. While they were mustered for this purpose, the hanging stairs leading to the Assembly Room of the Tontine buildings collapsed on the spot where the men would normally have been sheltering. (A reporter, writing in the contemporary *Glasgow Mercury*, provided the classic text-book example of the craft of non-reporting by commenting: 'had they been on the stair they could not have escaped being crushed to death'.)

About 1800, when for a second year a crop failure resulted in a grain shortage and widespread distress among the poor, a handloom weaver could earn the then good wage of £2 10s. a week. But thereafter wages fell to as little as 10s. as the factories gradually took over. Rum, cheaply available through Glasgow's West Indies trading connections at the close of the eighteenth century, had become unobtainable because of the Napoleonic War. Its place was being taken by whisky and gin. In these spirits, available at all hours in numerous drinking-shops, the poor sought a solace which also inflamed their grievances.

The war with Napoleon, which broke out in 1797, had at first found some support amongst liberal-minded people who still drew some inspiration from the ideals of *liberté, égalité, fraternité*. But when it became clear that 'Boney' posed

a practical threat of invasion with no such high-minded
beliefs attached to it, Glasgow responded to the patriotic call
to arms both with men and with money. There was a review
of the troops on Glasgow Green in 1804. Although
Glasgow's nine regiments were never called out on anything
more serious than rumours of invasions, the citizens took
much pride in the fact that the victor of Corunna, Sir John
Moore (1761-1809), the son of Burns's friend Dr John
Moore, was a Glasgow man commemorated to this day by a
statue in George Square. The British sea victory at Cape St
Vincent resulted in St Vincent Street receiving its name.

For Glaswegians, one of the worst features of the
Napoleonic War was the easy spread of rumour, news from
abroad taking so long to travel. Fortunately, most of the
alarming rumours eventually turned out to be false. 'Senex'
remembered that:

> During the time of the French war, it was quite exhilarating to
> observe the arrival of the London mail-coach in Glasgow, when
> carrying the first intelligence of a great victory, like the Battle of
> the Nile, or the Battle of Waterloo. The mail-coach horses were
> then decorated with laurels, and a red flag floated on the roof of
> the coach. The guard, dressed in his best scarlet coat and gold
> ornamented hat, came galloping at a thundering pace along the
> stones of the Gallowgate, sounding his bugles amidst the
> echoings of the street; and when he arrived at the foot of Nelson
> Street ... he there discharged his blunderbus in the air. On these
> occasions a general run was made to the Tontine Coffee-room to
> learn the great news, and long before the newspapers were
> delivered, the public were advised by the guard of the particulars
> of the glorious victory, which flew from mouth to mouth like
> wild-fire. The Coffee-room soon became densely crowded, the
> subscribers anxiously waiting the delivery of the newspapers,
> and every one repeating the information scattered abroad by the
> guard. When the papers were delivered, all was bustle and
> confusion to learn what the *Courier* said, or what the *Star* said.

It was after the victory of 1815 at Waterloo that men who
had been in the fighting services came back in numbers to a
Glasgow very different from the city they had left, perhaps as
long as twenty years before. Returning soldiers swell
unemployment. In 1815, a mob attacked Kirkman Finlay's
house in Queen Street, and had to be dispersed by soldiers.

As a Member of Parliament, he had voted for 'Prosperity'
Robinson's Corn Law, which had the effect of prohibiting
the import of corn until the price of home-grown corn
reached 80s. per quarter, a protective measure favouring the
landowning interest which caused the price of bread to shoot
up and forced the poorer people to rely upon potatoes. In
1816, some 40,000 people came together in Thrushgrove
demanding action to redress their grievances. By 1817,
indeed, the foundations of Glasgow's 'radical', later 'red',
reputation had already been laid, for a secret parliamentary
committee referred to the city in a report as being 'one of the
places where treasonable practices prevail to the greatest
degree'.

By 1819 the police and troops were daily to be seen in the
streets dispersing people who looked as if they might be
about to riot. On Sunday 1st April of that year, real trouble
broke out. There was desultory rioting, mostly by weavers
in the outlying districts affected by the shortage of work.
Eighteen men were arrested and tried for high treason.
Andrew Hardie, an ancestor of Keir Hardie, and John Baird,
both from Bonnymuir where they had been demonstrating
in favour of Parliamentary reform and the extension of the
franchise, were publicly hanged, and then beheaded at
Stirling, the executioner holding up Hardie's mangled,
illiterate head by the hair and crying: 'This is the head of a
traitor.' James Wilson, another of the eighteen, suffered a
similar fate in front of 20,000 spectators on Glasgow Green.
The remaining fifteen were transported for life.

In 1822, another hungry weaver, Richard Campbell, was
scourged through the streets by the public hangman, being
given twenty lashes with 'a formidable cat o' nine tails at four
separate stopping places', the last man to be publicly
whipped in Glasgow. Later in the same year John Provan's
factory in Great Clyde Street was wrecked, a mob having
erroneously got the notion that he was a resurrectionist or
digger up of the dead to provide university anatomists with
cadavers. Five men received sentences of transportation for
their share in this affair.

In 1825, the right to strike was recognized. The Catholic
Emancipation Act was passed in 1829. When the Reform
Bill, against which the dying Sir Walter Scott had so

disastrously campaigned in Jedburgh, received its majority in the House in 1832, there was a joyous demonstration on Glasgow Green attended by more than 70,000 people, Lord Provost Dalglish's house in West George Street being illuminated with 3,000 new gas jets highlighting the city's motto, 'Let Glasgow flourish'. Since 1817, the town council and the Glasgow Gas Light Company, whose chairman was Lord Provost Henry Monteith, had jointly brought gas to the city, so in a civic sense the Provost had a vested interest in letting the attractions of the new illuminant be seen.

There was to be another near–mutinous decade before the threat of riot receded from Glasgow. In any case, neither the weavers nor the textile industry had much cause to rejoice. The spinning and weaving of cotton soon ceased to be Glasgow's major job–opportunity provider, although for a time the factories went on growing in number.

By 1860 the peak of the cotton industry's prosperity was reached. In that year chimneys of some sixty cotton mills lacquered the sky with soot. They employed nearly 20,000 people, about three-quarters of them women, working on 20,000 looms. Two things happened to cut down this apparently flourishing industry to the point where, a century after its peak, it had all but disappeared from the city. One was the failure of the Western Bank in 1857. Although the Western Bank had an authorized capital of £4 million, four of the largest textile firms found themselves unable to pay their debts because of a commercial crisis in America. Soon after came a cotton famine, the American Civil War cutting off supplies from the Southern States between 1861 and 1865.

There were other less immediately obvious causes too, not least the fact that some of the countries which had hitherto been among Glasgow's best customers for the high-quality textiles the city produced, had begun to set up their own industries, which they protected by tariffs. Another cause was Glasgow's excessive concentration on high-quality muslins, which ceased to sell well after the bankruptcy following the Western Bank failure. To get rid of their high surplus stock, the manufacturers sold them at so low a price that even the workers were able to buy them. Consequently the ladies of fashion were no longer very keen to buy the material when normal production could be resumed. In any case, for reasons that have never been wholly examined, Lancashire, specializing in coarser but very cheap cotton cloths, was able to capture the market in Africa, India and the Far East, where there were no tariff barriers. Lancashire's cheap trade thrived as Glasgow's quality trade shrank.

Not many buildings erected during the earlier years of Glasgow's cotton period survive. The Assembly Rooms in Ingram Street, the centre portion of which was put up by Robert and James Adam in 1792, but the wings of which were added by Henry Holland in 1807, stood on the corner of George Square until it made way for an extension to the Post Office in 1890. Soon after, the centrepiece was rebuilt, with alterations, as the triumphal McLennan Arch on Glasgow Green. During the Assembly Rooms' century of useful life, the building housed many of the city's most glittering Victorian social functions, attracting them away from the Tontine.

Another vanished work by the Adams was the old Royal Infirmary, begun in 1792 upon the site of the ruined Bishop's Palace. Adam's Infirmary survived until 1912, when the present overbearing successor was put up, itself now under sentence of replacement.

The house which the brothers built for David Dale survived until the 1950s, when, in spite of protests, it was needlessly pulled down by the City's Education Department during a period when officially-sanctioned vandalism was almost the order of the civic day. Two houses by James Adam, situated on the corners of High Street and College Street, dating from 1793, and originally intended to accommodate university professors, were destroyed in 1973. Latterly their impressive columns rose above singularly tasteless modern shop fronts. The pleasing remains of a house by both Adam brothers at number 60 Wilson Street can still be seen, though its open arcade has gone and a mansard roof has been added.

The finest urban survivor of this renewal stage of Glasgow's prosperity is undoubtedly Robert Adam's Trades House in Glassford Street, built in 1791 and still serving its original purposes, though it now looks somewhat crushed in by what J.M. Reid called the 'tall insignificance of its southern neighbours'. James Sellars reconstructed the interior in 1887.

Since the loss of Garscadden House, only the remarkable Pollok House survives among former great country houses now engulfed by Glasgow. Designed by William Adam about 1737, it was finished by his son John in 1752, but it suggests a backward look towards the style of Sir William Bruce rather than the classicism which the other members of the Adam family were so successfully evoking. Sir Robert Rowand Anderson added the entrance hall in 1892 and the sympathetic wings and a terrace in 1896–1905.

Today, the house and its magnificent park around the White Cart, which is spanned by a delightful eighteenth-century bridge, are managed by Glasgow District and the National Trust for Scotland for the benefit of Glaswegians and those who visit their city. The fine collection of pictures includes an El Greco portrait, 'Lady with Fur Wrap'. Chamber-music concerts are held regularly during the winter months in the elegant drawing-room. A gallery to house the art collection bequeathed by the shipowner Sir William Burrell has been built in the grounds of Pollok House. The prize-winning design of Barry Gasson, it shows the remarkably varied range of pictures, sculpture, tapestries, coins and *objets d'art* to striking advantage. A visit to the Burrell Gallery has established itself as one of Scotland's leading tourist attractions.

During the period when cotton spinning and the manufacture of cotton textiles together formed Glasgow's staple industry – from 1780 to about 1830 – the population rose from 40,000 to 200,000. This rapid increase led to the expansion of the city through the creation of several 'new towns'.

George Square, which has already been mentioned, was 'West End' in relation to the old town around the cathedral, and when first put up housed such leaders in industry as the brothers W. and J. Coats, who had already a monopoly in the manufacture of cotton thread; Patrick Colquhoun, future Provost, founder of Glasgow's Chamber of Commerce, promoter of the Tontine Society, and with Cooksons of Newcastle the introducer of the first 'crystal manufactory' to Scotland, that at Verreville; and Thomas Dunmore, a founder partner of the Arms Bank.

During the reign of 'King Cotton', the city moved farther

The doorway from Hornby Castle, now housed in the Burrell Museum west still, as the lands of the Campbells of Blythswood began to be built upon. The Campbells of Blythswood, a family tracing their origins to Colin Campbell, merchant and trader in Glasgow in 1615, several of whose sons became Provost of the city in turn, possessed a splendid mansion in the Saltmarket which, according to 'Senex' in *Glasgow Past and Present*, had been built during the seventeenth century. Oliver Cromwell occupied it in 1650, and it survived until about 1829, though by then long since abandoned by the Campbells. They next occupied a mansion distinguished by 'five tympanny windows to the front with tappietouries', the front elevation of the property looking out on Bridgegait, the large garden rambling down to the Clyde. About the middle of the eighteenth century, the house was divided and let out, Provost Colin Campbell having by then acquired the lands of Blythswood for 'a mere wanworth' (approximately one farthing an acre, according to 'Senex').

In 1804 a large feu was taken by a Glasgow merchant, William Harley, who had made money by laying pipes from his property at Willowbank, where there was a spring, to the intersection of Bath and West Nile Streets, from where four-wheeled carts carrying tanks distributed the water for sale. In 1810 Harley built dairies, a 'Cowhouse' accommodating 100 cows which were fed by 'the operation of a wheel and pinion, placed on the outside portion at the transverse passage', baths,[3] and some houses in what became Bath Street. On the top of Blythswood Hill, Harley laid out an enclosed garden with a fountain, admission to which was open to anyone who bought a ticket. Harley thus founded one of Glasgow's cotton era 'new towns', though to no advantage to himself, for he overreached himself financially in doing so, and by 1816 was bankrupt (as soon afterwards, incidentally, were the trustees who took over his responsibilities). However, his pioneering development had suggested to others what could be done, and soon there was no lack of persons anxious to build upon the salubrious hilly site on the right side of the city to avoid most of the smoke from the growing number of factory chimneys. Among the most prominent of these speculative builders were Dugald Bannatyne, Dr James Cleland,[4] William Jack and Alexander Garden.

Cleland and Jack put up houses in Bath Street, Alexander Garden in St Vincent Street. From 1820, a descendant of Alexander Hamilton, William Garden, extended the family enterprise further up the hillside, though he too went bankrupt, his trustees continuing the work for a decade or so, until Garden hastily emigrated to America. To this series of financial failures, Thomas Burns added his name in 1827, though not before he had managed to build a substantial part of West Regent Street.

With this development, which J.R. Kellett has calculated increased the Campbells' income from £6,000 per annum to £300,000,[5] a Glasgow style of house emerged, all the Blythswood buildings being erected originally as elegant homes. In their definitive book *Architecture of Glasgow*, Andor Gomme and David Walker describe the basic unit of the Blythswood 'new town' as being:

> a fairly short terrace two or three storeys high, generally with centrepiece and end pavilions given considerable emphasis…. Pediments are rarely used, though pilasters appear at times where houses were individually designed. There is a fair number of porches of various orders regularly punctuating the smooth facades; cornices are generally heavy and emphatic; those on the windows and window surrounds especially so. The facing is of course all ashlar … now a darkish silver grey, but recent cleaning has revealed a lovely soft biscuity colour underneath.

They rightly deplore the recent widespread but misdirected custom of painting such stone, as a substitute for its proper maintenance and repair. They also comment on the solid, upstanding dignity of these well-proportioned buildings abounding in detailing that is often beautiful.

All the streets of this 'new town', which was built on the grid-iron plan later adopted by many American cities, still have examples of houses in this Blythswood Glasgow Style. Commercial pressures began to be exerted against them as long ago as the 1840s, when the first of them suffered the change to commercial use. Since then, there have been many intrusions, some of the Victorian replacement buildings being distinguished. Gaps are being torn in the old fabric so constantly that before long the 'feel' of the streets built in the

Blythswood Square, the centrepiece of Glasgow's 'New Town' (1823-9)
by John Brand

Blythswood Glasgow style will have been totally destroyed, taller newcomers outscaling the remaining houses with the dreary cosmopolitan glassy-eyed anonymity fashionable in our uncertain age.

It is therefore fortunate that Blythswood Square, on the summit of what was once known as Harley's Hill, has been designated a Conservation Area. John Brash was the architect for H.W. Garden in 1823. Unfortunately, the balanced sense of unity of the square depended upon the sympathetic corner buildings of the streets leading into it from each of its four corners. One of these was replaced by the glaringly hostile and thoroughly commonplace building originally built to house the offices of British Rail just after the 1939–45 war.

The show-piece of the square is the Royal Scottish Automobile Club, which occupies the whole of the east side. Here the unity of the window groupings, the balancing pavilions and the window astragals have been preserved. All the properties on the south side have recently been rebuilt behind the original façade. Many of the windows have been replaced with plate glass, or with more modern swivel devices. Without astragals, most buildings built before 1850 seem somehow to gape disconcertingly. Charles Rennie Mackintosh put a characteristic *Art Nouveau* door on number 5, where some internal reworking is reputedly by his disciple James Salmon junior, grandson of Brash's pupil, James Salmon, senior.

The Blythswood development spilled northwards up Garnethill, on the other side of the dividing valley of Sauchiehall Street. Many of the buildings here were originally flats, intended for humbler people. Unlike the square on the crest of its prouder neighbour, Garnethill has fallen on hard times, the unity of the area having been violated. Glasgow School of Art, itself a magnificent cuckoo in an otherwise shabby nest has now a few restored tenements around it.

Another direction in which development took place during Glasgow's cotton days was southwards, across the Clyde. In 1780 the village of Bridge-End or Gorbals lay just across the river. Beyond and around it was agricultural land divided into crofts with names like Trades Croft, Kirk Croft, Wellcroft, Windmill Croft, Stirlingfauld and Gushet Fauld –

land which was owned, for the most part, jointly by
Glasgow Corporation, the Trades House and Hutcheson's
Hospital.

When Glasgow officially extended its boundaries to take in
Gorbals, James and David Laurie got possession of some 47
acres of the old croft lands, and on a speculative basis
proceeded to plan a development 'according to one plan or
design, whereby it was in a manner set apart for houses of a
superior description'. David, who seems to have been the
leader of the partnership, in 1802 engaged Peter Nicholson to
design the two terraces of Carlton Place (so-named to honour
the Prince Regent), and Italian craftsmen were brought to
Glasgow to carry out the work of embellishment and
decoration, all at a cost of just under £10,000.

These dignified three-storey terraces with basements, each
of forty bays, have pavilions with Ionic porches and coupled
columns, with a double porch for the centrepiece. There has
been some damage to the group as a whole – the loss of two
pavilions and the addition of a mansard roof – but a
post-Second World War restoration has given some
indication of the kind of dignified waterfront Glasgow could
possess. Laurieston House, Nicholson's showpiece, was
intended by David for his own use. Indeed, the lavish Italian
plasterwork, now happily restored, was intended to impress
the Prince Regent, the future George IV, during a proposed
visit to the city. Because of rioting, however, the prince's
advisers decided to leave Glasgow out of his itinerary.

The two terraces are divided by the entrance to South
Portland Street, which John Laurie lined up with Buchanan
Street, across the river. Abbotsford Place, its continuation,
was for some time a favourite street with Glasgow's doctors.
Those four-storey terraces with their Ionic and Corinthian
porches, fronting on to broad streets, were latterly a forlorn
reminder of the imposing scale of the development which the
Lauries had hoped to establish.

But their plans went awry. Buchanan Street and
Abbotsford Place were not to be linked by a bridge. Then
there were the tolls to be paid by residents from the south
side using the other bridges, until a suspension bridge was
put up especially for their use in 1853, a toll of one halfpenny

Carlton Place (1802-4) by Peter Nicholson

being charged during the first few years it was in use. But what really overthrew the Lauries' ambitions for the area was the unplanned building which went on behind the north side of the central axis. The tenements put up by master builders like James Ballantine and John Binnie (whose relative, Thomas, built Monteith Row, which looked on to Glasgow Green, and features in Guy MacCrone's novels of Glasgow life, *Wax Fruit*) were sold as shells, to be completed to the customer's requirements. This was symptomatic of the unplanned approach that soon began to affect even land uses. What was intended to be a residential district became a jumble of housing and small industries, closely mixed. This was in large measure due to the fact that until almost the middle of the nineteenth century, Glasgow Corporation had no jurisdiction south of the river. Consequently, it could not prevent William Dixon, who since 1837 had owned the famous 'Dixon's Blazes' (which in time were to cast an orange glare over the surrounding district at night) building a trackway right across Laurieston's principal streets to the quay at Windmillcroft. Neither could the corporation stop the setting up of brickworks and coalfields on the outskirts of the district, nor the gradual proliferation of all sorts of small backyard industries. Gradually the wealthier residents moved out, the big houses were divided and sub-divided. After 1830 tenements were built subdivided from the start, and the course was set for Gorbals to become within half a century perhaps the worst, and certainly the most notorious, slum in Europe!

While the Lauries were ambitiously busy on the south side, new public buildings were appearing in and around the old town – William Stark's St George's Church went up in 1807 in what was once St George's Place,[6] a Wren-influenced building which is today one of the main adornments of Buchanan Street. We have lost most of Stark's other public buildings, including his Bell's Park Lunatic Asylum of 1809 (which survived for more than a century and was probably his masterpiece) and the original Hunterian Museum of 1804, famous for its Doric portico with Doric columns and domed interior, sacrificed with the rest of the old university. The Justiciary Court House facing Glasgow Green, also dating from 1807, was remodelled by J.H. Craigie in 1910, and is now a building of no particular interest.

Fortunately, more of the work of Stark's contemporary David Hamilton (1768–1843) has survived. Numbers 151 to 157 Queen Street give some idea of his earlier solid classical manner. Hutcheson's Hospital in Ingram Street, built in 1805 to replace the seventeenth-century original in the Trongate, also has obvious classical overtones, in spite of its slightly mannered detail. To most Glaswegians, however, Hamilton is best known for the work he did in 1827–9 on the Cunningehame mansion of 1778, to fit it out for its existence as Glasgow's Royal Exchange. The old house seems to have been cased in, while a powerful Corinthian portico was added to the east end, topped by a surprising but effective cupola. To the west stands Archibald Elliott the second's Royal Bank, put up in 1827, recently totally rebuilt within its shell in accordance with Glasgow Corporation's intention to conserve the original character of Buchanan Street. Royal Exchange Square, another of the corporation's Conservation Areas, which flanks the bank and the Royal Exchange (now Stirling's Library), is also Elliott's work.

Hamilton also rebuilt the Tolbooth behind the old steeple (now only the steeple itself survives); St Enoch's Church, now demolished; and in 1841 the ornate Western Club in Buchanan Street, also recently given a totally rebuilt interior. For the remarkable Kirkman Finlay, the textile manufacturer who successfully ran Napoleon's blockade to get his cotton goods into Europe, who sent Glasgow's first ships to open up both the India and China trades, and who became one of Glasgow's most distinguished early nineteenth-century Lord Provosts, a Member of Parliament and Lord Rector of her university, Hamilton built the spacious Castle Toward, on the Cowal shore.

A word should be said about the formation of Buchanan Street, since it remains in most respects the City's central axis. It was founded by Andrew Buchanan, who followed his uncle into the tobacco trade, made a fortune and lost most of it in 1777. He had bought four acres of ground immediately to the West of his father's house in Argyle Street and was already in the business of feuing it for building before the

Buchanan Street, begun in 1777 by tobacco merchant,
Andrew Buchanan

American Colonial crash came. Shops began to be built in Buchanan Street in 1820 and the arcade linking Buchanan Street with Argyle Street, built for the Incorporation of Wrights, was opened in 1828.

During the cotton phase of Glasgow's expansion, though

it never had the kind of overall plan which gives Edinburgh's New Town its unique grand design, Glasgow must still have been a very fair city. Several observant travellers visited it.

William and Dorothy Wordsworth arrived in Glasgow on Monday 22nd August 1803, in their Irish jaunting car. They were on their way to the Trossachs and the Highlands. They put up at the 'Saracen's Head', then 'quiet and tolerably cheap, a new building', according to Dorothy. Both brother and sister were tired, and glad to have a place of rest. But the observant Dorothy soon had out her diary and her critical pen.

> I shall never forget how glad I was to be landed in a little quiet back parlour, for my head was beating with the noise of carts which we had left.... But with my first pleasant sensations also came the feeling that we were not in an English inn – partly from its half-unfurnished appearance, which is common in Scotland, for in general the deal wainscots and doors are unpainted, and partly from the dirtiness of the floors. Having dined, Wm. and I walked to the post-office, and after much seeking found out a quiet timber-yard wherein to sit down and read our letter. We then walked a considerable time in the streets, which are perhaps as handsome as streets can be, which derive no particular effect from their situation in connexion with natural advantages such as rivers, sea or hills. The Trongate, an old street, is very picturesque – high houses with an intermixture of gable fronts towards the street. The New Town is built of fine stone, in the best style of the very best London streets, at the west end of the town, but not being brick they are greatly superior.

Dorothy Wordsworth then went on to record some lively general impressions. 'One thing must strike every stranger in his first walk through Glasgow – an appearance of business and bustle, but no coaches or gentlemen's carriages. During all the time we walked in the streets, I saw only three carriages, but these were travelling chaises. I also could not but observe a want of cleanliness in the appearance of the lower orders of the people, and a dullness in the dress and outside of the whole mass, as they moved along.'

Traditionally, the Scots were never very good innkeepers, and the dirt and disorder of Scottish inns and hotels was commented upon by travellers far into the nineteenth century. Temperament and a foolish sense of pride were – and to some extent, still are – responsible for a certain traditional lack of welcoming graciousness. More practical reasons were responsible for the dirty state of the Glaswegians seen by Dorothy Wordsworth. Cleanliness necessitates a plentiful supply of cheap water.

Glasgow's water at the turn of the century came from thirty public wells from which it was fetched by the water-bearers of those who could afford such help, and thirty other wells or pumps in the gardens of mansions in Buchanan, Queen and Miller Streets. Water was also drawn from various rivers and streams around the city. Cleanliness and hygiene, especially amongst the poorer people who had to fetch their own bucket-loads of water, cost a great deal of effort, since they could hardly afford to buy from the pony-carts at a halfpenny a stoup.

In 1806, however, the Glasgow Water Works Company was formed. It pumped water from the Clyde at Dalmarnock to reservoirs from which, after filtration, the water was then pumped to the city centre and to the new suburbs. In 1808, the Cranston Hill Company set up a similar operation at Anderston, but soon moved alongside its rival at Dalmarnock. These companies competed with each other until 1858, when they amalgamated. Even so, many Glasgow houses were to be without piped water for another three-quarters of a century!

In spite of the fact that piped water was at least available by the time Robert Southey, the Poet Laureate, arrived in Glasgow in the autumn of 1819, on his way back from a tour of the Highlands made in company with the Scots engineer Thomas Telford, inn conditions had improved very little. The hotel at which Southey stayed had been built in 1757 as the residence of Provost John Murdoch, though by 1790 it was an inn. It, and a neighbouring mansion of matching Georgian character and dignity, survived in Argyle Street until replaced by a 'Greek' Thompson building in 1863. Wrote Southey, under an entry dated 27th September:

> We drove to the Buck's Head in Argyle Street. Large as this house is, they had no room with a fire, when we arrived cold

and hungry, at ten o'clock on a wet morning.

The inns in large cities are generally detestable, and this does not appear to form an exception from the common rule. But it afforded what I cannot but notice as a curiosity in its kind unique, as far as my knowledge extends. In the *Commoditié*, which is certainly not more than six feet by four, there was a small stone, which as I learned from certain inscriptions in pencil on the wall, is regularly heated in the winter.

Southey, like the Wordsworths before him, set out to explore on foot.

A City like Glasgow is a hateful place for a stranger, unless he is reconciled to it by the comforts of hospitality and society. In any other case the best way is to reconnoitre it, so as to know the outline and outside, and to be contented with such other information as books can supply.

Argyle Street is the finest part; it has a mixture of old and new buildings, but is long enough and lofty enough to be one of the best streets in G. Britain. The Cathedral is the only edifice of its kind in Scotland which received no external injury at the Reformation.[7]

Southey found two faults with the cathedral. One related to the 'smeary appearance' of the painted-glass windows, which have long since been removed. The other belonged to 'the unclean part of the national character; for the seats are so closely packed that any person who could remain there during the time of service in warm weather, must have an invincible nose. I doubt even whether any incense could overcome so strong and concentrated an odour of humanity'.

The university, however, struck him as having 'an ancient and respectable appearance'.

Southey had come into Glasgow from Dunbarton, commenting that as he drove 'packed in a coach ... several steamboats were plying on the Clyde', and that 'yesterday morning when we rose, there was one smoking before the window at Arrochar on Loch Long'.

There had been experiment with steam-ships as far back as 1788, when, on 19th October, Robert Burns, among others, saw or possibly even sailed on a paddle steamer which crossed Dalswinton Loch at approximately 5 miles an hour. It had been built for Patrick Miller, an enterprising

Dumfriesshire laird, by William Symington. A year later, Symington built a large 7-miles-an-hour boat for Miller, which sailed on the Forth and Clyde Canal, a waterway constructed between 1768 and 1790, and on which passenger boats ran, latterly purely for pleasure, until the outbreak of the Second World War. In 1802, the *Charlotte Dundas* was built by Symington for towing purposes on the canal. The adjacent proprietors, however, complained of the damage caused by its wash to the banks, and it had soon to be beached and abandoned.

At the turn of the century, a still youthful engineer, Henry Bell, settled in the new town of Helensburgh, on the Clyde, becoming its first Provost. He had begun as a millwright, working with his uncle. Later, he worked as a shipmodeller at Bo'ness, from where he emigrated to London, where he served under Rennie, the engineer. In 1790, he was back in Glasgow, running his own carpenter's business, and in 1807 he moved downriver to Helensburgh. The problems and possibilities of steam navigation had been occupying his mind since 1786, but lack of money prevented him from developing his ideas in practice. In 1809, he built 'hot and cold Baths' at Helensburgh, and an adjacent hotel, now converted into flats.

An American, Robert Fulton, came to England in 1804, and ordered a steam engine from the Soho works of Messrs Boulton and Watts. In 1807 that engine was driving a little paddle steamer, the *Clermont*, between New York and Albany. Bell is known to have examined the unfortunate *Charlotte Dundas* and to have corresponded with Fulton. In August 1812 Bell advertised the first sailings of his own 'steam passage-boat *Comet*, between Glasgow, Greenock and Helensburgh, for passengers only'. The *Comet*, which took five hours to get from Glasgow to Greenock, had 'handsome carpeting … a sofa clothed with marone … twelve small windows, each finished with marone, curtains, with tassels, fringe and velvet cornices, ornamented with gilt ornaments, having altogether a very rich effect. Above the sofa there is a large mirror suspended and at each side bookshelves are placed, containing a collection of the best authors, for the amusement and edification of those who may avail themselves of them during the passage.'

Wellington Church (1883-4), University Avenue by T.L. Watson

The *Comet* was not herself a success, but by the time
Southey saw the steamers on the Clyde, more than forty of
these long-chimneyed wooden paddlers were sailing on
regular services at a profit. One of these, the *Marjory*, built by
William Denny of Dumbarton in 1814, was the first
steamboat to sail on the Thames. Another, and one that
presumably paid, was the *Waterloo*, built at Port Glasgow in
1816, a wooden steamship of 72 tons owned by a certain G.
Brown. It had the honour of featuring in a book by John Galt
called *The Steamboat*, a collection of tales told while in
passage down the Clyde by a certain Thomas Duffle, lodger
of Mrs MacLecket, Boyle's Land, Saltmarket.

The *Waterloo* had brought Mr Duffle and his garrulous
story-telling acquaintances from Glasgow to Greenock.

> After landing ... our cargo of Greenockians, the steam was
> again set to work, and the vessel, with all that orderliness and
> activity which belongs to the enginery, moved round, and,
> turning her latter end to Greenock, walked over the waters
> straight to Helensburgh. This is not a long voyage naturally,
> being no more than four miles, if so much, but it is not without
> its dangers; and we had a lively taste and type of the perils of
> shipwreck in crossing the bank, a great shoal that lies midway in
> the sea. For it happened that we were later for the tide than the
> Captain had thought; so that, when we were in what the jac-tars
> call the mid-channel, the gallant 'Waterloo' that had come all the
> way from Glasgow like a swan before the wind, stuck fast in the
> mud. Never shall I forget the dunt that dirled on my heart when
> she stopped, and the engines would go no further. Fortunately,
> as I was told, this came to pass just at the turn of the tide, or
> otherwise there is no saying what the consequences might have
> been.

A fellow-passenger from the West Indies distracted Mr
Duffle's anxieties from the potentialities of the Clyde winds
with a rumbustious tale about a Jamaican hurricane, talking
'until the steam-boat began to move, and in the course of a
minute or two ... was paddling her way towards
Helensburgh'. There, at Henry Bell's Baths Hotel, Mr Duffle
got 'a chack of dinner ... and a comfortable tumbler of old
double-rum toddy', after which he felt fortified enough to
inspect the 'hot and cold baths for invalid persons, and others

afflicted with the rheumatism and such like incomes'.

David Napier adapted the steamship for deep-sea routes, and in 1818 put the *Rob Roy* on the Greenock-Belfast route, though later she was sold to serve between Dover and Calais. Napier's cousin, Robert, played an important part in the development of river paddlers, mostly built by John Ward and Company at Greenock, and engined at the Vulcan Foundry, though the first of all iron ships, the *Fairy Queen*, came from the Garscube Road Foundry of John Neilson and Company in 1831.

With the development of the steamships, water, where available, became for a time the fastest, safest and most comfortable means of travel, a distinction it was to enjoy throughout Glasgow's cotton era, until the development of the railways.

Robert Reid (1773–1865), who used the pseudonym 'Senex' and from whose recollections of old Glasgow I have already quoted, has left an account of three holidays to the coast made by wherry in pre-steamship days when he was a boy, between 1778–82. A voyage to Dunoon was undertaken in a hired wherry in 1779, the family having first made arrangement to keep themselves in food throughout the summer, since they could 'put no dependence on getting provisions, not even fish, in such an out of the way place'.

When the day of departure came, the Reid family had 'a pretty fair passage down the river till the tide met us at Dunglass; our progress now became slow, and a little below Dumbarton Castle, we fairly stuck fast upon a sandbank. Here we remained for several hours till the tide flowed, when we again got under sail.'

The Reids were at least luckier than another Glasgow gentleman who, in 1817, mistrusting the new-fangled steamboats, hired a fast, shallow-draught sailing-wherry, known as a 'fly', to take himself and his family to Gourock for summer quarters. In their case, 'all the first day was occupied in making the passage to Bowling Bay, where we cast anchor for the night. Weighing anchor next morning, we proceeded down the Clyde, but were so buffeted by wind and waves that, after spending the whole day at sea, we were compelled to return to Bowling Bay. The third day we succeeded in making Port Glasgow in the afternoon.' Here, they abandoned the fly, hired post-horses, and so reached Gourock, the whole affair having cost the 'wet sick and exhausted' gentleman £7 14s. 3d. Had he trusted one of the new steamers, the *Marion* for instance, the journey would have taken about four hours, and cost him only a few shillings.

It would even have been possible for him to travel by stage coach virtually all the way, for the first regular stage coach service between Glasgow and Greenock began to operate in 1763, taking nine hours. By 1789, the journey time had been cut, and the service was twice daily every weekday.

Throughout the cotton era, there was a steady improvement in stage-coach services, both as regards speed and frequency. The first stage coach to Edinburgh, owned by one William Hume, had begun running as long ago as 1678. Not until 1749, when grants and subsidies were provided by Glasgow magistrates to ensure that the burgesses were given preferential treatment, was a regular service inaugurated, taking twelve hours. After 1758 there was a four-horse coach carrying the mail. By 1789 five stage coaches were running daily between Glasgow and Edinburgh.

The first regular London service, via Newcastle, began in 1758 and took seven days. In 1790, a link through Carlisle was formed, reducing the time to four days. The time for the London mail coach eventually came down to sixty-six hours, and by the year of Southey's visit, 1819, eight coaches drawn by four horses and seven drawn by two left Glasgow daily – one to London, three to Paisley, and one each to Hamilton, Kilmarnock, Ayr and Perth, in addition to the Greenock and Edinburgh services already mentioned. It cost a passenger travelling by four-in-hand stage coach from Glasgow to London – a journey which involved forty-five changes of horse – the sum of £40, a lot of money in those days.

In a private coach such as befitted the daughter of General Graham, Governor of Stirling Castle, under whose care the Bonnymuir martyrs had been held awaiting trial, 19-year-old Helen Graham travelled from Stirling to Glasgow, *en route* for Largs, on Monday 24th July 1826.

The day was beautiful, but very hot.... We changed horses at Cumbernauld, which retains its pristine bleak appearance.... We wended our way over moorland ground presenting no other aspect but green crops, reeds and rushes, till coming to the vicinity of Glasgow rich wood and cultivation rewarded appear. The harvest was completely begun; many fields were cut down, others filled with merry bands of reapers hard at work. The scene changes from this to clouds of smoke proclaiming the entrance to the western metropolis, and distilleries, manufactories, long ranges of buildings in succession, conducted us to the George Hotel, where we had an early dinner.

We then went out and surveyed the new buildings, Blythswood Place, Garden Square, etc., which are very handsome, but rather a steep ascent, for which one is, to be sure, rewarded by pure airs, comparatively speaking, and a fine view. From the heights above, we descended to the regions below, which presented a more bustling appearance, and here the Glasgow *belles* and *beaux* were parading. We saw our old servant, Anderson, in his shop and his little wife, buried in crockery ware and embosomed in hard fish and bacon hams. The town was rather dull, owing I suppose to the present state of the trade, and there were scarcely any equipages to be seen.

We took our departure from The George when the evening breeze began to blow. The streets on the bank of the Clyde I like better than the situation of Garden Square, being more gay and cheerful. After passing through the towns, the environs and country are very pretty, very rich, finely wooded and a pleasing variety of hill, and dale, numbers of very pretty villas extend a long way.

It was perhaps a pity that Helen Graham, who inherited something of her aunt, the novelist Susan Ferrier's, gift for racey character-drawing (as her *Parties and Pleasures*, covering the years 1823 to 1826 show), did not spend a night in Glasgow, for she was a keen theatregoer, and it would have been interesting to have had her comments upon whatever dramatic or operatic fare was being offered.

She could have had the opportunity of visiting the Theatre Royal, built by public subscription in 1804, and regarded as the most luxurious playhouse north of London, within a few yards of the Assembly Rooms in Ingram Street, and accessible both to Argyle Street and the Blythswood New

Argyle Street

Town. It was accidentally burned down in 1829. Glasgow's other theatre, the 'Caledonian' in Dunlop Street, had been built in 1782, after prolonged clerical opposition. It survived until destroyed by fire in 1863. The fate of these theatres, and of some of their successors, differed only from what happened to their primitive predecessors by the uncontrived nature of the conflagrations.[8]

Earlier efforts at establishing theatres had met with burnings 'inspired' by that religious mania which was so strong a feature of Scottish life from the triumph of the Reformers in 1560, to the 1770s, when the tyrannical arrogance of the pre-destined 'Elect' became so ridiculous that the prying domination of every aspect of life by the Kirk eventually produced a revolt against its authority. By the time Burns was writing 'The Holy Fair', 'Holy Willie's

Prayer', 'The Kirk's Alarm' and other satirical hammer-blows, the 'black craws' were already on the run. True, they made something of a come-back among the middle and upper classes in high Victorian times, three-quarters of a century later: but never again was their hold over ordinary folk to be what it had been in the seventeenth and early eighteenth centuries.

Most of the famous actors and actresses, from Mrs Siddons and Mrs Jordan to Kemble and Kean, appeared on Glasgow's stages during the cotton era, plays by Shakespeare, Dryden, Goldsmith and Sheridan rubbing shoulders with pieces like *Raising the Wind, Love Laughs at Locksmiths*, and *The Honeymoon*. There were also the operas of Mozart and Weber, keeping company with Sir Henry Bishop's musical versions of dramatized Scott novels, *Guy Mannering* and *Rob Roy* being the most popular.

The principal Glasgow newspaper was the *Advertiser*, published thrice weekly from 1783 to 1801, after which it became the *Glasgow Herald* (a daily only since 1859). Between 1791 and 1865 there was also the thrice weekly *Courier*. The first Glasgow daily paper, the *North British Daily Mail*, did not begin publishing until 1847.

For those who preferred to read at home, newspapers apart, there were the libraries. John Smith senior, founder of Glasgow's best and longest surviving bookshop, founded a circulating Library at the 'George Buchanan's Head', facing the Laigh Kirk, Trongate, in 1783. Five thousand volumes were available to the public for a yearly subscription of 10s. A rival, Archibald Colbrough, soon afterwards offered 4,500 volumes on similar terms at his shop in the High Street.

In 1791, Walter Stirling, merchant and magistrate, left his library of 804 books, £1,000 and some heritable property for the setting up of Glasgow's first public library, the books being kept at first in a room in the Surgeons' Hall, St Enoch Square, then in the Hall of Hutcheson's Hospital, and latterly in 48 Miller Street.[9]

There were also periodicals like *The Glasgow Magazine*, where in 1783 part of the Dumfriesshire poet John Mayne's poem 'Glasgow' first appeared. After serving his apprentice-ship as a printer with the Foulis Brothers, Mayne spent his adult life in London as a printer and part proprietor of the *Star* newspaper. In 1803, he was induced to complete his Glasgow poem. In its final form it provides a vital picture of life in the city at the turn of the century, as even a few stanzas show:

In ilka house, frae man to boy,
A' hands in Glasgow find employ;
Even little maids, wi' meikle joy,
    Flower lawn and gauze,
Or clip wi' care the silken soy
    For ladies' braws.

Their fathers weave, their mothers spin
The muslin robe, so fine and thin
That, frae the ankles to the chin,
    It aft discloses
The beauteous symmetry within –
    Limbs, necks and bosies....

Look through the town! The houses here
Like noble palaces appear;
A' things the face o' gladness wear –
    The market's thrang,
Business is brisk, and a's asteer
    The streets alang.

Clean-keepit streets! so lang and braid,
The distant objects seem to fade;
And then, for shelter or for shade
    Frae sun or shower,
Piazzas, lend their friendly aid
    At any hour....

Wond'ring, we see new streets extending,
New squares wi' public buildings blending,
Brigs, stately brigs, in arches bending
    Across the Clyde,
And turrets, kirks and spires ascending
    In lofty pride....

Wow, sirs! It's wonderfu' to trace
How commerce has improved the place.

Changing bare house-room's narrow space,
    And want o' money,
To seats of elegance and grace,
    And milk and honey....

Glasgow Fair apart, in the years between Mayne's first draft of his 'Glasgow' poem and the publication of it in its final form, there were other public pleasures and diversions: more than a dozen public executions, always a popular spectacle; a great frost in 1780, and an even more severe frost which lasted for four months in 1785, when the Clyde froze and carnivals were held on the ice; a flood in March 1782, when the Clyde rose 20 feet, forcing householders in Saltmarket to evacuate their houses by boat and drowning a woman in the Gorbals; a fire which burned nine houses in Gorbals in 1786, followed in the same year by what was thought to be an earth tremor; the introduction to Glasgow from Paris by the surgeon John Jamieson of the first umbrella in 1782; and in 1795 the balloon ascents of Vincent Lunardi from St Andrew's Square to Hawick, and from the Merchants' House Garden in the Bridgegait to Campsie. As Burns enthusiasts will remember, Lunardi lent his name to a certain style of lady's bonnet. But his ascents did not always inspire such charming flights of fancy. Up in Shetland, John Mill, a parish minister who kept a diary, remarked sourly of Lunardi's first ascent from Edinburgh a decade earlier: 'Oh! how much are the thoughtless multitude set on these and like foolish vanities to the neglect of the one thing needful!'

The obvious influence on Mayne is Burns, who himself visited Glasgow in 1787, and again in 1788,[10] when he stayed in the Black Bull Hotel, built for the Highland Society in 1758 (not to be confused with Old Black Bull Inn, on the other side of the road). But Glasgow cannot lay any real claim to Burns's loyalties in the sense that Edinburgh can. However, the novelist Tobias Smollett served his apprenticeship as a surgeon in the city, and both James Boswell and John Wilson ('Christopher North') studied at the university. Scott's friend Joanna Baillie – remembered now not for her unreadable and unactable verse dramas but for her little song 'Saw ye Johnie comin'?' – went to school in Glasgow. C.A.

Oakley thinks that she probably played some part in influencing her distant relatives and fellow natives of Lanarkshire, William and John Hunter, anatomist and surgeon respectively, to bequeath to the university their valuable scientific collection, still preserved in the Hunterian Museum at Gilmorehill.

Scott himself was often in Glasgow. He spent some days at Ross Priory, on Loch Lomond, where his friend the Principal Clerk of Session, Hector MacDonald Buchanan, lived. Scott's son-in-law, John Gibson Lockhart, also a Glasgow graduate, has left us a brightly painted verse-portrait of one of Glasgow's 'characters', Captain Archibald Paton, a retired military man renowned for his remarkable precision and dapper dress:

> His waistcoat, coat and breeches,
>   Were all cut of the same web,
> Of a beautiful snuff-colour,
>   Of a modest, genty drab.
> The blue strip in his stocking
>   Round his neat slim leg did go,
> And his ruffles of the cambric fine,
>   They were whiter than the snow.
> Oh! we ne'er shall see the like of Captain Paton no mo'e!

> In dirty days he picked well
>   His footsteps with his rattan
> Oh! You ne'er could see the least speck
>   On the shoes of Captain Paton.
> And on entering the coffee-room,
>   About two, all men did know
> They would see him with his *Courier*
>   In the middle of the row.
> Oh! we ne'er shall see the like of Captain Paton no mo'e!

Undoubtedly the most famous of Glasgow's men-of-letters, at least in his own day, was Thomas Campbell (1777–1844), the youngest of the eleven children of a Virginia tobacco merchant. After graduating at Glasgow, and leading a strenuous and varied literary life the main ornament of which in the esteem of his contemporaries was his long poem 'The Pleasures of Hope', Campbell was three times elected Lord Rector of his *alma mater*, on one occasion defeating Scott.

'Hohenlinden', 'Ye Mariners of England' and 'The Battle of the Baltic' have kept his fame alive among English schoolchildren, though the Scots may prefer 'Lord Ullin's Daughter'. I remember best his little poem, 'Florine', set to music by Francis George Scott; a poem not affected by considerations of nationality.

> Could I bring back lost youth again
>   And be what I have been,
> I'd court you in a gallant strain,
>   My young and fair Florine.
>
> But mine's the chilling age that chides
>   Devoted rapture's glow,
> And love – that conquers all besides –
>   Finds Time a conquering foe.
>
> Farewell! we're severed from our fate
>   As far as night from noon;
> You came into the world too late,
>   And I depart so soon.

In a city which relied on the classical teaching of its grammar school for over 200 years, continuing these traditions in the new school put up in 1787 on the north side of George Square, and where education was inevitably only available to the privileged few, the pleasures enjoyed by the ordinary more or less illiterate citizen were not exactly literary. Brutal sports like cock-fighting had their secret following. But many of the delights of Glasgow Fair were innocent enough, as recorded by the handloom weaver John Breckenridge (1790–1840).

> The carles, fu' cadgie, sat cocking
>   Upon their white nags and their brown,
> Wi' snuffing and laughing and joking
>   They soon cantered into the town.
> 'Twas there was the funning and sporting;

Eh, lord! what a swarm o' braw folk –
Rowly-powly, wild beasts, wheels o' fortune,
  Sweetie stan's, Maister Punch, and Black Jock.

Now Willock and Tam, geyan bouzie,
  By this time had met wi' their joes;
Consented wi' Gibbie and Susie
  To gang awa' doun to the shows.
'Twas there was the fiddling and drumming;
  Sic a crowd they could scarcely get through –
Fiddles, trumpets, and organs a-bumming;
  O sirs! what a hully-baloo.

Then hie to the tents at the paling,
  Weel theekit wi' blankets and mats,
And deals seated round like a tap-room,
  Supported on stanes and on pats.
The whisky like water they're selling,
  And porter as sma' as their yill,
And aye as you're pouring they're telling,
  'Troth, dear, it's just sixpence a gill!'

Says Meg, 'See yon beast wi' the claes on't,
  Wi' the face o't as black as the soot!
Preserve's! it has fingers and taes on't –
  Eh sirs! it's an unco like brute!'
'O woman, but ye are a gomeral
  To mak' sic a won'er at that!
D'ye na ken, ye daft gowk, that's a mongrel
  That's bred 'twixt a dog and a cat.

'See yon souple jaud, how she's dancing,
  Wi' the white ruffled breeks and red shoon!
Frae the tap to the tae she's a glancing
  Wi' gowd, and a feather abune
My troth, she's a brae decent kimmer
  As I have yet seen in the Fair!'
'Her decent!' quo' Meg. 'She's a limmer,
  Or, faith, she would never be there.'

' "She's a limmer", quo' Meg'; in other words, a comely
performer. Good Meg, if she but knew it, was merely
echoing that anti-pleasure principle firmly inculcated into the
Scots temperament by the Reformers, a principle the sterile

resonancing of which sounded down into the twentieth century. To be able to perform on the stage with professional skill may have indicated involvement with 'sinfulness' to the douce Glaswegians of the cotton era; strangely, however, to overeat, drink too much, and dance themselves into exhaustion was hampered by no such kirkly stigma.

> Now they ate and they drank till their bellies
>   Were bent like the head o' a drum;
> Syne they rase, and they capered like fillies,
>   Whene'er that the fiddle played bum.
> Wi' dancing they now were grown weary,
>   And scarcely were able to stan',
> So they took to the road a' fu' cheerie
>   As day was beginning to dawn.

Notes

1 The Carron Ironworks, some 3 miles south of Falkirk, has been founded by Dr. Roebuck of Sheffield in 1760. Burns turned up to visit them on Sunday 26th April 1787. On being refused admission, he scratched some harsh lines on the window of a Falkirk inn:

> We cam na here to view your works,
>   In hopes to be mair wise,
> But only, lest we gang to hell,
>   It may be nae surprise:
> But when we tirl'd at your door,
>   Your porter dought na hear us;
> Sae may, shou'd we to hell's yetts
>   come,
>   Your billy Satan sair us!

2 There were mills at 'villages', like Partick and Govan, on the outskirts of Glasgow, which have long since been engulfed by the city.
3 According to James Cleland's *Annals of Glasgow* (1816), cold baths for gentlemen, ladies, boys and girls, and hot baths including 'five stretching Baths for Gentlemen'. Similar arrangements were made for the ladies, 'the avenues to which are formed with shrubberies, and are quite distinct from those leading to the Gentleman's Baths'.
4 James Cleland LLD (1790–1840) was Glasgow's Superintendent Architect, author and the statistician who took the first classified census ever undertaken in the UK in Glasgow in 1819.
5 At 1972 values.
6 At the time of writing renamed Mandela Place.
7 Not quite true. St Magnus Cathedral, in Kirkwall, Orkney, sustained no damage at the Reformers' hands.

8 A timber shed adjoining the Bishop's Palace had housed performances in which the famous Digges and Mrs Ward, among others, had appeared from 1752. Two years later a sermon by George Whitefield caused the 'congregation' to set it on fire. Glasgow's first real theatre, built in 1762 and opened by Mrs Bellamy, was burned in 1780. It stood outside the city boundary, at Grahamston, where the Central Station now is.

9 The Stirling Library is now housed in the former Royal Exchange Building in Royal Exchange Square. It seems that so strong was Stirling's aversion to novels, he directed that the books to be bought after his death 'should be rather rare and curious than those of the common and ordinary kinds'. The Stirling Library has remained largely a 'technical' library.

10 A plaque on the wall of Marks and Spencer commemorates these visits.

5

The Years of Iron

Cotton and textiles continued to be manufactured in Glasgow in considerable quantity until the 1860s, after which the industry went into decline, partly, as we have mentioned, because of other investment opportunities, partly because of the cotton famine which resulted from the American Civil War, but more probably because the Lancashire mills had gone over to producing cheaper materials, increasingly in demand, while Glasgow stuck to quality production. This decline continued into the twentieth century, accelerating during the depression of the twenties, when 'rationalization' – the buying by an English firm of a Scots firm in order to close it – all but finished off the textile industry in the west of Scotland.

The textile industry in its hey-day did, however, encourage the development of a number of ancillary industries. Charles Tennant (1768–1838) – Burns's 'Wabster Charlie' – founded the St Rollox chemical works in 1800. Tennant manufactured a bleaching agent the success of which resulted in his becoming the largest firm of its kind in Europe, its 436-feet-high chimney – known as 'Tennant's Stalk', the tallest in Europe – depositing smoke over the city and greyish waste around the factory, neither of them by-products which improved the quality of the environment.

Another industrialist, Charles Mackintosh (1766–1843), a manufacturer of dyestuffs, discovered how to dissolve rubber and use it to waterproof fabrics. He set up a factory in Glasgow to produce mackintoshes in 1834, though later the business was transferred to Manchester, where it was owned by the Dunlop Rubber Company. There was also a growing demand for machinery for mills, collieries and the new steamships. But the industry, which, from about 1830 to

103

1870, occupied the dominant position in Glasgow's economic life, was the manufacture of cheap iron.

Iron smelted with charcoal had been manufactured in Scotland at the Lorn Furnaces, built on Loch Etive by the Argyll Furnace Company, since 1754, but the ore was shipped from England, and the iron was sent back there. Roebuck, Cadell and Company's Carron Works, founded in 1760, smelted with coke a mixture of Scots and English ores, but had to import bar iron from Sweden and Russia.

Thomas Edington, who had been a traveller with the Carron Company and later manager of the slitting-mill at Cramond, near Edinburgh, went into partnership with William Cadell in 1786 to promote the Clyde Ironworks, and with John Gillies of the Dalnotter Ironworks and William Robertson of the Smithfield Iron works, to promote the Muirkirk Ironworks in 1789. The Clyde works aimed at providing Carron with bar iron to remove the need, sometimes difficult to meet, to import it, while Muirkirk produced bar iron for general use. Other less successful ironworks came into being, notably at Cleland (Omoa) in 1789, and at Glenbuck, Calder, Shotts, and Markinch around the turn of the century. The trouble with the product of all the early Scottish ironworks was that it was too expensive, priced out of every market except that of Scotland.

As long ago as 1801 David Mushet had discovered the rich fields of blackband ironstone which lay more or less totally unworked in the west of Scotland – 'wild coal' it had been called when it was thought to be useless. The ironworks at Calder and Clyde did use a little, mixed with other ores, but found that its advantages were offset by the difficulty of smelting it in the small cold-blast furnaces then commonly in use.

In 1828, however, the manager of the Glasgow Gas Works, J.B. Neilson, while carrying out experiments at the Clyde Ironworks, discovered how to use hot instead of cold air in the blasting furnace. The combination of hot-blast furnace and blackband ironstone produced the recipe for cheap pig-iron which cut coal consumption by at least 50 per cent and enabled iron to be sent to England and sold there 15 to 20 per cent cheaper than the English product. Low mineral royalties, cheap coal and cheap labour, with a plentiful supply of jobless Highlanders or Irish always available to break strikes, were further factors which gave the Glasgow ironmasters their keenly competitive edge, especially after 1840, when a method of heating the blast with waste gases from the furnaces was discovered.

Between 1830 and 1843 the expansion of the iron industry was as startling as had been the rise of the cotton industry between 1780 and 1790. At Gartsherrie, the Bairds built their first furnace in 1830. Within a decade they had seven furnaces going and were the leading Scottish producers, responsible for about 25 per cent of Scotland's total output. Whereas in 1830 there had been twenty-five furnaces enabling Glasgow to produce about 40,000 tons, by 1843 sixty-two furnaces were producing upwards of 250,000 tons annually. In the peak year, 1870, approximately 120 furnaces were producing nearly a million and a quarter tons.

At the beginning of the 'railway mania', Scotland was thus well placed to supply railway iron throughout the United Kingdom; which was fortunate because, before 1830, with the notable exception of the Carron Works whose finished goods were internationally famous, Scotland was slow to develop the manufacture of malleable iron, in spite of the ready supply of cheap fuel to hand which might have encouraged its ironworks masters to try to do so. The fact was, however, that even Henry Bessemer, whose Bessemer Converter eventually led to the establishment of the steel industry, tried and failed to produce high-quality metal from Scottish ores during a visit to 'Dixon's Blazes'. By the 1850s, several ironmasters who insisted on using local materials were finding it difficult to produce the better grades of malleable iron needed for the propeller shafts of the bigger ocean-going steamships. By the 1870s, the ores found near Middlesbrough were enabling northern England to produce better iron so cheaply that it began to oust the Scottish product, even in Scotland.

Until the arrival of the railways, or at least their immediate predecessor the waggon-ways, heavy cargoes such as coal had to be shipped by water, if any quantity was to be transported. Canals like Telford's Caledonian Canal, and to some extent the Forth and Clyde Canal in which both Smeaton and Watt had a hand, were national in purpose. The

Forth and Clyde Canal shared with smaller connecting canals like the Monkland and the Union the primary purpose of exploiting more economically the natural resources of Central Scotland. By 1822, when the canal network was completed, coal could be sent from the Monkland coalfields to Port Dundas in Glasgow or to Port Hopetoun in Edinburgh. A canal intended to link Glasgow, Paisley and Ardrossan, however, never got beyond Johnstone.

Although a passenger use was developed for some of these canals, and a tourist industry use survived until 1939, they came upon the scene too late to be profitable for long. During the Forth and Clyde canal's first fifty years of operation it is reckoned to have carried up to 3,000 ships annually and to have been paying its shareholders a dividend of 30 per cent as late as 1837.

Shareholders gifted with foresight, or aware of what had been happening since 1824 at the Monkland coalfield, should have begun to think about getting rid of their canal shares by this time. A waggon-way had been constructed from Monkland to Kirkintilloch, leading from the Old Monkton collieries to the Forth and Clyde Canal. In 1826, locomotives supplanted horses on this line, and there is some evidence that passengers may also have been carried over the 10-mile stretch of the main track. In 1828 the Ballochney Railway added three branches to the Monkland to Kirkintilloch line, the result being a dramatic fall in coal prices, first in Edinburgh and later in Glasgow.

The real beginning of railroad travel in Scotland was on 27th September 1831, when the Glasgow and Garnkirk railway, which had opened for mineral traffic in 1827, first carried passenger at 7 miles an hour along its 8-mile length from St Rollox Station. It used steam locomotives from the beginning. Most of those early railways – though, curiously, not the Glasgow and Garnkirk – were phenomenally successful, the benefits they conferred leading not only to an upsurge in the mineral values of the areas they served but naturally, also to a substantial rise in the value of the owning company's shares.

In 1830, the Pollok and Govan Railway Company and the Rutherglen Railway Company were formed, the former with capital of £66,000, the latter with £20,000. These were small enterprises.

The second major Glasgow railway was also originally associated with coalfields. In 1837, the line to Paisley, Kilmarnock and Ayr was authorized, designed to serve the Ayrshire coalfields. (In 1869, the Glasgow and South Western Railway Company secured the unfinished Ardrossan canal and later built their link from Port Eglinton to Paisley along its bed.)

Thereafter, railway development was not tied so closely to coalfields. The Glasgow to Greenock line was authorized in 1837 and was opened for passenger traffic in 1841. The Edinburgh and Glasgow Railway Company, with a capital of £900,000 and a loan of £300,000, linked Glasgow to Edinburgh in 1842, the tunnel between Queen Street and Cowlairs, where a locomotive works was established, costing £40,000.

Since 1832, a railway line to connect Scotland and England had been talked of and some survey work had been carried through; but throughout the 1830s a dispute raged about the route to be followed. The route to connect Edinburgh with London through Berwick-upon-Tweed and Newcastle was obvious enough. The row which developed was over the Glasgow to London link. Should the line go over Beattock Summit, with all the engineering and subsequent operating difficulties this would entail? Or should the line traverse the flatter Ayrshire coalfields further to the west? A Royal Commission formed to investigate the proposals during the years of railway mania, which came to a peak about 1845, had actually favoured the Nithsdale route in preference to that via Beattock; yet in 1845, a Parliamentary decision was given in favour of the Caledonian Railway Company's Beattock route. It opened in February 1848, two years after the North British Railway Company's east-coast route had first crossed the border at Berwick.

Construction of the rival Nithsdale route was authorized in 1846, and the Glasgow, Paisley, Kilmarnock and Ayr Railway was, after an amalgamation, soon to become the Glasgow and South Western Railway Company, the third of the three big companies which dominated railway operation out of Glasgow throughout the nineteenth century.

To the north, the Scottish Central Railway ran up to Perth in 1840, its owners amalgamating eventually with the Caledonian Railway. Travel from Glasgow was further extended to Inverness and Nairn in 1855 – eventually to Thurso – along the track of the Highland Railway, and from 1852, to Elgin and Lossiemouth along the track of the Great North of Scotland Railway.

C.A. Oakley has pointed out that Glasgow had become the second city of the British Empire some forty years before the direct rail link with London was established. Even so, Glasgow Corporation was at first reluctant to allow the new means of travel to penetrate to the heart of the city. Both the Glasgow, Paisley, Kilmarnock and Ayr and the Glasgow, Paisley and Greenock companies had to be content with a station on the south side of the river; yet the owners of the Glasgow and Edinburgh line were able to build their terminal at Queen Street in the 1840s (reconstructed in 1878–80), and Buchanan Street station, the terminal for the companies running to the north, went up in 1849. Although in passenger-carrying terms the London link was by far the most important, the Glasgow and South Western Railway Company's station was kept out at Bridge Street. The St Enoch Station and hotel were not completed until 1880. It was 1879 before the Caledonian Company could bring their trains into Central Station, having previously used Buchanan Street Station or an inconvenient station at the junction of Cathcart Street and Pollokshaws Road. Both new stations necessitated the construction of separate railway bridges over the Clyde.

Both Buchanan Street and St Enoch Stations have been demolished and redeveloped. The levelling of the arches on which the agreeably Gothic St Enoch Station Hotel stood has removed a familiar Victorian Glasgow landmark, though James Miller's subway station of 1896 has survived. Queen Street Station, the work of James Carswell, though modernized internally, still carries its two great fanlights, one of them now obscured by redevelopment on the northern side of George Square.

It was from Queen Street Station that the first Sunday train ran from Glasgow, setting out for Edinburgh on 13th March

Central Station and Hotel by Sir Rowand Anderson

1842, 'filled with peaceful and respectable persons, gliding quietly away on its mission,' as a contemporary journalist gracefully put it. Such a smooth departure must have disappointed the Presbytery of Glasgow, who had denounced the running of Sunday trains as 'a flagrant violation of the law of God as expressed in the Fourth Commandment, a grievous outrage on the religious feelings of the people of Scotland, a powerful temptation to the careless and indifferent to abandon the public ordinances of Grace, and most disastrous to the quiet of the rural parishes along the line of the railway, by the introduction into them every Sabbath, of many of the profligate and dissipated who inhabit the cities of Glasgow and Edinburgh'.

In Edinburgh, a threatening battery of ministers, presumably unaware of the inclusion of their city in their Glasgow brethren's condemnation, lined the platforms and informed the detraining passengers that they had bought tickets to hell, a claim which does not seem to have deterred many of them from making their way towards Princes Street.

Janet Hamilton, a remarkable Lanarkshire woman (married in Glasgow by J.G. Lockhart's minister father), fifth in descent from John Whitelaw, a Covenanter executed at the Old Tolbooth of Edinburgh for his part in the battle of Bothwell Brig, herself unable to write until she was 50 and the mother of ten children, celebrated the occasion in 'The Sunday Rail', which rises to this indignant smoke-plume of a climax:

> Now range up the carriages, feed up the fires!
> To the rail, to the rail, now the pent-up desires
> Of the pale toiling million find gracious reply,
> On the pinions of steam they shall fly, they shall fly,
> To beauties of nature and art to explore,
> To ramble the woodlands and roam by the shore,
> The city spark here with his smart smirking lass,
> All peg-topped and crinolined, squat on the grass,
> While with quips and with cranks and soft-wreathed smiles,
> Each nymph with her swain the dull Sabbath beguiles.
>
> Here mater and paterfamilias will come
> With their rollicking brood from their close city home,

How they scramble and scream, how they scamper and run,
While pa and mamma are enjoying the fun!
And the urchins bawl out, 'Oh, how funny and jolly,
Dear ma, it is thus to keep Sabbath-day holy.'

Now for pipe and cigar and the snug pocket-flask,
What's the rail on a Sunday without them, we ask?
What the sweet-scented heather and rich clover-blooms,
To the breath of the weed as it smoulders and fumes?
So in courting and sporting, in drinking and smoking,
Walking and talking, in laughter and joking,
They while the dull hours of the Sabbath away.
What a Sabbath it is! Who is Lord of the day!

Mrs Hamilton, who wielded a powerful pen on behalf of
the temperance movement (which sought to remove the
palliative of the poor man's despair without doing anything
to alleviate the social causes of his distress), was not, of
course, on the side of the Sunday travellers; but irony
wielded in a losing cause is apt to end up wearing an
ambiguous edge.

The effect of the arrival of the railways upon the fabric of
central Glasgow must have been somewhat similar to that
caused by the construction of urban motorways in the
mid-twentieth century. For one thing, it settled the already
declining fortunes of Laurieston, the Laurie brothers'
housing development south of the river; for another, it cut
broad swatches through medieval and pre-Industrial
Revolution Glasgow. Much of what went had become an
overcrowded health hazard. Unfortunately – and this is not
simply the hindsight of a later generation with different
values – much that could have been conserved, using other
means to solve the social problems, was thoughtlessly swept
away. Up to a point it is fair to compare the way
mid-nineteenth-century Glaswegians treated the heart of the
city with what, say, contemporary Copenhageners or
Hamburgians did to theirs. Our Glasgow forebears do not
emerge with much credit on the environmental side,
however admirable their social promptings.

Their most disastrous decision was to demolish the
medieval university in order to make way for High Street
Goods Station. This had first been mooted in 1845, when a

move to Woodside had been proposed, but a powerful faction of magistrates and professors at that time took the view that a university should remain at the heart of a place and, by its influence, try to revivify it. In Glasgow, however, money has always talked loudly, and short-term economic gains have usually seemed more attractive than long-term environmental advantages. By the 1860s, when a second railway bid came in, the idealists had lost the battle.

There were other implications connected with the coming of the railways: physical implications such as the need for engine building and repair works, like those established at St Rollox and Springburn; and social implications arising from increasing opportunities for quicker and cheaper travel. Only the middle classes were able to make full use of this latter benefit, for the wages and holidays of the working classes did not allow more than an occasional day trip on the Clyde – or 'Doon the watter', to give this all-but-vanished pleasure its traditional local nomenclature.

The increasing number of paddle-steamers sailing from the Broomielaw was making the frequently-deepened upper river almost overcrowded. During the 1850s, the issue between the private owners of these Clyde steamers became one of speed versus comfort. For a time, speed won. The Clyde steamers of the mid-century years were mostly lean, rakish affairs, designed to paddle themselves up and down the Firth with the minimum water resistance, their decks as free as possible of luxury structures which might act as impediments against the wind.

An account of the days of cut-price steamer competition, of dangerous racing in order to snatch away a rival's potential passengers, of steamers banging each other at piers, of captains insulting their rivals through advertisements printed in local papers, and of the sturdy individuality which characterized many of the owner/skippers who operated throughout the Iron Years, has been written by Captain James Williamson, founder of the Williamson Line. Captain Williamson, in his later years a dandy with a white goatee beard, inherited the business created by his father, one of the earliest steamer operators on Loch Lomond who moved over to the Clyde. Captain Williamson himself served his apprenticeship as an engineer and then as a ship's master, qualifications not regarded as essential in the early days of steamboat operation. His book *Clyde Passenger Steamers* (1904) deals, as might be expected, with engineering and other technical developments, but also preserves for us fascinating social glimpses, in the writing of which he was able to draw on his own memories and those of his family.

Some of the fast but primitive steamers, which took the workers away for a few hours from the forges and the foundries and the grime of Glasgow to the mountainy loveliness of the Firth of Clyde at a cost of as little as a shilling for a day's outing, came to an untimely end. Huge prices were paid for the acquisition of vessels to run the Federal blockade in the American Civil War. Many of these frail paddlers were battered to pieces in mid-Atlantic before they could reach their new owners. Those that survived made large profits for their unscrupulous operators.

The railway companies were slow to appreciate the profitability of the steamboat business, and at first left the private operators to vie among themselves for the privilege of running to train connections.

Attempts in 1844 and again in the 1850s by the proprietors of the Greenock Railway (later amalgamated with the Caledonian) and in 1848 by the Wemyss Bay Steamboat Company Limited (an associate of the Greenock and Wemyss Bay Railway Company, also eventually amalgamated with the Caledonian) to run their own steamers failed. To travel by a privately owned steamer connecting with the train meant a more expensive journey than a sail 'all the way'. Even so, the obvious eventual threat of railway competition during these peak years of the private owner was clearly one which could not be wisely disregarded, especially after the North British Railway built a railhead pier at Craigendoran in 1883, and the Caledonian Company opened at Gourock in 1889.

One of the reasons for the provision of these increasing travel facilities between Glasgow and the Clyde Coast was the tendency for more and more wealthy Glaswegians to follow the example of Kirkman Finlay, for whom David Hamilton had built Toward Castle in 1821, and build holiday houses for themselves along the northern fringes of the estuary, turning little villages like Strone, Kirn and Innellan into water-front clusters of ornate Italianate villas with large gardens. When transporting the owners of these summer villas from their places of leisure to their city offices in the morning, and bringing them home again at night, the shorter the travelling time the better was likely to be the pressure of customers. One of the forms which competition took was steamer racing.

The practice of steamer racing came to a climax on 27th May 1861, when two new paddle-steamers, the *Ruby* and the *Rothesay Castle*, owned by rival companies, were both scheduled to leave Glasgow at 4 p.m. bound for Greenock and Rothesay.

Andrew MacQueen, another historian of the Clyde Fleet, has left us an account of this contest in his book, *Echoes of Old Clyde Paddle-Wheels* (1924).

It had been arranged that the steamers were to change berths at the Broomielaw on alternate days. On Monday 27th May the advantage fell to the *Rothesay Castle*.

> Right well she availed herself of it, for, having the lead, she kept it, travelling as never steamer had travelled on the river before. At twenty past five, the spectators on the Custom House Quay at Greenock saw her race past, with the *Ruby* in close attendance. Keeping up the pace, the *Rothesay Castle* finished at Rothesay Quay two and a half minutes ahead of her rival, having covered the distance in two hours twenty-eight minutes. The feat was suitably recognised, the awards being made the following Monday by Bailie Raeburn at the River-Bailie Court, where Captain Brown of the *Rothesay Castle* was fined a guinea for reckless navigation and Captain Price of the *Ruby*, in view of the reputation he had acquired for similar exploits, double the amount.

But Price, who had no doubt provoked Brown, was not to be cured by a mere 2-guinea fine. A few months later, he ran a neck-and-neck race with the *Neptune*, colliding with her twice and missing out Gourock, where he should have called, in order to maintain his lead.

'What right has this man, Price,' thundered the *Glasgow Herald*, 'to entrap people into his vessel for a safe summer-day sail and then subject them to the terror of a violent death by explosion or collision?'

This time the River-Bailie Court provided the answer. Price lost his command, and reckless racing came to an end.

While rail and steamer travel were mostly the concern of the well-to-do, in the city itself the horse-drawn omnibuses, which first appeared on the streets in 1834, carried a broader cross-section of the public. Working men of the poorer sort still preferred to walk to factory or foundry, for low-cost 'workers' tickets were not introduced until about 1894. The well-to-do relied for transport upon their own carriages throughout Victorian times, a status-symbol provoking the same sort of snobbery as the motor car was to inspire a hundred years later.

Robert Frame began running buses at 2d. the single journey between Barrowfield Toll, Bridgeton and Gusset-House, Anderston on 1st January 1845, and before long the magistrates had to lay down safety regulations to curb dangerous speeding by no less than four rivals. The famine of 1846, which raised the price of corn from 16s. to 35s. a boll (six bushels), bankrupted Frame and his rivals. After eighteen busless months, Forsyth, Craig and Mitchell tried running services. The 'father' of Glasgow's street transport system, however, was Andrew Menzies (1822–73), who took over many of the city's omnibus services early in the 1850s. His buses were painted in the Menzies tartan, those of his rival, Duncan MacGregor, in the tartan of Rob Roy. Gentlemen travelled on the exposed top deck, leaving the ladies the shelter of the straw-floored lower deck. Journeys in these vehicles can hardly have been pleasant experiences, especially in wet or steamy weather.

Menzies lived long enough to pioneer the introduction of the railway principle, thereby lowering wheel friction and giving faster and smoother running. After much opposition, his Glasgow Tramway and Omnibus Company was allowed by Parliament to run tramcars in 1870. The corporation laid the tracks, and in 1872 the first horse-drawn tartan tramcar ran from St George's Cross to Eglinton Toll. Menzies died soon after, but his pioneer plans were developed by John Duncan, a Glasgow lawyer. Tramcars eventually ran over eleven routes under private enterprise, the longest being from St Vincent Street to Dennistoun, before the corporation took them over in 1894.

In 1871 the Vale of Clyde Tramways received Parliamentary sanction to run steam cars from Paisley Road Toll to
Govan, but these were not very successful. Paisleyites may
still have remembered tales of the explosion of the boiler of a
prototype steam omnibus in 1830.

Changes were also taking place on the roads leading into
Glasgow. While the Statute Labour Act of 1772 laid an
obligation upon residents to maintain streets within the city,
the roads outside were developed by turnpike companies who
charged tolls to those who used them. The growth of the city
gradually engulfed some of these toll bars, so that some of the
new suburbs found themselves immediately on the wrong
side of them. This meant that suburban residents had to pay in
order to get past the toll bars to reach their offices in the city
centre, and pay again when they wanted to go home at night.
Squabbles constantly arose at the toll bars themselves. Force-
ful, though perhaps less violent, arguments were constantly
being put up by aggrieved industrialists to the Provost of
Glasgow and the turnpike trustees. Although it was not until
1878 that an Act of Parliament abolished toll rights on Glasgow's roads and bridges, an intermediate arrangement was
reached whereby the Statute Labour Trust, later the Police
Board, took over the cost of maintaining any road if two-
thirds of the area through which it ran had been built over.
The toll bar was then shifted out beyond the new suburb.

One of the advantages of the railways was that they cut out
the need to pay these irksome tolls. In a short time they drove
the lumbering stage-coaches off the roads and on to
Christmas cards and calendars. Until the development of the
internal combustion engine gave travel by road supremacy of
convenience over all other forms of surface transport, roads
had to take third place against the coastal shipping services
and the railways. Even trunk roads like that built by Telford
from Glasgow to Carlisle were intended only for light
carriage traffic, and for the driving of cattle to market
centres. Incidentally, the building of the Glasgow–Carlisle
road resulted in the construction of some fine Telford
bridges, notably at Hamilton and Elvanfoot, although
neither was as impressive as his bridge over the Dee at
Tongueland, in Kirkcudbrightshire, or his Cartlands Crags
bridge near Lanark, over the gorge of the Mouse Water.[1]

During the Years of Iron, Glasgow's population multiplied dramatically and the city continued to spread. In 1830 the population had been 200,000. By the 1870s, it had multiplied to half a million. There was a tremendous influx of Irishmen during the 1840s, reaching its climax in 1846 as a result of the disastrous potato famine of that year. Many of the immigrants crossed the Irish Sea on a deck passage costing only 6d. and were virtually paupers when they arrived. They found quick employment in the dirtier jobs which Glasgow's expanding economy was creating; but most of these jobs produced less than the mid-century average wage of about a pound for a sixty-nine-hour week. Irish immigrants were therefore forced to crowd into the cheapest accommodation available, old sub-divided narrowly spaced houses in the wynds and vennels of central Glasgow.

Being Catholics, they usually had large families. Infant mortality was high among them, and the problems of hygiene and health created by so dense a concentration of people in inadequate housing soon became considerable. The Irish also brought with them celebratory habits which did not exactly endear them to the dourer native Scots with the chill of Calvin sobered through several blood-generations. With what money they had, these new Glaswegians drank heavily and roistered heartily among themselves, wakes for the dead involving not only the usual disturbances associated with communal drunkenness but a risk of fire to close-packed properties and the spread of infectious diseases like cholera and typhus. So the basis of such antipathy as there is between Scots and Irish (who, after all, derive from one stock!), Scots-speaker and Gaelic-speaker, Catholic and Protestant, in part goes back to the inability of Glasgow to house adequately the influx of much-needed Irish labourers and their families in the 1840s.

The Irish influx also spread outwards from the old town, causing David Laurie to exclaim in the 1830s: 'We have been submerged by an inundation of Irish poor. They seldom have any furniture which the landlord can seize, and what they have they remove at night.' Under conditions such as Laurie describes the 'moonlight flittin'' was introduced to Glasgow, and there were sown the first seeds of the curious Scots belief that housing is a gift from God, who needs no

rent – a belief which was eventually to result for many years
in the acceptance of lower standards of council housing in
Glasgow than in comparable English towns, and which
latterly helped place on the city's metaphorical back a
staggering burden of debt.

In spite of this overcrowding of the older areas, building
for those who could pay at least some rent was going on at an
unprecedented rate. Tenements of a new style designed to
house the working classes were being put up from about
1830 onwards. These were sub-divided from the start, and
had no bathrooms. In later years, brick towers were run up
the back of these tenements, providing one 'stair-heid'
water-closet between two floors of dwellings, to serve six to
ten families. The inadequacy of such meagre sanitary
provision resulted in conditions of degradation and squalor
which no one who ever inspected them would readily forget.

Within two decades, even these tenements were becoming
so overcrowded that a system was devised whereby a metal
label or 'ticket' was affixed to the side of a house indicating
the number of adults and children (half-adults) permitted to
sleep there. Night-men were employed to carry out spot
checks that the number was not being exceeded, a practice
which had to be continued until after the First World War.

Until the Second World War the middle classes believed in
the adage 'safe as houses'. Most of these working-class
tenements were owned by people who had never seen them,
and were managed by a middleman or factor. They provided
their owners with a reasonable income until after 1920, when
mandatory rent restriction kept that income static, although
the cost of repairs went on mounting. As a result, not only
the old, overcrowded and insanitary tenements, worn out
and overdue for demolition by the end of the Second World
War, but also adequately appointed 'twilight' tenements
capable of modernization for a further useful lease of life in a
city which is chronically short of houses were, of necessity,
simply allowed to deteriorate beyond hope of economical
recovery, the owners of the title-deeds in many cases being
elderly great-great-granddaughters of the original investors
and living frugally on fixed incomes.

The four- and five-storey tenement became the characteristic architectural unit of Victorian Glasgow. Until

about the middle of the century, it was primarily a form of dwelling for the working classes, but after 1850 it was developed as a kind of extension of the middle-class terrace idea. Basically, both tenement and terrace derive from the medieval Edinburgh 'land'.

In order to try to overcome the various problems of balance and monotony which long lines of towering tenements create, certain stylistic characteristics became fairly generally adopted. Because each flat was to be self-contained, and each family would consider itself entitled to rooms having the accepted 12- or 14-feet-high ceilings, the Georgian practice of lowering the ceilings of the upper floors of a building and reducing the size of the windows accordingly, could not be applied. In an attempt to evolve a different kind of variety, the architects of the early tenement blocks usually marked off the first floor either with a heavy cornice or a series of pediments, sometimes with both. The top-floor windows carried no decoration, but a sense of graduation was achieved by putting rather less heavy pediments above the windows of the middle floors.

Avoiding horizontal monotony was a more difficult problem, and the architects of the earlier working-class tenements rarely achieved it. Pavilions were occasionally added, or advantage taken of turned corners to add pilastered decorative work, as on the now demolished corner of Minerva Street and Argyle Street, a block built in 1853 by Alexander Kirkland (the architect responsible in 1850 for the huge sweep of St Vincent Crescent). Later, especially in tenements intended to be occupied by what Sir W.S. Gilbert described as 'the lower middle classes', the tenements had often only three storeys. Experiments were also made with window spacing. The establishment in popularity of the bay window during the 1880s did more than anything else to solve the problem of horizontal monotony.

It is natural for us to think of Glasgow's cliff-like sootened tenements as the hemmers-in of much of the poverty, squalor and violence popularly associated with the city. Yet when these tenements, many now being refurbished, were new and honey-coloured, they must have been spacious, dry and weather-proof compared to the cramped but picturesque thatch-roofed old houses in central Glasgow.

There is perhaps little point now in trying to analyse in detail what went wrong. Many of the broad causes of decline are obvious. But the decline might have been less severe over the middle period of our own century had not political prejudice deflected any practical possibility of help being given to landlords to maintain acceptable housing standards. Many Glaswegians have yet to accept the fact that environmental quality has to be paid for by someone. Neither the now all-but-non-existent rich nor the central government can be expected to meet bills a larger share of which could, without hardship, be met by those who enjoy the benefits.

While the first spread of tenement building filled in the immediate environs of eighteenth-century Glasgow, building was going on further out for those in a position to pay for a fine new terrace house set among gardens. There were three areas in particular splendidly developed in this way. During the 1830s Sauchiehall Road, as it was then called, had 'for its sylvan charms ... long been the favourite promenade of the beauty and fashion of the city'. There was also Woodlands, the hill to the north overlooking Sauchiehall Street. And there was the long, straight Great Western Road, leading from the end of the Cowcaddens straight out towards the West Highland hills.

An Aberdeen architect, George Smith (1793–1877), was one of the earliest to have a hand in the laying-out of the first two of these areas, which together now make up Glasgow Corporation's Park Conservation Area. In doing so, he helped to evolve another characteristic Glasgow-style – that of the long terrace which contrives to achieve a clearly defined satisfying sense of entity.

Smith, whose practice was in Edinburgh, began in 1831 with Woodside Crescent, which once started at right angles from Sauchiehall Street at Charing Cross and curved round up the hill to become Woodside Terrace. Woodside Crescent has now been shorn of its first six houses to accommodate the western flank of the motorway which bisects Charing Cross. Some think it a rather severe terrace of identical three-bay two-storeyed houses, each with a Doric porch; but enough is left of the original curve to give it a graceful binding role at its lower eastern edge of the Park Conservation Area.

Queen's Park (1862), laid out by Sir Joseph Paxton

Woodside Terrace was built by 1842, straight along the hillside, looking south and facing Woodside Place, put up by Smith in 1838. Facing Sauchiehall Street, and back-to-back with Woodside Place, Smith's Newton Place is the simplest and most severe of all these terraces. Smith was also responsible for Lynedoch Crescent (1845), which makes clever use of the westward slope up which it is built. To the west of Woodside Terrace, John Baird built a great mansion about 1842. Wings were added in 1847 to make it into the present Claremont Terrace. These houses have large porches with Ionic columns, and the end-pieces of this terrace are pleasingly emphasized. In the same year, John Burnet senior (1814–1901) added Fitzroy Place, while Alexander Taylor, in Royal Crescent, provided what must surely be the most eclectic contribution to the splendid Sauchiehall Street series of terraces.

In 1854 Sir Joseph Paxton, the designer of London's Crystal Palace, was given a new commission in Glasgow. Already he had laid out Queen's Park, in the south side of the city, and the Botanic Gardens, run by a private company in the West End. Now, along with the architect Charles Wilson (1810–1863), he was invited to lay out a new park which would serve the Sauchiehall Street and Woodlands Hill terraces. Originally called the West End Park, its name has been changed for many years to Kelvingrove, after the river that flows through it. Wilson was also given the task of laying out the still unbuilt sections of Woodlands Hill.

Wilson (who, incidentally, had begun his career as Hamilton's chief draughtsman) was one of Glasgow's finest architects, though he was, and is, scarcely known at all outside Glasgow. The highly original building he put up in St George's Place in 1854 for the Royal Faculty of Procurators, a kind of Venetian palace rich in ornate decorative work, particularly in the lavishly magnificent library, has no equal of its kind and scale in Glasgow, and few anywhere in the United Kingdom.

The crowning glory of his Woodlands Hill scheme was Park Circus, not wholly circular in spite of its name but a flat centre-piece with curving wings and two quadrants separated by roads. The whole conception has proportions of Georgian

Park Circus (c. 1857-9) from Kelvingrove Park, by Charles Wilson

quality, though heavier in detail. The decorative work on the ground-floor masonry, part vermiculated, helps to give it its special character. The convex Park Terrace, with every third house a pavilion, almost French-like in character with steep mansard roofs, as if crowning the hilltop, creates distinction of another order. This terrace, which looks out across Kelvingrove Park, provides an impressive spectacle from Sauchiehall Street or Kelvin Way.

Wilson's final contribution to Woodlands Hill was La Belle Place, with the Queen's Rooms (1857), a classical temple carrying an inventive frieze. Once a recital hall, it is now a Christian Science church. Unfortunately it has had its fenestration altered and its stonework painted. The craze for painting stonework in areas such as this, though the outcome of a laudable urge towards improvement, is much to be deplored, since the paint cannot easily be removed and neighbouring buildings may have to be similarly treated in the interests of terrace conformity if practical conservation is to restore a sense of unity.

The Woodlands Hill scheme was not completed. Some tenements continued Park Terrace round towards the north, but the north face itself was never built upon. At present utilized as a playground for the Park School for Girls, it has for more than a century offered a challenge which no architect has thought fit to take up. Perhaps the time has passed when any kind of sympathetic completion could be evolved.

To Glasgow people, the Park Conservation Area is recognized as a landmark by its towers. Three of them belong to Wilson's Free Church College. As Trinity College, it became part of the university. Its towers and main façades now house luxury flats. The forward tower looks like an Italian campanile; the twin towers have been described as Lombardic. The building has certainly an Italian 'feel'. The tower that once belonged to Park Church is now attached to a contemporary office block.

Wilson built the first of the magnificent terraces which line Great Western Road between the Botanic Gardens and Hyndland. His Kirklee Terrace, originally called High Windsor, was begun in 1845. Standing on a raised bank above the road, it has been described as 'a grand Italiante palace'. Rochead's Kew Terrace – some say Decimus Burton's – (1849), which it faces, is, by comparison, severely plain, though it wears an air of quiet dignity.

Rochead, an Edinburgh man, like Wilson did his stint as chief draughtsman to David Hamilton. He practised in Glasgow for thirty years until he retired to his native city in 1870. Of his public works, the best known are the now internally reconstituted Western Club in Buchanan Street[2] (1841) and Northpark House, originally built in 1869 for two art-loving brothers, J. and P. Bell, to accommodate their pictures and *objets d'art*. The last brother to die, a misogynist and recluse, must have birled in his grave when, in 1883, his former home was bought by a pioneer of women's education, Mrs John Elder, and named Queen Margaret College after Malcolm Canmore's wife. Professors from the university had given 'Occasional Lectures for Women' since 1868, and in 1877 a Glasgow association for furthering higher education for women had been formed with Principal Caird as chairman. At first, Queen Margaret College operated separately, though using the lecturing services of some members of the university staff. By the 1930s, however, numbers and other factors made integrated teaching at Gilmorehill imperative. In 1935 the building was sold to the British Broadcasting Corporation, whose headquarters it thereupon became. The small addition to the back of the building by Charles Rennie Mackintosh was originally used by Glasgow's first women medical students. Later additions have been less happy. The BBC has really outgrown its Glasgow site, additional television studios crowding out the original buildings, while the cars of the enlarged staff have become a street nuisance to the residents.

Rochead's most original achievement was undoubtedly his contribution to the Great Western Road development, Grosvenor Terrace, which went up in 1855. He had already been responsible in 1852 for the eastern section of Buckingham Terrace, where he used cantered bay windows, then an innovation. The western section was completed in 1858. He has been credited also with Ruskin Terrace, but of this there is no proof.

Grosvenor Terrace has a Venetian appearance. Its large number of identical circular-headed windows repeated on

Grosvenor Terrace (1855) by John Thomas Rochead

each of its three storeys led David Walker and Andor
Gomme[3] to observe that it 'looks almost as if a design for cast
iron has been adapted for stone with as much glass and as
little masonry as could safely be allowed'. Unfortunately, the
Grosvenor Hotel, comprising the eastern half of the terrace,
was destroyed by fire during a fireman's strike in 1978. The
facing of the re-built façade has been modelled in fibre glass,
the largest building in the world to use this substance.
Grosvenor Terrace features in Guy MacCrone's Glasgow
saga *Wax Fruit*.

Hard by St George's Cross John Bryce, whose brother
David had been Rochead's teacher, built the charming but
now somewhat dilapidated Queen's Crescent in 1840. A few
years before, he had been responsible for some of the more
elaborate monuments in the Necropolis Cemetery set out on
the wooded area above the cathedral – notably, the Jews'
Enclosure, the Catacombs and the Egyptian Vaults. This
extraordinary conception, born in the mind of Provost James
Ewing in 1832 and fully approved and supported by the
Merchants' House, was intended to be an ornamental garden
as well as a cemetery, the idea being that quiet walks among
the illustrious dead would prove a source of uplift and
inspiration to the living by constantly reminding them of the
fleeting nature of human life. To make certain that these
heady delights should be tempered with the Scots belief in
the sinfulness of pleasure, a reproachful statue of John Knox
by Robert Forrest had already been erected on the highest
hillock.

During the Iron Years, there was also something of an
outburst of church-building, though less extensive than that
which broke out in later Victorian times. When Dr Thomas
Chalmers and 200 ministers walked out of the General
Assembly of the Church of Scotland in May 1843 over the
patronage issue to found the Free Church of Scotland, more
churches became necessary so that those who felt the
individuality of their sectarian approach to a common God to
be the major issue of the age could satisfy their consciences
through separate worship. The Ramshorn Church, around
which many famous Glaswegians lie buried, Lockhart's
Captain Paton among them, came down in 1824. It was
replaced by St David's, which still stands, the old name

frequently applied to it. Some new churches – like Boucher's and Cousland's Renfield Free Church, put up in 1851 but demolished in 1968, or John Carrick's Renfield Street Church (1842), demolished in 1965 to make way for British Home Stores – were familiar landmarks, if not particularly distinguished ones. Rochead's Park Church also went up during this spate of church-building. With the shift of population away from the areas served by central city churches, and the slowly dwindling numbers of regular church-goers, like so many others it became redundant. Unfortunately, an adventurous scheme to floor it internally and convert it to secular use, thought up by the architect Geoffrey Jarvis, came too late for practical consideration. The nave of the church was demolished to make way for an office block, and the tower alone has been conserved.

Another surviving relic of the period is Alexander 'Greek' Thomson's Caledonian Road Church, built for the United Presbyterians in 1856, but gutted by vandals, of whom Glasgow breeds a larger than fair share, in 1965. The corporation of Glasgow has conserved the splendid shell as a 'motorway monument'. Thomson's best work lies outwith the period of this chapter, and is therefore dealt with in the next.

Although many early Victorian Glasgow churches have been demolished – the population drift to suburbia began to gather momentum after the First World War – even the meritorious survivors are too numerous to mention.

The leaders of Glasgow business and social life were mostly bound up with church work in one way or another, and provided the money from which these new churches were built. However pleasing the exteriors of many of them, the thoughts and actions generated within their shelter were often less worthy. C.A. Oakley quotes G.M. Young's summing up of the English counterpart of Victorian inter-church wrangles: 'the stupid self-satisfaction of one side – the prurient self-righteousness on the other – the scolding, the melodrama the self-martyrdom.' For the second time in her history, the contentious antics of her churchmen reflected one of the least admirable aspects of Scotland's way of life. While it is undoubtedly true that the Victorian Church in Glasgow had in its ordained ranks many high-minded

ministers animated with zeal for improving the welfare
services and educational opportunities of the poor, even here
there are ugly blotches, like the story told by one of the
leaders of the reform movement in the city, Peter Mackenzie.
He described the plight of an Irish family destitute in the
street on a snowy January night in 1847, one child out of
seven dead, the mother herself dying of consumption,
victims of a Church ruling that soup kitchens for the destitute
were not to be opened on the Sabbath for fear of offending
the Lord.

Other sources of charity were available, however
imperfect in their operation. Once the Burgh Reform Act did
away with their traditional functions connected with the
running of the city, the Trades House and the Merchants'
House turned themselves into charitable institutions, which
they still remain.

Several circumstances encouraged the rise of the Chartist
movement, which had considerable support in Glasgow
from 1838 until it petered out in the 1850s. The post-war
slump which followed 1815 was succeeded by frequent
'slacknesses' of trade, years such as 1819, 1825-6, 1829, 1832,
1837 and 1840–3 bringing waves of hopeless distress to
industrial towns like Glasgow. There was also the realization
that the Reform Bill of 1832 had enfranchised the middle
classes, but not the workers.

In 1837, the London Working Men's Association collected
the six points which formed the basis of radical agitation into
one document, the People's Charter. These points were:
equal electoral areas, universal suffrage, payment of
members, no property qualifications, vote by ballot, and an
annual parliament. All except the last have come to pass.

'Missionaries' came up to Scotland to organize Chartism
throughout the country. By 1839 Glasgow had five large
associations, mainly based on delegates from trades, factories
and districts. Henry Vincent and Feargus O'Connor, the
most eloquent and the fiercest of the Chartist leaders, both
visited Glasgow.

The disenfranchised, through the Chartist associations,
elected members to an anti-Parliament known as the
Convention, which was to present to the Commons a
petition signed by the masses of the working classes, for the

enactment of the principals of the Charter, If the Commons refused, then there was to be a general strike (the 'Sacred Month'). The Commons did refuse, preparations were put in hand for the 'Sacred Month', and the convention then discovered that it had no organization to carry through its threat.

A petition calling for a 'National Assembly' was presented on 10th April 1848, the year of European revolution. The Government packed London with troops and police, and the procession to accompany the petition was abandoned.

The disappearance of Chartism from the United Kingdom scene was due in part to the prosperity following the repeal of the Corn Law (1846) and the enforcement of Lord Shaftesbury's factory reforms.

In Glasgow, Chartism was riven down the centre almost from the start by arguments as to whether or not physical force was justifiable, the Scots remaining, in general, firmly against any such ultimate action. There were later squabbles over the desirability of allowing middle-class interests to merge with those of the Chartists (who particularly disliked the 'shopocrats', and in a few places founded Chartist stores), and on whether or not to support Corn Law repeal without a demand for universal male suffrage. One of the most influential of the short-lived Scottish Chartist newspapers came out in Glasgow, *The Scottish Patriot* (1839–41). *The Glasgow Argus* (1833–47) was sympathetic to the Chartists' aims.

Although nothing like the Welsh insurrection led by John Frost happened in Glasgow, Chartists were suspected of having encouraged the riot of 6th March 1848. So much distress was prevalent at this time that the magistrates engaged large numbers of men to break stones until more purposeful work could be found to occupy them. A free distribution of food from soup kitchens had been promised by Bailie Stewart, the acting chief magistrate. A mob ostensibly made up of the unemployed gathered on Glasgow Green to listen to a series of speakers urging the people to demand food or money as a right, without any return in the shape of labour, and to 'do a deed worthy of the name of France'.

There was apparently no direct incitement to violence. As

the mob dispersed, some people moved towards the City Hall to find out what further measures for their relief the magistrates proposed to take. On the way there, they broke into a gunsmith's in the Trongate and armed themselves. Rioting then broke out in Ingram Street and soon spread to many other parts of the city. Thieves made off with watches and jewellery, while hungry men and children seized food and clothes. As the soldiers moved in and the Riot Act was read, barricades made out of carts were set up in the streets. Ordinary well-fed citizens were rapidly enrolled by the magistrates as special constables. In the end it took cavalry charges and the arrival of reinforcements from Edinburgh to restore order. There was further rioting at Bridgeton the next day, when six people were shot. *The Scotsman* of 8th March thought it 'unjust in itself' to call these disturbances Chartist riots. They had nothing political about them, and it is unfair to attach their disgrace to any political party, however, rash and violent.' Thirty-five men thereafter received sentences ranging from eighteen years' transportation to one year's imprisonment.

Grim though conditions were for those at the lower end of the social order during the Iron Years, many people found means and opportunity for enjoyment of one kind or another. Glasgow was slow in taking to itself the visual arts. Bailie Archibald McLellan presented his collection of pictures to the city and commissioned James Smith to build his McLellan Galleries, which opened in 1854. When the city heired the collection on his death, the gift was so little valued that some of the pictures were offered for sale at absurdly low prices. Those that were left had to wait for another generation to appreciate the bequest, by which time the practice of picture-buying by individuals to adorn the walls of their own homes was becoming widespread amongst those with money to spare for luxuries.

Literature perhaps fared rather better than painting, although the serious reading public at the time of Scott's death was probably not more than four or five thousand throughout the whole of Scotland. The popularity of Scott among people in the West of Scotland, for whom *The Lady of the Lake* and *Rob Roy* had done so much to encourage tourism, continued after his death in 1832, the young Queen

Victoria being one of his most devoted readers. Thomas Hamilton (1789–1842) produced his novel *The Youth and Manhood of Cyril Thornton*, from which I have already quoted; and John Galt (1779–1839) though born in Greenock, depicted middle-class small-town life in *Annals of the Parish* and Glasgow life in parts of *The Entail*.

William Motherwell (1797–1835), born in a house at the corner of College Street and High Street, the son of an ironmonger, was once thought by some to 'rank close after Sir Walter Scott and the Ettrick Shepherd'. No doubt the tearful 'Jeanie Morrison', which carries the Burns tradition into that slough of sentimentality where it oozed and splashed with feeble but persistent motion throughout most of the nineteenth century, was much to the taste of some Glaswegians.

> I wonder, Jeanie, aften yet,
>   When sitting on that bink   [school-bench]
> Cheek touchin' cheek, loof locked in loof,
>   What our wee heads could think!
> When baith bent doun ower ae braid page,
>   Wi' ae bruik on our knee,
> Thy lips were on thy lesson, but
>   My lesson was in thee.

Despite an interest in Nordic balladry, Motherwell was a member of the group concerned with the publication of a post-Burnsian anthology, *Whistlebinkie* (1835), which brought poetry in Scots almost down to its nadir. The group met regularly at David Robertson's bookshop, 108 Trongate, and in Mrs Anderson's Sun Tavern, in the Saltmarket. 'At the head of them all,' wrote James A. Kilpatrick,[4] 'sat Motherwell, short, stout, and muscular of build, a man of fine poetic sympathies ... a very considerable personality in Glasgow.'

Among the others was William Miller (1810–72), described by Robert Buchanan as 'the laureate of the nursery'; with some justice on the strength of one poem known to every Scots child:

> Wee Willie Winkie rins through the town,
> Up stairs and doon stairs in his nicht-gown,

Tirling at the window, crying at the lock
'Are the weans in their bed, for it's now ten o'clock?'

'Hey, Willie Winkie, are ye coming ben?
The cat's singing grey thrums to the sleeping hen,
The dog's spelder'd on the floor, and disna   [sprawled]
   gi'e a cheap,
But here's a waukrife laddie that winna fa' asleep!'

Another Whistlebinkieist, Alexander Rodger (1784–1846),
neatly summed up the curiously false values generated by
watered-down Calvinism, which were common among
Glasgow's respectable middle-class circles, with

   Behave yoursel' before folk,
   Behave yoursel' before folk,
And dinna be sae rude tae me,
   As kiss me sae afore folk.

It wouldna gie me muckle pain,
Gin we were seen and heard by nane,
To take a kiss or grant you ane;
   But gudesakes! no before folk
   Behave yoursel' before folk,
   Behave yoursel' before folk,
Whate'er you do when out o' view,
   Be cautious aye before folk!

If further proof of such false gentility were needed, there is
the story Charles Mackay (1814–89) tells of the occasion
when the great actor Macready was brought to Glasgow by
J.H. Alexander in 1846. The Lord Provost invited him to
dine, then went to Mackay in a panic for advice when the
actor suggested a Sunday meal.
'What am I to do?' inquired the Lord Provost in much
perplexity, and speaking broad Scotch. 'I'm not that
strait-laced mysel', and wad just as soon gie him his dinner
on the Sabbath as on ony other day; but then I'm Lord
Provost, ye ken, and bound to set a good example. If I were
to gie a dinner on the Sabbath, and to a player too, I should
raise such a hullabaloo in a' the pulpits of the town against
me, as I culdna stand against. If I were no' the Provost, I

wadna mind; and if the man were no' a player, it wouldna look half so bad against me. What's to be done?'

Mackay offered to take over the role of host, and invite the Lord Provost as a guest.

'Ou aye!' said the Provost, 'I'll come, and bring my friends. But ye maun let me pay for the dinner and the wine. I shall bring ten friends, and Macready and mysel' will just mak up the dozen. And you'll just invite as mony as your table will hold. Not a word of contributing; the dinner will be at my expense; but ye mustna' let ony body ken it.'[5]

Mackay, who knew the Whistlebinkieists and had no doubt sunk his pint with the rest of them at the 'Sun', was a brilliant journalist of his period who spent most of his life in the South, although he edited *The Glasgow Argus*, which appeared between 1833 and 1847. In some of his own popular verse he reflected something of the then prevailing British optimism that the millennium was at hand:

> There's a good time coming, Boys, a good time coming,
>   And a poor man's family
> Shall not be his misery
>   In the good time coming.
> Every child shall be a help
>   To make his right arm stronger.
> The happiest he, the more he has,
>   Wait a little longer.

Another of his songs provides an early example of the 'wider still and wider' variety of ballad, though no doubt it found a warmer reception with the wealthy Lowlanders who stayed at home than among the dispossessed Highlanders whom poverty and the Clearances were then forcing to emigrate:

> Cheer, boys, cheer! the steady breeze is blowing,[6]
>   To float us freely o'er the ocean's breast,
> The world shall follow in the track we're going,
>   The star of empire glitters in the west.

The poet hailed as the most promising of mid-Victorian Glasgow writers was Alexander Smith (1830–67), a native of Kilmarnock, whose *Life Drama* (1853), an incredibly uneven performance, caused him to be labelled a 'spasmodic' by his critics, and induced the witty W.E. Aytoun to parody it mercilessly in *Firmilliam*. But Smith achieved one good poem, 'Glasgow', in which he captured vividly the sights and sounds of the city at the height of its mid-Victorian iron power:

Draw thy fierce streams of blinding ore,
Smite on a thousand anvils, roar
   Down on the harbour-bars;
Smoulder in smoky sunsets, flare
On rainy nights, when street and square
   Lie empty to the stars.
From terrace proud to alley base
I know thee as my mother's face.

When sunset bathes thee in his gold,
In wreaths of bronze thy sides are rolled,
   Thy smoke is dusky fire;
And, from the glory round thee poured,
A sunbeam like an angel's sword
   Shivers upon a spire.
Thus have I watched thee, Terror! Dream!
While the blue Night crept up the stream.

The wild train plunges in the hills,
He shrieks across the midnight rills;
   Streams through the shifting glare,
The road and flap of foundry fires,
That shake with light the sleeping shires;
   And on the moorlands bare,
He sees afar a crown of light
Hang o'er thee in the hollow night.

At midnight, when thy suburbs lie
As silent as a noonday sky,
   When larks with heat are mute,
I love to linger on thy bridge,
All lonely as a mountain ridge,
   Disturbed but by my foot;
While the black lazy stream beneath
Steals from its far-off wilds of heath.

And through thy heart, as through a dream,
Flows on that black disdainful stream;

All scornfully it flows,
Between the huddled gloom of masts,
Silent as pines unvexed by blasts –
   'Tween lamps in streaming rows.
O wondrous sight! O stream of dread!
O long dark river of the dead! ...

It is interesting to compare this picture of mid-Victorian Glasgow with Mayne's verse-picture[7] of the city seventy years before. Eighteenth-century Edinburgh had Robert Fergusson to celebrate her attractions, but otherwise the Scots tradition has never been particularly rich in urban poetry, and these two pieces by Mayne and Smith are almost the only effective poems of their kind to come out of the West until John Davidson began to prelude the arrival of the Scottish Renaissance writers.

Glasgow had one strange literary lodger between 1841 and 1843 in Thomas De Quincey (1785–1859), who lived in solitude at 110 Rottenrow, his room stuffed with papers, before returning to Edinburgh where he remained until he died.

The pursuit of music was also much more chequered in Glasgow than in Edinburgh. Andrew Thomson, who apparently organized concerts in Glasgow's College Hall during the second decade of the century, mounted a performance of work called *The Intercession* in 1819. This, he claimed was 'the first time that an entire oratorio had been attempted' in the city. A festival was held in Glasgow in 1821, and another in 1823. But the gentlemen's subscription concerts, a late eighteenth-century institution, apparently had to be wound up because of lack of support in 1822. The opening of the City Hall in 1841, and the Queen's Room in 1857, provided fashionably suitable premises.

The first complete performance of Handel's *Messiah* to be given in Scotland took place in the City Hall in 1844, when one of the soloists was the popular tenor Sims Reeves.

Two music societies – the Glasgow Musical Association, founded in 1843, and the Glasgow Harmonic Society, dating from 1853 – amalgamated in 1855 to form the Glasgow Choral Union, thus encouraging and fostering a love of choral-singing applied to serious works, a tradition still happily with us. Glasgow held what is subsequently described as its First Festival (the two previous efforts not counting, since they did not include choral works) in the City Hall in 1860. During the four days for which this festival ran, *Messiah* was again given, along with Mendelssohn's *Elijah* and *Gideon*, an oratorio by one of Mendelssohn's English pupils, Charles Edward Horsley.

It would be wrong to suppose that those musical occasions were of interest to more than the cultured minority of Glasgow's prosperous middle class. A broader cross-section of the community attended the Glasgow theatres of the Iron Years, though, as with music, the drama depended on middle-class patronage. The Christmas pantomime matinee, for instance, had become an institution by about 1850.

The splendid Theatre Royal in Queen Street, at the corner of what is now Royal Exchange Square, went up in flames in 1829, nine years after a performance of Mozart's *Don Giovanni* had marked an innovation. An advertisement for this performance promised that the 'Grand Crystal Lustre of the front Roof of the Theatre, the largest of any of this time in Scotland, will in place of the Wicks and the Candles and the Oil Lamps be Illuminated with Sparkling Gas'. The previous illuminants were certainly a big enough fire risk, but leaking joints in the pipes carrying the 'sparkling gas' were to result in further theatre conflagrations.

The old Caledonian Theatre in Dunlop Street had fallen on evil times after its Queen Street rival opened. By 1807, its boards were given over to third-rate variety artists like 'Bauldy Cochran, with mouth of alarming dimensions, who would on a pasteboard horse sing "Greenock Post", and "Duncan McCallaghan" to the great delight of a discerning audience'. Unfortunately, neither of these pieces has survived in the recorded annals of Scots song, so we are unable to judge their merits.

By 1825, the 'Caledonian' was up for sale, and the most colourful of all Glasgow's actor-managers, John Henry Alexander, described by an unappreciative contemporary as having had 'a somewhat varied career as tragedian, low comedian, character actor, and heavy gent', tried to buy it, only to find that Seymour, the manager of the Queen Street theatre, had forestalled him. So Alexander bought the cellar underneath the 'Caledonian', and on the night when Seymour opened upstairs with *Macbeth*, downstairs, Alexander opened in the basement (which he advertised as 'The Dominion of Fancy'), with a piece called *The Battle of Inch*. Walter Baynham, in his book the *Glasgow Stage*, wrote of that opening night: 'Macbeth was acted nearly throughout to the tuneful accompaniment of the shouts of the soldiery, the clanging of dish covers, the clashing of swords, the banging of drums, with the fumes of blue fire every now and then rising thro' the chinks of the planks from the stage below to the stage above. The audience laughed, and this stimulated the wrath of the combating managers.'

The magistrates then allocated the contending managers different night for their performances, but when it was the turn of 'The Dominion of Fancy' to put on its production, Seymour hired a brass band to play for his private entertainment above.

A further instruction by the magistrates that 'neither party was to annoy the other' led to Seymour's upstairs audience lifting floorboards and pouring water on Alexander's audience beneath, and later to both houses mounting productions of the same pieces simultaneously. There was a final flurry when the two theatres offered simultaneous productions of Weber's *Der Freischutz*. On Alexander's first night, Seymour's supporters lifted the stage planks during the incantation scene, grabbed the dragon by the tail, and prevented him extinguishing his fumes, to the great consternation of that inflamed monster. However, a piece called *Tom and Jerry* ran successfully in both houses for over a month, ending this cat and mouse rivalry.

When the Queen Street theatre went up in flames, fired off by leaky gas, Seymour opened a new Theatre Royal in York Street with *The Merchant of Venice*, billing Edmund Kean as Shylock. J.H. Alexander then acquired the Dunlop Street, 'double' theatre and rebuilt it as one establishment in 1840, offering in his first season Diamond's *Royal Oak, or the Days of Charles II. Paul Pry, Cramond Brig, Guy Mannering* (with Mackay as Bailie Nicol Jarvie), Edmund Kean in *Othello* and Charles Kean in *Richard III* were only a few of the varied selection of plays with which Alexander regaled Glasgow audiences in the ensuing years of his theatrical reign.

Two other places of entertainment further broadened the Glaswegians' choice of theatrical fare. D.P. Miller, a former showman at Glasgow Fair, made so much money with his penny-a-time Great Gun Trick that in 1842 he was able to open a new theatre, the 'Adelphi', in the Saltmarket. He was the first to bring another famous Victorian actor, Phelps, to Glasgow in the title role of *Hamlet* in 1843. 'The Adelphi' went up in flames in 1848. In 1838 Edmund Glover, a member of a famous London theatrical family, opened 'The Prince's', a converted exhibition hall in West Nile Street, so salubrious that the Western Club booked a box permanently for the convenience of its members. Incidentally, the Prince's was said to have been the first theatre in Scotland to have the stalls separate from the pit.

In 1845, another actor–manager, Anderson, known as 'the Wizard of the North', built the largely wooden City Theatre at the foot of Saltmarket opening with Balfe's opera *The Bohemian Girl*. It went up in spectacular flames in 1845, the embers carrying west to George Square.

Tragedy became all too real at the Dunlop Street Theatre one Saturday in 1849. During the performance of *The Surrender of Calais*, flames flickered around a leaking gas joint in the lower part of the house, but were quickly put out. Panic, however, broke out in the upper gallery, and the occupants rushed for the stairs. Although the street doors were open, some of those first to reach the bottom stumbled and fell, and within seconds the whole stairway was a compressed fallen throng. As the *Glasgow Herald* put it the following Monday: 'The weak were trampled down by the strong – the latter only to be trampled down by the furious crowd in the rear. The noise of the cries and groans, and the struggle for bare life, was most agonizing.' Sixty-five people died, causing especial 'grief among the working classes.... One poor lad in Dunlop Street was the picture of woe. He had taken his sweetheart to the theatre. She was carried away from him in the rush; and in his attempt to save her he had only been able to grasp her bonnet and shawl. With these still in his possession he often exclaimed to the by-standers – "How can I go home to her parents without her, and tell them of this!" '

But the Dunlop Street theatre really did go up in flames

after a performance of the pantomime *Bluebeard* in 1863. We are again indebted to the *Glasgow Herald* – the leading newspaper of the time, together with, after 1847, the *North British Daily Mail* (forerunner of today's *Daily Record*) – for the information that 'the appearance of the conflagration was awfully grand' and that 'sixty thousand gallons of water derived from our noble Highland lochs' were poured into the flames during the course of an hour, providing a spectacle which was eagerly watched by an appreciative crowd, most of whom would probably never have been inside any theatre doors. Patched up after the fire, the Dunlop Street theatre functioned for a further five years until it was pulled down to make way for part of the approaches to St Enoch Station.

If the working man wanted dramatic diversion, he might find his simple tastes more adequately catered for at Mumford's penny 'geggie' which was located at the foot of the Saltmarket. Mumford, a Bedfordshire man who first came to Glasgow with a travelling marionette show, from 1835 offered heavy melodrama at his roughly put-together booth. J.H. Alexander managed to get an injunction against Mumford's 'geggie', forcing it to close. But Mrs Mumford carried on and other 'geggies' were in due course set up, flourishing at least into the seventies and for long making a regular appearance on the Green during Glasgow Fair, along with travelling circuses.

In the Iron Years, the music halls had not yet established themselves, the kind of fare they were later to provide being then offered by public houses. There were also crude and prolonged bouts of fisticuffs, ruffians like Deaf Burke killing Simon Byrne in the ninety-ninth round, Byrne having some time previously killed Sandy MacKay in the forty-seventh round. It was an age of 'characters', too, like The Juggler Malabar; Hawkie, a dwarf with a turn for four languages; and Fesa, who spat on people's backs and then exacted a tip to clean off the spittle from their clothes: the uncouth products of illiteracy and deformity.[8]

Drinking shops abounded, and, as there was no really effective restrictive legislation regarding the sale of drink until 1854, gutter-sprawling drunkenness abounded. Indeed, beer was commonly served by the quart until the 1840s.

Better taverns, like Jamie Begg's in Hutcheson Street, or

the nearby MacArthurs, served food as well as drink. It was also the age of the club, particularly well known being the City Club, a literary-minded gathering which met in the Bank Tavern, Trongate. Its members included the journalist Hugh MacDonald, whose enormously popular book *Rambles Around Glasgow* (1854) makes fascinating, if somewhat wordy period reading. Even better was his *Days at the Coast* (1857), a delightful evocation of the pleasures of the Firth of Clyde soon after its exploitation as a leisure playground for Glaswegians. The Garrick Club, which met in MacLaren's in Dunlop Street, had amongst its members J.H. Alexander and Carlisle-born Sam Bough, then a theatrical scene-painter but later a Glasgow water-colourist and much admired ben-and-glen painter in oils, and Sir Daniel McNee, known in his day as 'the prince of portrait-painters'. A few years ago you could pick up a Sam Bough for the price of the frame. Today, with the renewal of interest in Victorian achievement, his reputation and the price his work fetches have both risen.

Only the middle-class folk had houses spacious enough to allow them to entertain. Enormous dinners were consumed in their homes in the fine new terraces and crescents. The working classes, living in single rooms or, at best, in but-and-ben accommodation, existed on porridge and milk washed down by pennywheep or small beer for breakfast, and on broth and cheap dishes like sheep's head, pig's trotters or salted herring for the rest of the day. They had no inducement to stay at home, and many of those who were not drinking simply stood about the streets.

The class structure was rigid. The upper class comprised the titled aristocrats, who kept very much to themselves. The middle classes divided into upper (professional men and leaders of trade and industry), middle (small merchant and shopkeepers), and lower (respectable working men).

One tenth of the city's population lived in absolute poverty – deservedly, according to the upper- and middle-class Victorian view, probably because they drank or were idle. Liberal Victorians believed strongly in the rights of the individual to dispose of his energy and his property as he saw fit. Charity, however welcome to the recipients, was often bestowed with such cold self-righteous hauteur that it has looked to later eyes like conscience salving.

While bare-footed children played their singing games, their peever and their peeries and bools, in the streets of Glasgow into the twentieth century – they still have nowhere else to play in some of the worst of the poorer districts, though since the Second World War some streets have been pedestrianized and they need no longer go without shoes – at least by 1860 most children were getting some kind of primary education, albeit in wretchedly overcrowded schools. Knox's system of education for all children, involving the provision of a school for every parish – laid down originally so that children might recognize 'the Trewth' as he understood it – as maintained by the Scottish Education Acts of 1684 and 1696, would probably have broken down in Glasgow under the pressure of the Irish influx but for the work of David Stow (1793–1864). Stow had met and been influenced by Dr Chalmers, who, with others, had been instrumental in founding Sunday schools which tried to provide basic secular education for poor children. Stow not only founded his own weekday school for 100 pupils in Drygate, but took the first steps towards overcoming the teacher shortage by founding in 1836 his Normal School for the Training of Teachers in Cowcaddens.

Secondary education, except through the grammar schools, was non-existent. Even so, with one out of every 205 pupils in Scotland receiving a secondary education compared to one out of 1,300 in England during the 1860s, the post-Reformation tradition of the superiority of the Scots educational system was clearly still holding its own.

Technical education was advanced with the founding in 1796 of the Andersonian University, which provided evening classes in arts, law, theology, physics and chemistry, held in the rooms of the grammar school in George Street. A brilliant but bad-tempered professor of Oriental languages and then of natural philosophy, John Anderson, had sensed the desirability of relating the teaching of scientific subjects to the needs of industry, and on his death had left his fortune for the setting up of a university for 'mechanics'. Unfortunately his 'fortune' proved to be much less ample than he must have imagined. However, out of one of these grammar school evening classes which his Will inspired, taught by a Dr Ure, eventually came not only the Mechanics Institute, which was to provide technical classes in many parts of the city, but also eventually, built in Edwardian times on the site of the Andersonian University, the Royal Technical College. This in turn developed in our own day into Glasgow's second centre of learning, the University of Strathclyde. It now incorporates not only the Royal Technical College building, but also the former Scottish College of Commerce, a development of the Glasgow Commercial College which had first been set up to educate aspiring business men in 1845.

Inevitably there were public events and spectacles to provide talking points throughout the three decades of the Iron Years. The Jamaica Bridge of 1772 proved to be inadequate and was replaced by a new one in 1833. The old Glasgow Bridge at the foot of Stockwell Street was widened by Telford in 1819 and replaced in 1851–54 by the Victoria Bridge. Two years later, a different kind of spectacle was the sensational trial of Madeleine Smith, daughter of the architect James Smith, designer of the McLellan Galleries. The family lived in Blythswood Square. Madeleine, by all accounts a pretty girl, too intelligent to be readily confined within the semi-literate female conventions of the age, took to herself a lover, handsome Pierre Emile L'Angelier, a clerk from the Channel Islands working in Glasgow. Three years later an eligible suitor appeared, but L'Angelier was unwilling to give Madeleine up. He was thought to have died of arsenic poisoning after drinking a cup of cocoa prepared by Madeleine. At her trial she was deserted by all her family, except for one brother. She was shown by the prosecution to have purchased arsenic. Because of this, and because she admitted that L'Angelier had been her lover, the public at large pre-judged her guilty of murdering him. Doubtless there would be much tut-tutting in middle-class families, especially those with nubile daughters, when the jury returned the Scots verdict of 'not proven'.[9] Madeleine eventually went to America where she began a new life, surviving into her nineties. Her story has continued to exert a fascination on writers and playwrights, possibly because she was the first Victorian London-finished 'miss' to rebel, in however unorthodox a manner, against social beliefs which did not admit that women had the right to possess either intelligence or the capacity for physical passion.

Next year there was another scandal, less titillating but more serious in that it affected a large number of small savers. This was the failure of the Western Bank, the second[10] of the three major failures in the history of Scottish banking. The Western Bank had been founded in 1832, seven years before the City of Glasgow Bank. Both banks sought to break the restrictive arrangements imposed on Scottish banking by the system of 'closed shop' consultation practised by the chartered banks, whose head offices were in Edinburgh. In order to be able to pay a half per cent higher rate of interest than their Edinburgh rivals, the Western Bank did not invest as high a proportion of their deposits in safe low-yielding government stock as did the others. Also, unlike the older banks, the Western Bank used a large proportion of its resources in discounting ordinary trade bills. Under such working circumstances, clearly, any sudden call for funds through the failure of several clients at once could pose a threat to financial stability. The Western Bank's shareholders and directors included the best known and wealthiest of Glasgow's industrialists, men like the Bairds of Gartsherrie, and James Dunlop of the Clyde Ironworks.

Although for a time the Western Bank prospered, achieving deposits of over £5 million and having paid-up capital of £1½ million and an extensive network of branches some of which pioneered late-night opening in Glasgow, the failure in 1857 of four of the leading firms who were its clients produced exactly the kind of strain under which it was vulnerable. Even so, all might have been well had the Edinburgh banks come to its assistance as some of the other Glasgow banks did. But Edinburgh's banking community chose to risk discrediting in the public mind the whole Scottish banking system rather than rescue its non-conforming rival. The refusal of the Edinburgh banks to accept the Western Bank notes, though well secured by the personal fortunes of those behind it, was merely the most widely publicized aspect of an incident which left a stain upon the history of Scottish banking.

Many famous writers visited Glasgow in these years. Dickens came on the invitation of the Sheriff of Lanarkshire, Sir Archibald Alison, and again in the following year, when the great novelist appeared on the stage of the Dunlop Street theatre as Master Shallow in a production of *The Merry Wives of Windsor* designed to raise money to pay for a curator to look after Shakespeare's birthplace in Stratford. He also gave readings in 1858, when he noted gleefully that three evenings and one morning netted him £600. On 25th February 1869 he made his last appearance in Glasgow.

Thackeray first came in 1851, and in 1856 lectured on the humorists and on the Four Georges in the Athenaeum in Ingram Street. This was the former Assembly Rooms, rented then acquired by the Athenaeum proprietors. It was demolished in 1890 to make way for an extension to the General Post Office, by which time the new Athenaeum in St George's Place (now part of the Royal Scottish Academy of Music and Drama) had been opened.[11] Trollope was a postal surveyor in the Glasgow district during the winter of 1857–8, his Glasgow experiences being reflected in *The Three Clerks*.

Several travellers set down their reactions to Glasgow during the Iron Years. At the beginning of this period, the composer Mendelssohn, on his way back from that Hebridean journey which resulted in the Overture 'Fingal's Cave' and the 'Scotch' Symphony, reached the city in company with his friend and travelling companion Karl Klingemann, Secretary to the Hanoverian Legation in London. On 10th August 1829 Klingemann recorded their arrival from Inveraray.

> In Glasgow there are seventy steam-boats, forty of which start every day, and many long chimneys are smoking. An excellent inn refreshes us; the waiters minister to us with two hands and as many feet, as steam-service in hotels has not yet been invented.... We have seen and admired, Glasgow. This morning we were in a stupendous cotton mill as full of maddening noise as the falls of Monass. What is the difference to the ear? One old work woman wore a wreath of cotton, another had tied up her aching tooth with it. Hundreds of little girls toil there from their earliest days and look yellow. But there will ever exist poetry about it. Systematic order becomes sublime, and the whole swallows itself up in succession, like seasons and vegetation.

Twenty years later, on 14th August 1849, Queen Victoria and Prince Albert spent a day in Glasgow, the first visit of a reigning monarch since the arrival of James I and VI. An enormous triumphal arch was built for the occasion at the northern end of Jamaica Bridge.

Next day, safely back in Balmoral, the Queen recorded her own impressions of that day in *Leaves from the Journal of Our Life in the Highlands*, her artless style strangely capturing her pleasure in the occasion.

Now I must describe the doings of yesterday. We embarked on board the *Fairy*[12] at a quarter to nine o'clock, and proceeded up the Clyde in pouring rain and high wind, and it was very stormy till after we had passed Greenock. We steamed past Port Glasgow, then came Dumbarton and Erskine. The river narrows and winds extraordinarily here, and you do not see Glasgow until you are quite close upon it. As we approached, the banks were lined with people, either on esplanades or on the sea-shore, and it was amusing to see all those on the shore take flight, often too late, as the water bounded up from the swell caused by the steamer.

The weather, which had been dreadful, cleared up, just as we reached Glasgow, about eleven, and continued fine for the remainder of the day. Several addresses were presented on board, first by the Lord Provost, who was knighted (Colonel Gordon's sword being used), then one from the county, the clergy (Established Church and Free Kirk), and from the House of Commerce. We landed immediately after this, the landing-place was very handsomely decorated. We then entered our carriage, with the two eldest children, the two others following, Mr Alison[13] (the celebrated historian, who is the Sheriff) rode on one side of the carriage, and General Riddell (the Commander of the Forces in Scotland) on the other. The crowds assembled were quite enormous, but excellent order was kept, and they were very enthusiastic. Mr Alison said that there were 500,000 people out.[14] The town is a handsome one with fine streets built in stone, and many fine buildings and churches. We passed over a bridge commanding an extensive view down two quays, which Albert said was very like Paris. There are many large shops and warehouses, and the shipping is immense.

We went up to the old cathedral, where Principal MacFarlane,[14] a very old man, received us, and directed our attention, as we walked through the church gates, to an immensely high chimney, the highest I believe in existence, which belongs to one of the manufactories. The Cathedral is a very fine one, the choir of which is fitted up as a Presbyterian Church. We were shown the crypt and former burial-place of the bishops, which is in a very high state of preservation. It is in this crypt that the famous scene in Rob Roy is laid, where Rob Roy gives Frank Osbaldistone warning that he is in danger. There is an old monument to St Kentigern, commonly called St Mungo, the founder of the Cathedral.

We re-entered our carriages and went to the University, an ancient building, and which has produced many great and learned men. Here we got out and received an address. We only stopped a few minutes, and then went on again towards the Exchange, in front of which is Marochetti's equestrian statue of the Duke of Wellington, very like and beautifully executed. We got out at the railway station and started almost immediately.

From the new Queen Street station the royal couple went to Perth, where they spent the night at the George Inn, now the Royal George Hotel, and next day arrived back at Balmoral.

In 1858 Theodor Fontane, the German realist novelist, poet and drama critic (in which capacity he was one of the first to defend Ibsen), made an extensive tour of Scotland. Hutcheson, the predecessor of David Macbrayne, had already linked the Highland lochs and islands with paddle-steamers, and Fontane's *Across the Tweed* is a delight to those who relish descriptions of early steam-boat journeys. It may not prove quite such a delight to those who love Glasgow, for Fontane was one of the earliest writers to make comparisons between the cities more favourable to Edinburgh.

Disembarking from the Loch Lomond steamer at Balloch, Fontane recorded:

An hour later the express took us first to Bowling then eastwards with growing speed towards Glasgow. The sun had long set when we approached the rich capital of the Scottish west, but the dark masses of the houses were still clearly visible in the grey evening light. The question was: Should we stay or should we not? The descriptions with which a Glasgow resident, inspired by strong local patriotism, had entertained us during the journey had not failed to touch the heart and the ear of my travelling companion. For my own part I longed to return to the Canongate and to Edinburgh High Street. By way of answer, I pointed to some of the three-hundred-feet-high factory chimneys, of which a number were to be seen rising to heaven like pillars of petrified steam. The chimney is the most characteristic thing in Glasgow.

This gesture sufficed. From one side of the railway station, we hurried over to the other, where the Edinburgh train was already impatiently waiting, and was giving vent to its impatience by grumbling and hissing. Then there was a long whistle, and, passing Falkirk and its battlefields and without any kind of greeting for Linlithgow, which disappeared like a shadow picture as we passed, we were, after barely an hour's journey, describing an arc around Edinburgh's Castle rock, and could see the city's houses rising to the right and to the left of us – as always misty and fantastical.

Whilst noting that the actual journey time between Glasgow and Edinburgh seems scarcely to have improved in rather more than a century, we Glaswegians may perhaps take some comfort from this evidence he provides of Glasgow's slipping image at the end of her Iron decades, with the reflection that, for all its romantic appeal to him, nevertheless he thought Edinburgh 'a city of clouds broken by flashes of light'.

Notes

1 He also built the original Jamaica Bridge (1833–36), Blyth and Westland's (1884–90) rebuilding largely preserving the appearance of the original structure.
2 Built while he was working for the Hamiltons.
3 *Architecture of Glasgow* (1968).
4 *Literary Landmarks of Glasgow* (1898).
5 *Forty Years Recollections* (1877).
6 Credited by J.H. Millar in his *A Literary History of Scotland* (1903) to Mackay, but by Harold Scott in his *English Song Book* (1938) to Henry Russell.
7 See page 96.
8 Some of them commemorated in a Victorian poster, reprinted in 1970.
9 Which has been said to mean: 'We know you did it but we can't prove you did!'
10 That of the first, the Douglas, Heron and Company Bank in Ayr in 1773, does not directly concern us here, although some prominent Glaswegians suffered severely as a result of its fall.
11 The St George's Place frontage dates from 1886, the Buchanan Street section from 1891–93. The original decision to form an Athenaeum arose out of a meeting held in Steele's Coffee-House on 10th January 1847.

Having taken in the former Liberal Club, it became the Royal Scottish Academy of Music and Drama, which, in 1987, moved to new purpose-built premises at the top of Hope Street, opposite the Theatre Royal.

12 The Royal Yacht, anchored in Rosneath Bay, in the Gareloch.

13 Sir Archibald Alison (1792–1867) was the author of *A History of Europe*, which in its day was widely read.

14 The Sheriff was evidently a believer in royal flattery! *The London Illustrated News* gives the figure of 40,000.

15 Duncan MacFarlane was principal of Glasgow University from 1823–58.

6

Steel into Ships

As the century of the internal combustion engine moves towards its close, the world has been sharply reminded of the finite nature of the supply of fossil fuels, especially oil. Even although in these islands there are believed to be reserves of coal to last three hundred years, the political cost of mining it may prove an intractable factor. Victorian prosperity was built upon the availability of very cheap coal. 'Coal,' a late Victorian, Stanley Jervis, put it, 'stands not beside but entirely above all other commodities.' It is therefore perhaps strange that in human terms the working conditions of the collier should have been the worst imaginable.

Until an Act of 1775, miners were bound for life to a particular colliery, serfs wearing a collar with their owner's name upon it, unable to get employment elsewhere and certain to be returned if they escaped. Such powers of enforced recall, which operated most strongly when there was the most widespread distress among miners, were finally removed by a further Act of 1799. When the report of the commission appointed by Lord Ashley, later Earl of Shaftesbury, came out in 1842, it was found that the most frightful conditions of employment existed in the east of Scotland, where women and very young children were still being employed to haul coal to the pithead, up to two tons a day being surfaced in this way for a daily wage of less than 2s.

During the eighteenth century the mines in Glasgow, on the banks of the Kelvin, round Jordanhill and elsewhere, merely supplied local domestic needs. The rise of the iron industry on Glasgow's doorstep greatly stepped up the demand for coal. While in the west the industry was organized, broadly speaking, on more up-to-date social lines than in the east, the construction of miners' rows – but-and-ben dwellings built as cheaply as possible and in close proximity to the pitheads – tended to make miners a race apart, and to create both human and environmental difficulties which have still not been fully overcome.

The earliest known figure for Scottish coal production was recorded for the year 1854, when just under 7½ million tons were mined, of which about probably one-third went to the iron works. As the iron industry declined, its share of coal consumption came down to 16 per cent by the early 1870s. By then, many of the iron masters were also coal masters, firms like William Baird[1] and Company and Merry and Cunninghame owning substantial coal interests. After a boom in the early 1870s, particularly after production began to rise as coal was won from new pits sunk in anticipation of a continuing boom, Scottish coalmasters both in the east and the west found themselves competing against each other for export markets.[2] From about 1873 onwards, the industry was no longer able to rely on the ironworks as its major customer and was forced to adapt itself to the needs of foreign markets, at a time when international competition was growing and coal production in Germany was steadily increasing. That it only partially succeeded in doing so has been attributed variously to the coalmasters for failing to produce in sufficient quantity the kind of coals European customers wanted, and to the Scots miners for adjusting their output in relation to wage fluctuations, thus making it difficult for the industry to take advantage of periods of increased demand.

It was in mid-Victorian times, too, that the forerunner of the fuel which was eventually to challenge coal began to be produced. James 'Paraffin' Young, born in 1811, had learned cabinet-making in Glasgow but attended the chemistry lectures of Professor Graham at Anderson's College to such advantage that, in the easy-going academic fashion of the day, Young became assistant at University College after Graham had gone there in 1837. Later he was appointed assistant to the Professor of Chemistry at University College, London, and Chemist at Tennant's Chemical Works, Manchester. In 1848 Professor Lyon Playfair consulted Young about a petroleum spring found in a Derbyshire coal seam. Young erroneously decided that the oil was produced by the natural distillation of coal and coaly substances. In 1850, while following through his investigations at Boghead, near Bathgate, from where a sample of coal had been sent to him by the manager of Glasgow Gasworks, Hugh Bartholomew, Young discovered an oil shale which yielded 120 gallons of oil per ton. He therefore took out a patent for the production of oil from bituminous coal, and started distilling near Bathgate.

For a time the Scottish shale-oil industry flourished in this region mid-way between Glasgow and Edinburgh, but the winning of the shale from deep mines and the crushing and subsequent distilling made it a laborious process. The industry survived well into the twentieth century, but from 1870 onwards American competition began to tell against it, and paraffin eventually became a by-product from imported crude oil produced in the refining of petrol.

However, the development which opened up a new wave of prosperity for Glasgow depended not upon shale oil, but upon coal and iron. Malleable iron has the advantage over other forms in that it can be bent, twisted, welded or riveted. Steel was to offer malleability together with the strength of the hard but brittle cast iron.

Attempts to produce steel in Scotland began in 1857, but the unsuitability of Scottish pig-iron had defeated even Bessemer himself. Then in 1871 the Siemens-Martin acid open-hearth process – and during the 1880s, the improved Gilchrist-Thomas process, which enabled Scots pig-iron to be used with the Bessemer converter – was adopted at Hallside, Newton, this time with success, and the Steel Company of Scotland was formed. Two years later, it acquired the Blochairn works at St Rollox, Glasgow, a year after William Beardmore set up his works at Parkhead. Soon there were other Scottish steel producers, including David Colville and Sons at Motherwell, the Glasgow Iron and Steel Company at Wishaw, and Merry and Cunninghame at Glengarnock, where, after 1885, Bessemer steel was produced. By 1900 there were 115 open-hearth furnaces in or around Glasgow, producing just under 617,000 tons of finished steel in various forms.

From the beginning, the steel industry became closely linked with shipbuilding on the Clyde. These two industries together sustained much of Glasgow's prosperity until the First World War, while the iron industry declined in the face of the continuing importation of raw materials from the Cleveland field, and the increasing international competition facing the 'finished' product.

Because of its nearby mineral deposits and the advantages of a great waterway, Glasgow was well suited for development as a major centre of the shipbuilding and marine engineering industries. Coal, iron ore, and the technique of producing iron and steel lay to hand. At first the Clyde was not deep enough to receive imports such as copper ore from Sweden, Spain and other countries, to bring large ships up to the city or to carry the launching burdens of Clyde-built tonnage. But a series of deepening operations, beginning with the invention of piers built into the river to induce a self-scouring deepening action by the Chester Engineer John Golborne in 1768, and continuing with further deepening and widening operations in the early years of the nineteenth century, turned Glasgow into a port and changed Port Glasgow into an engineering and manufacturing town.

These were not, of course, overwhelming advantages so long as ships were constructed of wood; but Bell's *Comet*, built by John Wood of Port Glasgow and engined by David Napier, secured for the Clyde a national lead which was in due course turned to good advantage.

The early steamboats did not at first venture beyond the Clyde estuary. They then began to extend their range down the English coast, across to Ireland, and over the English Channel. The first steamship to cross the Atlantic, the *Sirius*, was built in Leith, but it was engined by Wingate and Company of Glasgow.

The Clyde came fully into its own when iron was substituted for wood in the construction of ships. The first two Clyde-built iron ships were the *Vulcan* (1818) and the *Fairy Queen* (1831), built for service on the Forth and Clyde Canal. The Clyde's first seagoing iron ships were the *Royal George* and the *Princess Royal* both built by Tod and MacGregor for service between Glasgow and Liverpool.

In 1840 the founding of the Cunard Company, whose

purpose was to maintain a regular service across the Atlantic, proved to be an enormous stimulus to Clyde shipbuilding. Early Cunard paddle-steamers like the *Britannia*, the *Caledonia* and the *Columbia* had wooden hulls. The *Great Britain* – a wreck for many decades on the Falkland Islands but recently salvaged and brought back to her native port of Bristol for conservation – was built in 1844 with a single screw instead of paddles. The advantages of screw propulsion over paddlers soon became apparent, particularly after 1850, when the Inman Line challenged the Cunard Company by putting two screw steamers on the run, the *City of Glasgow* and the *City of Manchester*. As a result, the Cunard Company adopted the iron hull in 1855, and in 1862, went over to screw propulsion with their ship the *China*.

There was much disputation at first over the relative advantages of the two methods of propulsion but, as a contemporary writer put it: 'Situated as it is at the stern of the vessel and fully immersed, the screw acts upon relatively a much larger volume of water in a given time than paddle wheels, and its efficiency is not impaired by the rolling and pitching motions of the vessel or completely nullified by variations in the ship's draught as with paddles.'

Paddle steamers continued to be built for river work, or where care in manoeuvring in and out of piers was essential, as in the competitive short-haul circumstances of the Clyde Estuary, where the last British sea-going paddle steamer, the second *Waverley*, was launched as recently as 1946. But in wider waters, screw propulsion quickly gained the mastery. Coasters and cargo ships continued to be built with single screws. By 1889 Clyde-built passenger ships were being equipped with twin screws.

The first steel ship was produced by Denny of Dumbarton in the 1870s for the Union Steamship Company of New Zealand. The first steel Cunarder, the *Servia*, one of many of her line to win the Blue Riband, came from Clydebank in 1880.

John Elder, developing ideas derived from James Watt, invented the first compound, as opposed to single-action, engine in 1854, reducing coal consumption by from 30 to 40 per cent. Elder's invention of the surface condenser, which made unnecessary the use of sea water, damaging to boilers,

followed in 1858. The perfecting of the triple expansion
engine in 1886, and the quadruple in 1896, reduced coal
consumption still further, and made possible the use of three
or four propellers, with consequent gain in size of ship and
speed.

The inability of the early steamboats to carry sufficient coal
to enable them to undertake long hauls resulted in the
continuing construction of sailing ships, particularly for the
East India and China trades with Glasgow and other parts.
Alexander Stephen built the first Clyde clipper at Linthouse
in 1862. Clippers were still being built on the Clyde – as
many as 185 of them, between 1890 and 1894. After that
year, there was a rapid fall in their construction rate.

This was due in some measure to the invention of the
turbine engine by the Honourable C.A. Parsons. The
Turbinia the prototype of a method of propulsion described
by Lord Kelvin as 'the greatest advance in steam-engine
practice since the days of Watt', was followed by the
construction of two steamers for Clyde service by Denny of
Dumbarton in 1901 and 1902. In her prime the *King Edward*
reached a speed of 20½ knots and was extremely economical
in coal. She saw service on the Clyde until 1951, and to her
last sailing maintained a smoothness, an absence of vibration
few ships of her size have since equalled. Her engines are now
preserved in the Kelvingrove Art Galleries, Glasgow.

The Cunard Company thereupon adopted turbine engines
for their *Carmania* and more famous *Lusitania*, built at
Clydebank in 1910 and the taker of the Blue Riband from a
German rival with an Atlantic crossing time of 4 days, 10
hours, 41 minutes, a far cry from the eighteen days taken by
the *Sirius* in 1838 from Cork to New York. The *Lusitania*,
however, was sunk by a German torpedo during the First
World War, taking with her, among many others, the
Spanish composer Granados.

Naval orders did much to help swell the total of Clyde
shipbuilding in Edwardian days. By the outbreak of the 1914
war, Clyde yards were building about half the world's
tonnage, and employing not far short of 100,000 workmen,
including those engaged in the ancillary trades.

Up to and including the development of the steam turbine,
the Clyde had consistently led the way. The distinction of

building the first oil-fired diesel ship went, not to the Clyde but to Denmark, where the *Selandia* took to the water at Copenhagen in 1912. This was, in a sense, the harbinger of bad times for Clyde shipbuilding; but the days of decline belong to a later chapter.

Throughout the decades when steel-making and shipbuilding were the dominant Glasgow industries, the range of manufactures and industries was constantly widening. An enthusiastic Glaswegian of the late 1870s, declared that nothing any civilized man could want was then not manufactured in or around the city. This was partly because the fitting out of ships also called for many of the products associated with domestic or hotel use.

Opinions might differ as to the reasonable wants of a civilized man. Certainly in 1804 Dr John Strang, the City Chamberlain and author of *Glasgow and Its Clubs*, was able proudly to claim that:

> Glasgow unites within itself a portion of the cotton-spinning and weaving manufactures of Manchester, the printed calicos of Lancashire, the stuffs of Norwich, the shawls and mousselines of France, the silk-throwing of Macclesfield, the flax-spinning of Ireland, the carpets of Kidderminster, the iron and engineering works of Wolverhampton and Birmingham, the pottery and glass-making of Staffordshire and Newcastle, the shipbuilding of London, the coal trade of the Tyne and Wear, and all the handicrafts connected with, or dependent on, the full development of these. Glasgow also has its distilleries, breweries, chemical works, tan-works, dye-works, bleachfields and paper manufactories, besides a vast number of staple and fancy handloom fabrics which may be strictly said to belong to that locality.

One of these 'fancy fabrics' was the Paisley shawl, woven on hand-looms and using designs of Indian origin, including that cone-like fertility symbol, the cornucopia; no doubt one of the reasons why, between about 1830 and 1875, a Paisley shawl was considered an appropriate gift for a bride. Cheap printed imitations costing about a quarter of the price of the genuine article, along with changing ideas on dress, eventually destroyed the fashion for these beautiful local products.

Another form of decorative production came from the Saracen Head Foundry at Possilpark, owned by Walter McFarlane and Company, who had originally begun their operations beside the 'Saracen's Head' in the Gallowgate. Their delicately designed cast-iron ornamental railings were used by architects all over the world; but their range of products included bandstands, ornamental lamp-posts and gates, garden-seats, fountains and many other elegant objects regarded as essential outdoor 'furniture' in Victorian and Edwardian times, but despised during the neo-Georgian years and often destroyed. Today, the little that survives is being reinstated for its period charm.

Carpets, mentioned by Dr Strang, are both useful and decorative. Three Scots inventions made in the 1820s and 1830s established the industry in Ayrshire, Edinburgh and Glasgow: the discovery by a Kilmarnock engineer, Thomas Morton[3] of a way to produce three-ply fabrics, and later the more colour-versatile two-ply, which also wear better; the discovery by Richard Whytock in Edinburgh of a new method of weaving which resulted in 'tapestry carpets'; and the discovery by James Templeton in Glasgow of how to apply the chenille shawl principle to the making of Axminster carpets.

Templeton set up a Glasgow factory, which was burned out in 1856. After carrying on business for a time in an old mill, expansion made necessary the construction of a new factory in 1889. Because it faced Glasgow Green, the city fathers rejected several proposed designs. In exasperation, the directors of Templetons told their architect, William Leiper[4] (1839–1916), to copy any building which was generally accepted as a masterpiece. The result was the re-creation of something similar to the Doge's Palace of Venice, in colourful poly-chrome tile with stone dressing. Unfortunately, the engineer's dislike of the architect resulted in the collapse of part of the structure while it was going up, and caused the death of twenty-nine weavers who were in an adjoining shed. However, the building has outlived its unlucky beginning, and although it is not exactly one of Scotland's more native architectural treasures, at least its brilliant bizarreness has won itself a place in the affections of Glaswegians. Today, it is incorporated in a centre for small business.[5]

The tradition for fine printing in the production of books

founded by the Foulis brothers in the eighteenth century reasserted itself, though adapted to suit a changed demand. Firms like William Collins, Sons and Company, Blackie and Son and Robert MacLehose and Company provided books for the general reader rather than for scholars or connoisseurs. George McCorquodale, who hailed from Argyll, set up a printing factory in Glasgow in 1854, and established a reputation for stationery, boxes and posters. Paper-making also flourished in and around Glasgow.

While soap-making seems to have been established at Greenock in 1667, and soap was one of Glasgow's staple industries by 1700, its manufacture for exports was begun by Charles Tennant in 1803 at his St Rollox Chemical works, which also specialized, in the production of the acids and alkalis necessary to every centre of industry, and produced most cheaply locally.

It was surely ill-luck for Glasgow that the Leblanc method of alkali production was displaced by the more efficient Solway process, which involved the action of ammonium bicarbonate solution on strong brine, and therefore made Cheshire, with its salt-beds, a more natural location for this method of production than Scotland. As a result of this switch of emphasis, amalgamations occurred which led to Scottish closures, the Irvine and Eglinton Chemical Companies and the St. Rollox company forming the United Alkali Company.

Other firms specialized in producing chemicals like phosphates, cyanide (used extensively in South African gold-mining) and later in the manufacture of iodine from kelp. Here, too, ill-luck befell. In the 1860s and 1870s, Whiteinch Chemical Works produced virtually all the iodine for the United Kingdom. The opening up of foreign deposits of potash resulted in a decline in the value of potash salts, and the collapse of the Scots iodine industry in the ensuing competition. The company founded by Alfred Nobel in 1873 introduced the manufacture of explosives, though necessarily away from Glasgow, among the sand-dunes of Ardeer, Ayrshire, and with the opening of subsequent branch factories soon became a major employer. It is now a division of Imperial Chemicals Industries.

American industries began to arrive in the Glasgow area

during the high Victorian period. Singers, the makers of sewing-machines, started their Scottish operations with a factory in Glasgow in the early 1880s and soon afterwards moved out to Clydebank. Babcock and Wilcox, the industrial 'child' of an American parent company, started their British operations at Renfrew in 1895, and in 1910 acquired premises at Dumbarton. The arrival of Swedish and American firms in the Glasgow area was hailed at the time as a Scottish triumph. No doubt it was, in the short term. Some of these companies are still with us. The influence of foreign-owned enterprises in the long term, however, was to prove a different proposition.

In pottery, Glasgow delft won itself a high reputation. The clay came from Devonshire, the ships that brought it returning south laden with coal. The craftsmen originally came from Holland, hence the name. Firms like the Verrefield Company, the Glasgow Pottery Company and the Britannia Pottery Company produced characteristic domestic and decorative ware, some of which, including the famous 'wally dugs' (china dogs) have now become collectors' pieces. Incidentally, in 1890 Glasgow received one of the most remarkable pieces of pottery ever devised, the Doulton Fountain symbolizing Victoria reigning over her people. It was designed by A.E. Pearce for Messrs Doulton to display at the exhibition of 1888, presented to the city and re-erected on Glasgow Green.

But for all this diversification developing alongside steelmaking and shipbuilding from 1870 onwards, the accent of economic importance was upon the heavy industries. Pipes and tubes were manufactures in Glasgow in the mid-Victorian period, and A. and J. Stewart, a firm founded in the 1860s, eventually became the largest manufacturers of butt and lap-welded tubes in the United Kingdom, amalgamating with Lloyd and Lloyd of Birmingham to become Stewart and Lloyds. The production of steam locomotives, as well as the rails for them to traverse great tracts of the world upon, became another Glasgow speciality. In the early days, the manufacture of locomotives was generally combined with marine engineering, but in the 1850s the industries began to go their separate ways. A son of the inventor of the hot-blast furnace founded Neilson and

Lord Kelvin (1913) by A. Macfarlane Shannon, in Kelvingrove Park

Company in 1836, the first Glasgow firm to specialize in locomotive building at their Hyde Park Works, Springburn. They were one of the three firms which merged to form the North British Locomotive Company in 1903.

Throughout the final decades of Queen Victoria's reign, Glasgow concentrated successfully on its heavy engineering, but so exclusively that for the first time in its commercial and industrial history, no major new industry was coming along behind, so to say, to take over the next phase, as cotton had succeeded tobacco, iron had succeeded cotton, and steel and shipbuilding had succeeded iron.

Some light industries were introduced to Glasgow. Just before the middle of the century, Kelvin and Colville – later Kelvin, Hughes Limited – began, through its association with Lord Kelvin, the manufacture of electrical instruments, some of which were used in the laying of the first Atlantic cable. Two other industrially minded academics, Professors Barr and Stroud, started to produce range-finders in 1890, founding the instrument-making firm which still bore their name into the present century. Mavor and Coulson began experimenting with electrically-driven coal-cutting machinery in 1897, and eventually specialized in it. And there were others.

Unfortunately, Glasgow missed out on the two industrial developments which were to prove most significant in the early part of the twentieth century, the motor-car and the aeroplane. Glasgow's attempts to introduce these new industries were also subjected to ill luck.

The first all-Scottish car, based on the Daimler, was produced by George Johnston, whose Mo-Car Syndicate, later the Arrol-Johnston Company, began to manufacture vehicles commercially in 1896. Fire destroyed the Glasgow foundry in 1901, but production moved first to Paisley and then to Dumfries, where it survived into the 1920s. The Beardmore company produced a car in the former Paisley works of Arrol-Johnston. The A.B.C. Company and the Bergius Company also tried their hands at car production, the latter soon abandoning the motor-car in order to develop their Kelvin engine for marine use. None of these companies survived the slump years as makers of motor-cars.

The two most successful car producers were the Albion

Company, founded in Glasgow in December 1899, and the Argyll Motor Company founded in 1905. In 1912, Albion abandoned the production of cars to concentrate on making lorries, and was eventually absorbed by British Leyland. Alexander Govan's Argyll car, modelled on the French Darracq, which in turn was modelled on the Renault, was first produced at Bridgeton.

Govan realized the potential of his product, and built an imposing red-sandstone factory at Alexandria, Dunbartonshire, which opened in 1906. Unluckily, Govan died a few months later, in his fortieth year. His company struggled on, concentrating on the development of the single-sleeve valve engine, a course which led to prolonged litigation with the Daimler company, who claimed infringement of patent rights, and led to the liquidation of Argyll Motors in 1914. A new company formed to continue production at Bridgeton also went into liquidation in 1920. Incidentally, the Glasgow inventor of the single-sleeve valve engine, Peter Burt, founded the firm which later became the Acme Wringer Company. They also built airships, including the R.34, the first airship to cross the Atlantic.

An unlucky death also removed the man of vision from the Scottish aeronautical scene at a crucial stage of development. Percy Pilcher, a lecturer in naval architecture at Glasgow University who achieved the first successful glider flight at Cardross in 1895, had made considerable progress in designing a powered aircraft when he was killed in a glider accident in 1899. Both the Argyll Company and Beardmores designed aero-engines, the latter providing more engines than any other company for the Royal Flying Corps machines between 1914 and 1916. Here again, there was apparently no realization of the need for a follow-through, the market for Scotland's ships and heavy engineering products creating a false sense of prosperity given temporary buoyancy by replacement needs after the end of World War I in 1918.

Men of vision had seen the dangers of concentration upon too narrow an industrial front for long enough. As early on in Glasgow's steel and shipbuilding era as 1886 Dr John Oswald Mitchell, author of *Memoirs and Portraits* and *Old Glasgow Essays* was writing:

Glasgow has lived through many a trying season, and probably
she has still vitality to revive now. But the *felix arbor* is not sound
at the roots. Chicago and Glasgow have been likened to each
other, for their rapidity of Growth. But Chicago depends on
wheat, which grows, and Glasgow every year more and more
depends on minerals, which do not grow. Here and there grass
grown blocks of slag tell where a great iron-work once blazed
that has blazed its iron-stone all away; or a weather-blown heap
of shale tells where the pant-engine has sent up its last batch of
coal. As the exhaustion of minerals advances, our industry, and
with it our commerce, must fall back, and the general suffering
can only end when the population shall have shrunk in keeping
with the reduced power of production.

These were to prove prophetic words; though not
immediately, for job opportunities multiplied between 1878
and 1900, and the population expanded accordingly from
about half to three-quarters of a million.

The city spread its acres still wider. In 1891, the
independent burghs of Govanhill, Crosshill, Pollokshields
East, Pollokshields, Hillhead and Maryhill were brought
within Glasgow's boundaries, along with the districts of
Mount Florida, Langside, Shawlands, Kelvinside, Possilpark
and Springburn. Kinning Park came in in 1905, and in 1912
the burghs of Govan, Partick and Pollokshaws, as well as the
districts of Shettleston, Tollcross, Cathcart, Dawsholm,
Temple and North Knightswood.

So many buildings were put up between 1870 and 1900
that it is possible to mention only the most distinguished.
More than 100,000 tenements were built between 1860 and
the end of the century. After 1900, commercial companies
lost interest in building homes for letting, there being more
profitable ways of investing money.

Whatever may have been its good intentions, the Rent
Restrictions Act of 1915 turned out to be a death warrant for
much of Glasgow's stock of tenements. Landlords who had
no way of shielding themselves against rises in the cost of
repairs brought about by inflation (which, after several
decades of more or less stable prices, gathered momentum
during World War I) eventually had no money at all to spend
on routine maintenance, and the builders' equivalents of
moth and rust were left to do their corrupting will.

United Presbyterian Church (1858), 265 St Vincent Street,
by Alexander Thomson

But these days of decline were still far off when Glasgow's buildings were striving to beat the housing shortage by covering acre after acre with tall grey or golden ashlar tenements, using stone from local quarries until it began to run out during the early 1890s, and then turning to the red sandstone quarries of Arran and Dumfriesshire to provide material for their late-Victorian and Edwardian successors.

The fact that these builders simply could not keep pace with the housing needs of Glasgow during its flowering Victorian years – for such, indeed, they were, the industrial canker which had already fastened upon the vital stem of her major industries producing few apparent blemishes on the bloom of the city's prosperity before 1900 – meant that more and more people took to letting rooms, and the old early-nineteenth-century problem of overcrowding began to repeat itself in the rebuilt heart of the city, and in the older areas of the cotton era New Town and its suburban extensions.

The bloom of prosperity also resulted in the construction of so rich a profusion of public and commercial buildings that Glasgow became, and to some extent still is, not only the repository of a major part of the United Kingdom's Victorian stone-and-mortar heritage, but as J.M. Reid put it, '*the* Victorian city'.

The most exciting contribution to Glasgow's built environment in the 1860s and 1870s undoubtedly came from Alexander Thomson (1817–75), dubbed 'Greek' because of his fondness for classical detail. The most obvious feature of Victorian architecture is that it evolved no real style of its own, the 'battle of the styles' being really an argument as to whether this or that ancient manner, Greek or Gothic, was the more appropriate to copy for an age whose upper and middle classes enjoyed a degree of affluence never before experienced, but which nevertheless felt sufficiently insecure to believe that the physical reflection of that affluence should be based upon the greatness of past ages.

Thomson was born at Kippen, Stirlingshire, the seventeenth child of John Thomson, an upholder of the United Presbyterian Kirk who came of Covenanting stock. Alexander Thomson came to Glasgow with his brothers and sisters after their father's death in 1824. He was employed as a clerk in a lawyer's office, where he attracted the attention first of Robert Foote, then of John Baird, whose chief draughtsman he became. Thomson married a daughter of Peter Nicholson, the designer of Carlton Terrace. With another John Baird, no relation to Thomson's former boss, he set up in architectural practice, later to be joined by brother George, who was not himself an architect. Thomson rarely went to London, preferred Arran to anywhere else for his holidays, and so far as is known never left the shores of the United Kingdom.

He was highly regarded even in his own day, becoming President of the Glasgow Institute of Architects in 1871. His presidential address included consideration of the question: 'How is it that there is no modern style in architecture?' He was enormously prolific, and at his death sufficiently wealthy for his wife to be able to endow a travelling scholarship for young architects, one of the recipients of which was to be a young man called C.R. Mackintosh.[6]

Thomson gave a series of lectures in the Glasgow School of Art in 1874. In one of these lectures he declared the fundamental qualities of Greek architecture to be 'Beauty and symmetry of form, and harmony of relative perspective ... the only style of architecture which harmonizes with the higher class of sculpture and painting'. In another lecture given the same year he declared his antipathy to Gothic: 'Every part of a Gothic building looks as if it was trying to stand on end.... Gothic does not express greatness; it is only great where it is actually of large dimensions.' To him, it suggested the Dark Ages. He rightly observed that it was no more native to Scotland than Greek or Renaissance, and in his view, to call it a 'Christian' style was an impudent assertion, since the early Christian buildings were Greco-Roman.

Such were the beliefs which earned Thomson his sobriquet. J.M. Reid, however, perceptively suggests that 'memories of the Old Testament surely coloured his mind and work', pointing out that he would borrow 'as readily from ancient Egyptian models as from Greek ones – Egyptian columns, pylon-like openings, lotus forms and even Greco-Egyptian chimney-pots'. Though he was no more the innovator of a true Victorian style than any other

nineteenth-century architect, his 'borrowings' were so
thoroughly assimilated and his rich invention so consistent
and contained that he at least achieved an immediately
recognizable personal idiom in his best work, whether
churches that were temples, spacious villas, large-scale
terraces, commercial buildings or tenements.

Thomson is best known today for his churches and his
terraces. Caledonian Road Church, his first, went up in 1856,
and, as has already been remarked, its beautiful shell stands as
a motorway monument to twentieth-century mindless
vandalism. His St Vincent Street Church, built in 1859 for
the United Presbyterians and subsequently occupied by
another sect, occupies a dramatic hillside site, rendered
somewhat less so by Heron House, which dominates and
partly obscures the church from certain angles. A plinth
contains basements and the ground floor of the church carries
the temple, columned at its ends with square columns down
either side between the aisles. One of Thomson's most
remarkable steeples, suggesting Indian rather than Greek
inspiration, crowns this noble building. Its interior has a deep
pillar-supported gallery, banked as in a theatre. 'One can
almost see the blind Samson laying his hands on one of those
climbing pillars,' wrote J.M. Reid, 'cast iron beneath the
paint though these are, to bring down the Philistines about
his head;' a pleasant fancy, for no Samson has yet been found
who might undertake what would be in Glasgow so
encompassing a task.

Thomson's third major church, built at Queens Park and
also for the United Presbyterians, with 'its sloping
Phoenician doorways, its Greek ornament, its dwarf
Egyptian columns and its Assyrian-looking high door', to
quote William Power, must in some ways have been the
most exciting of all his churches, Indian and Egyptian
inspiration predominating over Greek. It was struck by
German bombs in 1942 and totally destroyed, one of the
most serious of British architectural losses sustained in the
Second World War.

Thomson, great creative artist that he was, no more
repeated himself in his churches than in his terraces. Walmer
Crescent, begun in 1857, is scarcely classical at all. As David
Walker and Andor Gomme remark, 'the tremendous and

Great Western Terrace (1867) by Alexander Thomson

nearly unbroken sequence of large square mullions on the top storey' form a kind of 'residual colonnade'. There are twice as many 'columns' on the top floor, an effect Thomson developed in Moray Place, built in 1859, which, with its imposing end pavilions, inspired Professor Hitchcock to dub it 'the first of all Greek Terraces'. If one ignores the non-Greek detail, and apprehends the Greekness rather than subjects it to technical analysis, one sees what he means.

The most famous of Thomson's terraces is undoubtedly the serenely imposing Great Western Terrace, begun in 1869, in number eleven of which this book was first drafted. A two-storeyed terrace on a raised mound set back from Great Western Road, its basements concealed by ornamental railings, it achieves a balanced dignity. This is no doubt due in part to the fact that its two pavilions are placed not at the ends of the terraces, but six bays in from each end, and have each an extra storey.

Thomson's last terrace,[7] Westbourne (1871), now numbering 21 to 39 Hyndland Road, has a highly characteristic ground floor, but the inclusion of oriels or bays, apparently forced upon Thomson by the taste of his clients, introduces a discordant feature which detracts from the overall balance.

Thomson's personal accent can be read even in his tenements. The finest of these blocks was Queens Park Terrace, Eglinton Street, the ground floor of which carried a row of shops. The decorated pediments on the first and second floors, the little columns between the top-floor windows, and the arrangement of the chimney heads were highly characteristic.

Thomson built houses and villas throughout most of his career, not all of them yet documented. He was influenced to some extent by the German architect Karl Friedrich Schinkel, both in his linked bands of windows, and in the so-called 'round arch' style, the latter manifesting itself in some of his houses in the vicinity of Kilcreggan, on the Clyde Coast, and in Pollokshields. 'The Knowe', 301 Albert Drive, is certainly his, dating from 1853, as is 200 Nithsdale Road, Pollokshields. The most complex of Thomson's houses is probably Holmwood, Netherlee Road, Cathcart, now a convent, which also has an exceptionally fine interior.

Of Thomson's public buildings, the most frequently looked at, but the least seen, is the Grosvenor Building opposite Central Station, which went up in 1860. It was owned and let by Thomson and his brother, but a continual worry to them. In 1907 J.H. Craigie, an architect of distinguished tastelessness, added an overpowering additional storey in Renaissance style. As the Grosvenor Restaurant, the grotesque Edwardian Assembly Hall, its roof supported by muscular men and generously-breasted maidens stripped to the waist, the whole slaistered in gilt, was the scene of innumerable Glasgow dinners and wedding receptions before it was badly damaged by fire in 1969. It is now offices.

The Buck's Head replacement building, which went up in 1863, is an iron-frame structure of considerable interest, though suffering from the fact that the two sides are of

different lengths (not, of course, Thomson's fault), and that
the attics seem fussy. It is much less successful than the first
and finest iron-frame building to be put up in Glasgow,
Gardner's Warehouse in Jamaica Street, the work of John
Baird I, finished in 1856.[8]

Of the remainder of Thomson's surviving public
buildings, the most fantastic is the Egyptian Halls in Union
Street (1873) with its powerful cornice, its increasing number
of windows on each ascending storey, and its vigorous
decorative details. More delicate are the Grecian Buildings in
Sauchiehall Street (1865), with shops at ground floor level.
Presumably one has to accept that in modern times when
ever-increasing consumption is regarded as an end in itself,
shop-fronts are likely to go on being shoutingly tasteless,
paying scant regard to the nature of the buildings they
disfigure. Developers should be severely discouraged from
laying hands on either of these fine buildings in order to
replace them with prefabricated arrangements of undistinguished clichés varied by 'faceless' towers, producing higher
plot ratios and richer rateable returns.

By the nature of their work, architects are, or should be,
part artist, part technician. It is easy to condemn them for
giving in to a client's insistence, though the technician
persona in some cases seems to have put up singularly little
resistance to assaults against the conscience of the artist. It is
interesting to note that with Thomson in mind, his
contemporary and fellow architect Campbell Douglas –
builder in 1878 of what is now the Citizens' Theatre, Gorbals
(but whose columns came from Hamilton's Union Bank in
Ingram Street) – should say: 'In my experience I have only
known one man who confined himself to one style, and if his
proposed employers insisted on building in a different style,
why, then, he let them go elsewhere. That architect was a
great man, who probably made less money than some others
did, but he left behind him monuments more worthy of his
genius.'

Thomson prepared a plan for the university on
Gilmorehill. The first disaster of the Senate's decision to
abandon their medieval university was succeeded by a second
disaster – their failure to choose what must surely have been

the most distinguished entry submitted to them for the
design of the new buildings. Alas! They preferred the farrago
of imitation Gothic by Sir George Gilbert Scott (1810–78),
who, in 1870, four years later, built the much more chaste
and restrained St Mary's Cathedral. His son, John Oldrid
Scott (1841–1913), added spires to both buildings in 1887 and
1893 respectively, the fretwork nature of the university spire
being the result of Lord Kelvin's calculation that the weight
of a solid spire could not be borne by the central tower.

Of Thomson's successors, the most obvious classicist was
James Sellars (1843–88). His St Andrew's Halls, in Berkeley
Street (1873), with its magnificent columned west front, had
a splendidly panelled interior, resulting in it being, according
to the BBC, acoustically the finest hall in Britain. It was
destroyed by fire in 1963. When the decision to incorporate
the shell of it in an extension to W.B. Whittie's rather heavier
Renaissance-style copperdomed Mitchell Library (1911) was
taken, it was decided to conserve the Granville Street
ornamental elevation, but only three of the bays on the
returns, a sad error of taste on someone's part.

Sellars was also responsible for Kelvinside Academy
(1877), which is reminiscent both of Thomson's work and of
Hamilton's much more sympathetic Edinburgh Royal High
School. Perhaps Sellars' finest work was his City of Glasgow
Bank (1878), a Renaissance delight (though never given its
intended top storey), which, sad to say, was demolished in
1959. Some of his other good things, like the Queen
Insurance Building (1879) in St George's Place, have also
gone. His churches rarely represent him at his best.

John Honeyman (1831–1914), on the other hand, has three
of Glasgow's finest churches to his credit: Barony North
Church (1878), in Cathedral Square, richly inventive with a
suggestion of the eighteenth century; Lansdowne (1862), a
delicate exercise in Gothic Revival with a slender spire of
breathtaking poise; and the beautiful classical Westbourne
Church (1880). Comparing the three, it becomes obvious
that Honeyman was the gifted Victorian imitator *par
excellence*, with, unlike Thomson, no identifiable 'voice' in
stone of his own, yet able to create masterly buildings in
whatever manner he turned his hand to. The gay, Italianate

Ca d'Oro (1872) in Gordon Street, once a furniture warehouse then a restaurant (though with a hideous slamming-down mansard attic added in 1923–24 by J.G. Gillespie), provides yet further evidence of his stylistic versatility. It was destroyed internally by fire in 1986, but the façade was saved and the building subsequently reconstructed and restored to its original elegance.

One or two other Glasgow classicists ought to be mentioned. Thomas Lennox Watson (1850–1920) showed his disapproval of Gothicism-run-riot by building the Roman temple with its massive Corinthian portico that is Wellington Church (1883) on the north side of University Avenue. St Georges-in-the-Fields (1886), by Hugh and David Barclay, is Ionic, more obviously Thomsonian, but with rich figure sculpture by Birnie Rhind. The Barclays were also the builders of Glasgow Academy (1878), Kelvinbridge, though the addition of large attic windows has distorted its proportions. Elgin Place Congregational Church (1856), an earlier example by John Burnet senior, brings us to the work of a father and son who together gave Glasgow many of its most spectacular later Victorian, Edwardian and even neo-Georgian buildings.

John Burnet (1814–1901), born in Kirk o'Shotts, began life as a carpenter, but rose to be President of the Glasgow Institute of Architects for two years from 1876. Fitzroy Place, Sauchiehall Street, an early work dating from 1847, was his contribution to what is now the Park Conservation Area. The Merchants' House in George Square is also his, being fitted in to the Italianate pattern already begun by Rochead with his Bank of Scotland building in 1869, further added to in 1874 by Sellars, who provided a matching central building. Burnet's tower, however, somewhat disturbs the balance of the range as a whole, the additional two storeys added later by his son completing the 'ogee' appearance, rising up by steps from the St Vincent Street end to the tower on the Queen Street–George Street corner of George Square.

The elder Burnet's three main public achievements stand within a few yards of each other. The head office of the Clydesdale Bank (1870) provides a fine white sandstone Italian-influence Baroque flourish, even although the east range was never finished, the *Evening Citizen* securing the site for their building. Lanarkshire House (1876) in Ingram Street, now High Court offices, is a Venetian palazzo originally built as a house, made into a bank by Hamilton, and given its present façade by Burnet. Splendid sculptured figures by John Mossman fill the niches between the columns on the top floor. It is thought that the original magnificent coved banking hall may still exist behind later plasterboard partitioning. Finally, there is the Stock Exchange Building (1875) in Buchanan Street, Franco-Italian Gothic of high inventive originality, though re-using sections of William Burges's unpremeated London Law Courts competition design. It now wears a totally new structure within its shell, and provides a fine example of how to conserve irreplaceable façades.

Burnet's contribution to the Great Western terraces was Cleveden Crescent, Kelvinside (1876), a simple and dignified series of houses stepping down a gentle slope.

His son, Sir John James Burnet (1857–1938), was born in Glasgow, and, after an extensive education and apprentice-ship that included three years in France, joined his father's firm in 1878. He visited America in 1896.

His first notable work was the classical Fine Art Institute in Sauchiehall Street, which became part of Pettigrew and Stephens, but regrettably was destroyed by fire in 1964 and subsequently demolished. The fantastic, Frenchified Charing Cross mansions (1891–7) with chateau-like roof detail, sweeps round what used to be Charing Cross but now dominates the eastern cliff of the inner ring motorway. In 1980, the building was cleaned, restoring the warm red glow to its sandstone. It was then discovered that the splendid clock was without machinery, the money apparently having run out before this could be provided.

The Athenaeum (1886), later part of the Royal Scottish Academy of Music and Drama, and the related former Athenaeum Theatre (1891) in Buchanan Street are the younger Burnet's, as is Waterloo Chambers (1899) in Waterloo Street; similar to, though less assured than, his Atlantic Chambers in Hope Street, dating from the same year. Both these buildings rise up from narrow Georgian

Charing Cross Mansions (1891) by Sir John James Burnet

frontages, and cope admirably with the problems set by this ground restriction.

American influence, particularly that of Louis Sullivan, was reflected in the construction methods employed by Burnet in his Alhambra Theatre (1910) – now alas demolished! a victim of changing fashions in entertainment – and in the magnificent balance of McGeoch's Warehouse (1905) in West Campbell Street which became a victim of the former Glasgow Corporation's failure to produce overall practical plans for the post-war conservation of its finest central area buildings, and the failure of successive governments to match conservation legislation with appropriate grant-assisting cash.

Burnet's lesser buildings are too numerous to detail here, although one must note that they include the Cenotaph in George Square, Glasgow (1922), the ornamental Forsyth's buildings in Princes Street, Edinburgh (1907),[9] and Kodak House, Kingsway, London (1911).

Working at the same time as Burnet was J.A. Campbell (1859–1909), who joined forces with Burnet in producing the Athenaeum Theatre. Campbell's masterpiece is the Northern Insurance Building (1908) in St Vincent Street, with its soaring lines of windows and its functional but impressive steel-frame fenestration at the rear elevation.

Another contemporary was Sir Robert Rowand Anderson (1834–1921). In Govan Old Parish Church (1884) and the Pearce Institute (1903) he provided Govan with two of the very few public buildings of quality to survive the comprehensive redevelopment of the area. Pollokshaws Burgh Hall (1897) is a delightful reinterpretation of Scottish Baroque. Anderson's main Glasgow achievement is the Central Hotel (1884), curiously Scots in feeling yet, as many people have remarked, bringing successfully together a Swedish tower, Amsterdam gables and both Florentine Renaissance and English Jacobean windows. In a sense it is the most spectacular embodiment in Glasgow of that assimilation of, and variation upon, foreign styles which was the deliberate achievement of Victorian architecture.

The most obvious visual sign of the confidence that Glasgow felt in itself as it sailed upon its high tide of

Victorianism was the new City Chambers, built upon the site of Alexander of Ballochmyle's[10] town house and opened in 1888 by the Queen herself. A London Scot, William Young (1843–1900), won the competition to build it. It, too, is an astonishing amalgam of styles, capped by a great tower abounding in Renaissance detail. The noble central staircase, its ceiling and the interior decoration and furnishings of the public rooms put one in mind of a Renaissance nobleman's palace. As a boy I used to laugh at it; but I had not then lived long enough to experience our age of prefabricated design, staining concrete and shoddy finish. There is never likely to be another palace like the sumptuous City Chambers built again in Glasgow. For its sheer magnificence of craftsmanship alone it should be highly valued. The arches which link the additions at the rear of the building are by Watson, Salmond and Gray, and date from 1923, and there is a further acceptable modern extension eastwards.

A word should perhaps be said here about Glasgow's statues, particularly those in George Square. A favourite quiz test on Glasgow invites the contestant to name them. Few can, which is hardly surprising in an age out of sympathy with the Victorian belief in permanence and the consequent fondness for bronze Valhallas. The taste for such things had passed even by Edwardian times, for Neil Munro makes 'Erchie', his 'Droll Freen', report King Edward VII to have said, on first arriving at Queen Street Station from Edinburgh: 'Whit 'na graveyaird's this?'

The dominating statue of Scott (1838) is by A. Handyside Ritchie, to a design by John Greenshields, a self-taught Lesmahagow man. Sir Walter Scott visited him in his cottage by the Clyde, the last visit taking place a year before Scott died. Greenshields was on his own deathbed when he learned that his statue had been accepted to stand on top of David Rhind's tall fluted Doric column on a plinth at the centre of George Square. By then the statue of Sir John Moore of Corunna by John Flaxman was already a familiar landmark, having been erected in 1819, and reputedly made from smelted-down cannon. Once surrounded by railings, as were all the statues, it was the object of an attempt by Glasgow hooligans to destroy it, according to a drawing published in

City Chambers (1883) by William Young

The Northern Looking Glass in 1825. Colin MacIver who took his uncle's name of Campbell and served under Moore, became first Sir Colin Campbell and then Lord Clyde, for services during the India Mutiny. His statue, the work of J.H. Foley, joined the George Square bronze set in 1867.

James Watt's statue by Sir Francis Chantrey went up in 1832. Three former rectors of Glasgow University are represented. The statue of Sir Robert Peel (1859) is also by Mossman. Peel, whose repeal of the Corn Laws won him wide popularity in Glasgow, had a banquet given in his honour in a marquee erected in a Buchanan Street garden when he was elected Lord Rector in 1837. Another politician, William Ewart Gladstone, whose statue is by Hamo Thornycroft and went up in 1904, was a speaker at that dinner. Gladstone delivered his rectorial address in the Kibble Palace, a fascinating structure originally erected by the engineer John Kibble at his Clyde Coast home in Coulport about 1860, but sold to Glasgow and re-erected in the Botanic Gardens in 1873. It contains tropical vegetation interspersed with romantic white-marble statues by Hamo Thornycroft, Goscombe John and others. The Botanic Gardens, originally open only to private subscribers, were taken over by the Corporation in 1887 and opened to the public in 1891. The gardens were bought at a cost of £59,531.

The statue of the third rector, the poet, Thomas Campbell, another of Mossman's contributions to George Square, went up in 1877. It was he who, in *The Pleasures of Hope*, pointed out to us that:

'Tis distance lends enchantment to the view,
And robes the mountain in its azure hue

and is said to have coined a phrase popular with authors:

Now Barabbas was a publisher.

Thomas Graham (1805–69), a friend of David Livingstone, was lecturer in chemistry in the Mechanics' Institute, and successively Professor of Chemistry at Anderson's College and University College, London. In 1855 he became Master

The Kibble Palace (1872) in the Botanic Gardens

of the Mint in London. His representation joined the George
Square Valhalla in 1872 and was the work of William Brodie.
Marochetti was responsible in 1855 for the likeness of James
Oswald, his hat in hand an ageless temptation to small boys
to lob things into it. Oswald was a Reform Bill supporter and
a Glasgow Member of Parliament twice – from 1832 to 1837
and from 1839 to 1847. He is said to have been in his day 'one
of the most influential Scottish members in the House of
Commons'. That the mere suggestion of erecting a statue to
any Glasgow member of the House of Commons in our own
day provokes instant risibility may not wholly be due to the
twentieth century's lack of enthusiasm for statuary.

Robert Burns arrived in 1876, the year before his fellow
poet, Campbell. His statue, by C.E. Ewing, was paid for by
more than 40,000 shilling subscriptions, and unveiled before
a crowd of 30,000.

Finally, there are the equestrian statues of the Prince
Consort and the Queen herself, both by Baron Marochetti of
Turin and Vaux. They arrived together in 1864, the Queen's
statue having come from Charing Cross, where she had been
since 1849.

Other notable examples include Mossman's represen-
tations of David Livingstone, the explorer,[11] and the
Reverend Dr Norman Macleod, an eloquent minister of the
Barony Church, which went up in Cathedral Square in 1877.
Alexander Skirving's monument to the Battle of Langside
was erected at Battlefield in 1887. Lord Kelvin, pensive, went
up in Kelvingrove in 1813, the work of Macfarlane Shannan,
three years after Paul Montford's figures on Kelvingrove
Bridge. Ernest Gillick was responsible for the lions that flank
Burnet's Cenotaph of 1922.

To complete our survey of the fabric of late Victorian and
Edwardian Glasgow, several rather more minor figures who
provided an exciting flourish or two should be mentioned.
James Salmon senior (1805–88) built the first Langside
College (1870), originally a Deaf and Dumb Institute, but
superseded by Boissevain's and Osmond's new college in
1965. Salmon's famous grandson, also James Salmon
(1874–1924), built 'The Hatrack', 142 St Vincent Street
(1899), an exuberantly-detailed realization of another narrow

The 'Hatrack', 142-4 St Vincent Street (1899) by James Salmon, jun.

Georgian frontage drawing inspiration in many respects from Art Nouveau. It contrasts with his more severe Lion Chambers (1906), 170-72 Hope Street, the first building in Glasgow to have a reinforced-concrete frame. His number 12 University Gardens (1900), in which J.G. Gillespie may have had a hand, has been restored amongst the complex of new university buildings of which it now forms a part.

Because the former Liberal Club (1909) was incorporated with the former Royal Scottish Academy of Music and Drama in what in its day was one of Glasgow's most architecturally exciting precincts, its builder, Alexander Nisbet Paterson (1862–1947), who worked with the firm of Burnet Son and Campbell, perhaps also deserves mention.

There remains John Keppie (1863–1945), whose main claim to our interest here is that Charles Rennie Mackintosh (1868–1928) joined the firm of Keppie and Henderson as a draughtsman, and Keppie had the young Mackintosh working in association with him in the former *Glasgow Herald* Building (1893) in Mitchell Street, the annexe to Northpark House (1893), now Broadcasting House, Queen Margaret Drive, and, in the same year, formerly Martyrs Public School at Townhead.

Mackintosh is generally hailed as the founder of twentieth-century design. Although his father was a Police Superintendent of Highland extraction, Glasgow provided the environment of Mackintosh's formative years. After five years of apprenticeship to a Glasgow architect, John Hutchinson, during which period he studied at the Glasgow School of Art, Mackintosh joined the firm of Honeyman and Keppie. In 1890 he won the 'Greek' Thomson scholarship, which took him to France and Italy. During the nineties, he became associated with Herbert McNair and the sisters Frances and Margaret Macdonald – he later married Margaret – who, as 'The Four', exhibited graphic and craft work in the then novel Art Nouveau manner. At the age of 28, perhaps as a result of some influence upon the governors by its director, Fra Newberry, Mackintosh won the limited competition for the Glasgow School of Art.

This building, his masterpiece, went up in two sections, the eastern in 1897, the western in 1907. Between these years,

Mackintosh built two inventive houses, both with his belief in total design carried through to include the furniture: Windyhill, Kilmacolm, Renfrewshire in 1901, which has had its interior altered and is no longer equipped with all its original furniture; and the still intact Hill House, Helensburgh, Dunbartonshire – now owned by the National Trust for Scotland – the following year. Queen's Cross Church went up in 1897, its interior a minor instance of Mackintosh's remarkable skill in manipulating spatial relationships in the way that a composer must. It has a Gothic influenced exterior. Scissored by motorways and roads, and deprived of its church hall, it went out of use for worship and has now been taken over as the headquarters of the Charles Rennie Mackintosh Society. It is used for public meetings and as the venue for appropriate exhibitions.

Scotland Street School, with its two Gropius-like glass-fronted towers, was built in 1904. No longer needed for teaching, it is to be converted for re-use, perhaps as a museum. The buildings which formerly obscured it have been cleared away, and it now looks over the M8 motorway.

Additions to the School of Art have not impinged upon Mackintosh's building. Even today, let alone in 1896, it is truly astonishing. Thomas Howarth, Mackintosh's most considerable biographer, speaks of its 'synthesis of traditional craftsmanship and twentieth-century engineering', and rightly calls it 'the first important architectural monument to the new movement in Europe'. Whereas all Mackintosh's Victorian predecessors had synthesized combinations of the five basic architectural styles, achieving excellences that, with the exception of Thomson's work, had no continuing personal 'thumbprints', Mackintosh synthesized feelings and achieved a new and instantly recognizable individuality. Even the greatest of artists show their influences from time to time, since art, like life, is a continuing process, and – contrary to the ill-considered dogma circulated by our late-twentieth-century drop-outs – we cannot disown our ancestry. The tower of the former *Glasgow Herald* Building may, as Gomme and Walker suggest, have been inspired by J.M. MacLaren, who built a farmhouse and the hotel at

Glasgow School of Art (1897) by Charles Rennie Mackintosh

Fortingall, Perthshire, at the turn of the previous decade. Certainly, the names of Voysey and Halsey Ricardo have been commonly mentioned as other possible influences. Yet what ultimately matters in art is not which influences show but what asserts its own life. A Scottish cliff-cum-castle feeling shows itself in the eastern and southern façades of the art school, while possibly the northern façade, as J.M. Reid puts it, catches 'a faint reminiscence of the old University building, transformed in a mind that was re-thinking everything for itself'. The detail, including the 'iron gates that hint at portcullises', adds satisfaction to the whole conception, inside and out, in a curiously integral way. The finest interior is undoubtedly that of the library. Here, the spatial relationships that were Mackintosh's speciality, the strength of creative power yet of containment, call to my mind Beethoven's late String Quartet, opus 132, where there is displayed the same absolute mastery of a great mind operating economically and effortlessly at full stretch, for its own satisfaction.

Mackintosh left Glasgow when he was 48, and, with the exception of the house he built for Basset Lowke at Northampton, his creative days were virtually over. A difficult temperament not helped by too great a reliance on drink may have hampered the getting of further major commissions; or he may, as some suggest, though with no evidence to support them, simply have been played out, the delicate French and other water-colours of his last years providing a kind of therapy against decline.

I have devoted considerable space to the buildings which went up in the steel and shipbuilding era of Glasgow and the men who created them, because, in spite of depredations already made upon our stock of them, they form a major part of the United Kingdom's stone-and-mortar heritage. The inevitable limbo into which newly-dead artists and just-passed eras are necessarily plunged as their successors strive after original variations on the basic themes of life has now released the Victorians and their achievements from the darkness of its contempt, and a fresh realization of the measure of these achievements has developed.

One aspect of Mackintosh's work which unfortunately has

not re-emerged from the decades of neglectful limbo, being by its very nature fashionably ephemeral, had considerable social significance. This was his association with Miss Kate Cranston, to all intent and purpose the inventor of the Glasgow tea-room.

Stuart and Kate Cranston, members of the family who owned the Crow Hotel in George Square, where the Merchants' House now stands, were responsible for this innovation. Stuart Cranston opened his tea-room in Argyle Street, while Kate had her first tea-room in Ingram Street. Mackintosh began designing for her in 1896, along with his wife Margaret Macdonald: furniture – his chairs offered greater visual than physical satisfaction, but perhaps the intention was to discourage patrons from staying too long! – interior decor, cutlery, and, in the case of 'The Willows' (inspired by Sauchiehaugh, 'the willow meadow', on which Sauchiehall Street was built), the whole tea-room. It survived incorporation in a fashion house, and has now been well restored. The Ingram Street tea-rooms, with their Oak and Chinese rooms, were in the possession of Glasgow Corporation for almost a quarter of a century. For a time they did duty as a warehouse store. Mackintosh's interiors have now been stripped for assembly elsewhere, and the building itself demolished.

That composite writer James Hamilton Muir[12] claimed a major reason for the success of the tea-rooms to be the fact that women, who were not then popular in Glasgow pubs, were able to go to a Cranston's tea-room on their own. Wrote Muir: 'It is believed (and averred) that in no other town can you see in a place of refreshment such ingenious and beautiful decorations in the style of new art as in Miss Cranston's shop in Buchanan Street.'

A Glasgow man's overheard commentary on an uncompleted building is quoted: 'It is so kind o' artistic, ye know, wi' a' that sort o' light paint. Oh, it'll do! It's quite Kate Cranston-ish.'

The design sense of successive generations of Glaswegians was widened by a series of exhibitions which flowered out of the city's sense of prosperity, and its belief that at last it had something to show off to the world.

The first of Glasgow's International Exhibitions was held in Kelvingrove Park during the summer of 1888. The theme of the exhibition was oriental, and white stone palaces with domes and minarets went up to house the various objects on show. A replica of the Bishop's Palace was built on the Gilmorehill slopes, and extra bridges were thrown across the Kelvin on whose waters gondolas glided up and down.

J.J. Bell, whose autobiography *I Remember* provides a vivid account of the day-to-day lives of what he calls 'Little Victorians', remembered a festive glimpse of Victoria herself.

> Bank Street led to the University and it was therefore a thoroughfare of some little importance, but in August 1888 it attained, for a few minutes, honour and glory, by the progress of Her Majesty passing through it to Kelvingrove Park, there to visit Glasgow's first International Exhibition;[13] a little elderly lady in a bonnet, sitting erect in a big landau, giving every now and then a nod – so she passed by, looking severe and not bored. A year ago, the land had acclaimed her Jubilee – fifty years on the throne yet with, as reigns go, many years to come. The Exhibition had been opened in May by the Prince and Princess of Wales, her Royal Highness wearing a tight-fitting costume with a very decided 'bustle', a floral bonnet, with a veil to the tip of her nose, and carrying a prim little muff.
>
> Not long after Queen Victoria and her retinue had passed, and the pavements and windows had become vacant, an aged Italian with barrel-organ and monkey appeared. Possibly he knew nothing of the importance of the hour of Glasgow's first International Exhibition, of the august Personage who had so lately preceded him. It was his day for Bank Street, and calmly he began to grind the 'Carnival of Venice', lifting peering rheumy eyes to the windows.

There was, indeed, a cosmopolitan feeling in the air, a feeling even more apparent when the exhibition of 1901 opened on the same site. The profits of the previous exhibition had been used to help provide a red sandstone wedding-cake of an art gallery,[14] built by Sir J.W. Simpson and Milner Allen on the apparent assumption that the more variegated the detail the greater the effect of sumptuousness. It is said that Simpson wanted his gallery built the other way round, and that because he did not get his own way he committed suicide. Simpson, however, lived to a ripe old age, and the myth probably arose because of the early death of Allen. In any case the gallery put on a notable opening show of painting.

The 1901 exhibition, known as 'The Groveries', was both more extensive and more ambitious than its predecessor. Its architect, James Miller – who built the Royal Infirmary which replaced the Adam Infirmary – laid it out over 73 acres, intending it to wear a Spanish air. Its purpose was to demonstrate the development of art, industry and science during the century that had just ended, particularly during the reign of Queen Victoria, who died while it was in progress. There were numerous innovations; an industrial hall with a dome crowned by a Statue of Light balanced on one toe, several Russian pavilions and a display of motor-cars. The railway companies, who in 1888 had cut an hour off their journeys from London, this time enticed the southern British to the exhibition with tempting excursion fares. The occasion was marked locally by the introduction of electric tram services,[15] powered by the new generating station at Pinkston. This innovation harmonized with other electrical manifestations at 'The Groveries'. Electricity apart, the weather was magnificent, and a new generation of Glaswegians relaxed and enjoyed themselves.

The 1911 exhibition had the purpose of raising money to found and endow a Chair of Scottish History and Literature at Glasgow University. It was smaller in scale, if more ingenious in the range of its delights, which included a Highland village, a 'Scottish Toonie', a West African village, a Palace of History that housed the most comprehensive collection of bits and pieces out of Scottish history ever brought together, an aerial railway, a mountain slide, and motor boats instead of gondolas on the yet unfouled Kelvin, where a flotilla of model ships also floated. German and Hungarian bands in immaculate uniforms flapped the tunes of the day against the summer air, and there were sessions of massed hymn-singing, to placate the god of prosperity. A great storm blew up on the final day of this last Glasgow exhibition before the First World War, carrying the roof of the Aviation Pavilion up to Park Terrace and damaging many of the others.

Exhibitions apart, regular opportunities for Glaswegians to enjoy themselves had both improved in quality and multiplied in quantity between 1870 and 1914.

For one thing, the theatre-going habit had spread. Glasgow acquired further scarcely less inflammable theatres, to say nothing of music-halls, a zoo and a skating palace, which stood on the site of what became the first building to show films commercially in Glasgow, later the Regal Cinema in Sauchiehall Street and now three small cinema theatres.

For those whose tastes did not reach the higher flights of dramatic fancy, there was the Scotia Music Hall, which later became the 'Metropole', a house of barn-storming melo-dramas like *Maria Martin* and *The Face at the Window*. Its burnt-out façade until recently faced the Goosedubs, allegedly so-called after a goose-keeping bailie who had a house in Stockwell Street with a garden stretching to the Briggait, the goose-puddles providing the name for the lane that later connected these two streets. Among the many famous artists who appeared at the 'Scotia' was the young Harry Lauder, facing his first audience as a professional entertainer.

The Britannia Music Hall, newer than the 'Scotia' and located in the Trongate, near Glasgow Cross, was another popular haunt of our ancestors, though by Edwardian days it was reputed to have become a known rough house, where bad fruit and rotten eggs were sold outside, so that patrons could arm themselves before entering in case a performer turned out not to be to their taste. 'The Britannia' and its neighbour, MacLeod's Waxworks, both came into the hands of an eccentric Yorkshireman, A. E. Pickard, who turned the 'Britannia' into the 'Panopticon', which then alternated films with variety acts, and MacLeod's into Pickard's Waxworks, beneath which he ran a zoo of sorts. Neither of these establishments managed to survive the slump between the wars.

The Theatre Royal had been rebuilt in Cowcaddens when the Dunlop Street Theatre Royal went up in flames in 1863, after a performance of the pantomime *Bluebeard*. Fire removed this theatre in 1879, and badly damaged its successor in 1895. However, the third rebuilding carried the 'Royal' over two wars and into the television era, when it became the studios of Scottish Television Limited. Splendidly restored, it was re-opened as a theatre in 1975, the home of Scottish Opera.

The Royal Princess's (now the Citizens') Theatre in the Gorbals, and the 'Grand' in Cowcaddens (burned down in 1917), specialized in melodrama and pantomime. Indeed, the very essence of Glasgow pantomime lived on into the 'Citizens'' occupancy through pantomime with such traditional thirteen-letter titles as *Gaggiegalorum* and *Bletherskeite*.

For East End folk, the Queen's Theatre at Watson Street, which had begun life as the 'People's Palace', provided good strong music-hall fare. 'The Gaiety', later rebuilt as the 'Empire', provided music-hall fare for posher customers. It was mostly a mixture of Scots comics like Neil Kenyon and such popular artists from England as Nellie Wallace and Bill Bennett, who filled these halls, as well as the smaller 'provincial' theatres, which, by the nineties, had sprung up in Partick, Anderston and Govan.

Music-hall artists also appeared at both the City Hall and St Andrew's Halls. Charles Coburn was a popular favourite with Glasgow audiences, singing such hits as 'Two Lovely Black Eyes', 'If you want to know the time, ask a P'liceman' and 'The Man who Broke the Bank at Monte Carlo'. Albert Chevalier was amongst those who came to St Andrew's Halls about 1890, delighting audiences with 'Mrs 'enry 'awkins', 'The Nipper's Lullaby', and 'My Old Dutch'.

Scots comics such as J.C. Macdonald and W.F. Frame, did not emerge into popularity until the late eighties. The line of Scots comics that burgeoned from them included Will Fyffe (who, like Lauder, came from the east coast, in spite of his famous song 'I belong to Glasgow'), Tommy Lorne, George West, Tommy Morgan and in our own day, Duncan Macrae, Jimmy Logan and Stanley Baxter, Macrae and Baxter versatile actors as well as comedians. Sir Harry Lauder openly acknowledged Macdonald's influence on his own later successful career.

Many of the early Scots comedians relied heavily on songs

and jokes about drink. J.J. Bell quotes a typical example of
early Scotch comic lyricism, obviously dating from the end
of the beginning of the new century:

> Oh, my, I'm thenkfu that it's by –
> That dreidfu Exhibeetion, ma temper it did try,
> For every time oor Jock gaed there
> He cam' hame roarin' fu,
> And he always blamed it on the tea
> He got at the Bungaloo.

I remember an uncle of mine quoting the verse of a song
by Frame which ran:

> The River Clyde is verra wide
> Especially whaur it's narra.
> There's mony a chiel stauns at the bar
> That couldnae wheel a barra.

though whether this inability was due to drink or sheer
absence of skill I was never really sure.

Even Lauder on occasion, used drunkenness as a theme for
his melodious humour.

Edwardian Glasgow, fonder even than the nineties of
foot-tapping tunes, had more theatres and a wider range of
'shows' to choose from. 'The Alhambra' ran variety, the
'Royalty' (later the 'Lyric'), 'rep'. 'The Pavilion', the 'Savoy'
and the 'Coliseum' also catered mainly for the music hall
public. The new King's Theatre, opened in 1904, vied with
the 'Royal' in offering plays and opera. To most people,
Lehar's operetta *The Merry Widow*, with its languorous waltzes
and its saucy gaiety, symbolizes the leisured side of
Edwardian life. The *Widow* made her first Glasgow curtsey in
the King's Theatre on Christmas Eve 1907. By then
internationally famous, she had a tremendous reception.
Robert Turnbull, the music critic of the *Glasgow Herald*,
deplored the liberties taken with the music in the interest of
laugh-raising by George Edwards and his cast, but was
otherwise full of praise for the performance. 'Last night the
piece, presented by an entirely capable company, never
flagged for a moment. The singing, both solo and concerted,

was always good; there was plenty of verve in the dancing; and in matters of setting, dresses etc., "The Merry Widow" left no room for criticism.'

The famous waltz in the second act had to be repeated three times. While Glasgow's middle and upper classes were not nearly as sophisticated as London society – it is doubtful if many copies of that clandestine publication *The Pearl*, from which respectable Victorian gentlemen were able to draw pornographic sustenance between the rigours of appearing to be upright pillars of society and generous dispensers of charity, sold in Glasgow[16] – the 'Golden Age with the gilt off', as J.B. Priestley calls Edwardian England, would have sufficiently affected Scotland for that King's Theatre audience of bosomy women and moustachioed men to experience something of the cosmopolitan sensuousness of Lehar's measures, before driving back to their West End houses, still well staffed with servants to stoke up their coal fires.

Incidentally, the prices of the seats for that performance on Christmas Eve 1907 were: orchestral stalls, 5s.; dress circle 4s.; upper circles, 2s.; pit, a shilling; and gallery, 6d.[17]

In the 1880s, orchestral concerts moved from the City Hall to St Andrew's Halls, and chamber concerts were held in the Queen's Rooms. Glasgow had a second Festival of Music in the City Hall in 1873. It lasted five days, during which the celebrities included the singers Tietjens and Santley and the conductor Sir Michael de Costa. The choral works on this occasion included Mendelssohn's *Elijah*, at which the audience was requested not to applaud for religious reasons, and Costa's own oratorio *Eli*. Beethoven's *Pastoral* and Schumann's *Spring* symphonies were the main orchestral items.

This festival seems to have given the necessary encouragement for the creation of a new and 'permanent' orchestra, proposals for which had been mooted nine years before. From 1874 to 1891, the Glasgow Choral Union's orchestra gave concerts all over Central Scotland under such conductors as Sir Arthur Sullivan, Hans von Bulow, and Augustus Mann. A group of music-lovers then engineered a break-away. While the Choral Union continued to give their concerts, the Scottish Orchestra Company Limited ran a rival series. By 1894 the two bodies had merged to become the Choral and Orchestral Union. A long series of foreign conductors and foreign leaders then dominated the musical scene, Glaswegians believing, in common with most British audiences, that a musician who was not a Herr, a Monsieur or a Signor could not possibly be any good, although informed British opinion thought otherwise. As long ago as 1914, the *Musical Times* greeted the appointment of Max Bruch to the conductorship of the orchestra with a brave nationalistic protest: 'What becomes our boasted progress in music if important appointments ... are not to be filled by native musicians? Cannot we raise the article on our own soil? Are we always to import it? Would such a stigma be tolerated in any other European country?'

The answer, of course, was 'no': but tolerated it was in Glasgow. Even the providers of light music for balls and dinners had to have names like Monsieur Claude Jaquinot and Herr Wilhelm Iff. Until the appointment of Alexander Gibson as musical director of the Scottish National Orchestra – the permanent successor from 1950 to the peculiarly impermanent old Scottish Orchestra, whose season at most never stretched to more than six months of the year and for much of its existence lasted for only three – this dreadful unmusical snobbery resulted in preference being given to a third-rate mittel-European rather than to even a first-rate English conductor.

The taste for painting greatly increased during the seventies, the leaders of city life having homes with plenty of wall space and money to spend on pictures they liked. The work of the Barbizan group and their Dutch followers was much sought after in the seventies and eighties, imported to Glasgow by the art dealers John Forbes White and Alexander Reid. The *plein-air* method of painting – setting the easel in front of the subject and painting direct from nature – had brought home to Glaswegians the excitement of light. The influence of Whistler on young painters was also considerable. Revolt was in the international air.

The Glasgow Group of painters came together about 1880. The 'father' of the movement was W.Y. Macgregor (1855–1923), a powerful painter 'glorifying in the quality of the medium for its own sake', to quote Ian Finlay: 'deriving inspiration from it, in stark contrast to the infilling of colour upon careful drawings which had become the established tradition in the academies'.

Not all 'The Boys' who gathered in Macgregor's studio were Scots. Joseph Crawhall (1861–1913), was a Northumbrian hunting man, the delicacy of whose birds and beasts still seem remarkable. Sir James Guthrie (1859–1913), who caught fleeting moments at tennis parties or on the golf course, and whose early portraits abound in character, came from Belfast. E.A. Hornel (1864–1933) was influenced by the decorative qualities of Japanese painting, and created his rosy-cheeked children in laid-on daubs of sheer colour. George Hendry (1858–1943) also visited Japan, and produced what has come to be regarded as the key-picture of the movement with his *Galloway Landscape*. The others included E.A. Walton, Stuart Park, Alexander Melville and, a younger recruit, D.Y. Cameron.

A show at the Grosvenor Gallery in London, where they were welcomed by the followers of England's rebels against the academies, the New Art Club, brought the Glasgow Group its first major success. Other successes followed in Munich, Dresden and Vienna, where the German Secessionists welcomed them.

They were never really a 'school' in any unified sense, and the nearest they came to having a manifesto was the short-lived *Scottish Art Review*, which included as fellow contributors characters as diverse as James Matthew Barrie, then still full of unfulfilled Kirriemuir ambition; that inverted Calvinist rebel-poet from Greenock, John Davidson, whose later plays hammered home with Knoxian obstinacy his belief that God was dead; and the Russian revolutionary writer Kropotkin.

All that 'The Boys' had in common was a freshness of approach, a certain emphasis on colour,[18] and chance that brought them enthusiastically together at a moment when the rich Philistines were ready to buy. By the turn of the century, they were going their own diverse ways, Hornel to Kirkcudbright to repeat his coy little girl-pictures so endlessly as almost to suggest a psychological obsession, and Guthrie to become the fashionable President of the Royal Academy. But for about twenty years they produced a remarkable range of impressive pictures, as an exhibition of the work of the movement mounted by the Scottish Arts Council in the Kelvingrove Gallery in 1968 clearly demonstrated.

Interest in Art Nouveau perhaps helped to make the movement seem old fashioned by Edwardian times. Of the Scottish Colourists who succeed them, Peploe and Cadell had no real Glasgow links, only the lyrical Leslie Hunter (1879–1936) belonging to and drawing inspiration from Glasgow and the West, whose citizens on the whole neglected him.

In literature, the latter part of the Victorian era in Scotland was dominated by Robert Louis Stevenson (1850–94) and James Matthew Barrie (1860–1937), the novelist who, so to say, preceded the playwright with such things as *Auld Licht Idylls* (1888) and *The Little Minister* (1891), part of which is set in Glasgow. Neither of these men had Glasgow connections, any more than had the Kailyard, or back-green cabbage-patch school of Gallovidian S.R. Crockett (1860–1914) and the Reverend John Watson, 'Ian MacLaren' (1850–1907), whose novels *The Lilac Sunbonnet* (1894) and *Beside the Bonnie Briar Bush* (1895) showed a coy archness of sugar-sweet sentimentality never before achieved, though doubtless devoured avidly by many Glasgow readers, to whom the novel that jerked the fashionable validity out of such saccharine literary pietism, Ayrshire-born George Douglas Brown's (1869–1902) *The House with the Green Shutters*, must have come as a disagreeable shock.

The darling of the circulating libraries in the seventies and eighties was undoubtedly Trongate-born William Black (1841–98), who took the journalist's road to London. After two false starts he produced *The Daughter of Heth* (1871), a love story painting contrasts of manners and conventions through the arrival of a French girl at a country manse in the West.

Into almost all his novels, Black contrived to introduce his native city. Thus in *The Daughter of Heth*, Coquette, the French heroine of the book who captures the fancy of the minister of Airlie's eldest son (known by his nickname, the 'Whaup'), comes up from Ayrshire by train to see him, chaperoned by Lady Drum, one of the minister's aristocratic parishioners.

As Coquette and Lady Drum drew near to Glasgow, the impatience of the girl increased. Her thoughts flew on more swiftly than the train; and they were all directed towards the Whaup whom she was now about to see.

'Will he be at the station? Does he know we are coming? Or shall we see him as we go along the streets?' she asked. 'Dear me,' said Lady Drum, 'Ye seem to think that Glasgow is no bigger than Saltcoats. Meet him in the streets? We should scarce see him in the streets if he were dressed in scaurlet.'

It was growing towards dusk when the two ladies arrived. Lady Drum's carriage was waiting at the station; and presently Coquette found herself in the midst of the roar and turmoil of the great city. The lamps on the bridges were burning yellow in the grey coldness of the twilight; and she got a glimpse of the masses of shipping down the dusky bed of the river. Then up through the busy streets – where the windows were growing bright with gas, and dense crowds of people were hurrying to and fro', and the carts, and waggons, and carriages were raising a din that was strange to ears grown accustomed to the stillness of Airlie.

'Alas!' said Coquette, 'I cannot see him in this crowd. It is impossible.' Lady Drum laughed and said nothing.

And so they drove on – the high, old-fashioned chariot which ought to have been kept for state purposes down at Castle Cawmill,[19] swinging gently on its big springs – up to the north-western districts of the city.

For those who really cannot bear not to know what happened, Coquette never married the 'Whaup', for she fell in love with a dashing earl who perished when his yacht *Caroline* was run down by a steamer bound for Ireland. Coquette, after visiting the spot where his body had been washed ashore, fell ill with one of these fatal 'fevers' which Victorian doctors could not accurately diagnose, and for which they knew no cure.

Black's other successes included *The Strange Adventures of a Phaeton* (1872) and *MacLeod of Dare* (1878), after which, as J.H. Millar put it, he merely repeated his stock effects, 'impulsive tomboys, Highland seas, polychromic sunsets'. There is perhaps an air of contrivance about all the tales which has no doubt militated against their survival. Nevertheless, *The Daughter of Heth* could well bear reprinting as a period piece.

Nor was the output of the verse department in Glasgow much more distinguished. Throughout the seventies and eighties, Robert Buchanan (1841–1901), Staffordshire born but brought up and educated in Glasgow, was thought by some to be the equal of Browning; but the rhetoric of such pieces as 'Judas Iscariot' has worn decidedly thin, and he is really better remembered now for his onslaught on Rossetti and his friends of the so-called 'Fleshly School of Poetry', and for thus providing W.S. Gilbert with the theme for the Gilbert and Sullivan opera *Patience*, than anything he achieved during his London career as a somewhat pugnacious Man of Letters.

Glasgow-born Sir James George Frazer (1854–1941) produced between 1890 and 1914 his enormous Spencerian attempt to unify life through the interpretation of myth and legend. It aroused considerable interest, and was still spoken of in tones of hushed awe by *savants* when I was a boy, though more recent scientific inquiry has discredited some of its conclusions.

Bret Harte, the American writer, was American consul in Glasgow for four years from 1880, during which time he lived at 113 West Regent Street, where he wrote his Glasgow tale *Young Robin Gray*.

Edwardian prose-writing was dominated by the remarkable popularity of *Wee MacGreegor* (1902) and *Wee MacGreegor Again* (1904) by James Joy Bell (1871–1934) which began to appear in the *Evening Times* in 1901. Its humorous portrayal of Glasgow working-class life won it a popularity which even spread to America. The novelist who best captured the atmosphere of Edwardian Glasgow was Frederick Niven (1878–1944) with *The Staff at Simsons*, though there is also real merit in *The Setons* by Anna Buchan (1877–1948). Neil Munro (1864–1930) succeeded to the Stevenson tradition with romantic historical novels like *John Splendid* (1898), *Doom Castle* (1901), and many others still popular. He became editor of Glasgow's *Evening News*, lived latterly in a house next the building that had once been Henry Bell's hotel in Helensburgh, and endeared himself to Glaswegians and many others, with his *Para Handy* tales of the West Highland skipper of a Clyde 'puffer' or coal-boat, and his pawky crew; tales that have achieved a wider popularity through television, even if becoming over-extended and temporarily devalued in the process. Munro's autobiographical reminiscences *The Brave Days* do for middle-class Edwardian Glasgow life what Bell's *I Remember* did for the late Victorian city.

The *fin de siécle* nineties and most of the Edwardian decade had John Davidson (1857–1909), the Barrhead-born Greenock-bred writer, as Glasgow's nearest *Yellow Book* literary representative. He taught in various schools, including Kelvinside Academy, before going south, where he battled with the usual odds against making a living as a poet and essayist, odds stacked high by depressions stemming from the strain of insanity in his family.

While his best poem, 'Thirty Bob a Week', which powerfully influenced both T.S. Eliot and 'Hugh MacDiarmid', is couched in Cockney terms, the hopeless position of the struggling London clerk he depicts was probably little different from that of his Glasgow counterpart.

> And its often very cold and very wet,
>   And my missis stitches towels for a hunks;
> And the Pillar'd Halls is half of it to let –
>   Three rooms about the size of travelling trunks.
> And we cough, my wife and I, to dislocate a sigh,
>   When the noisy little kids are in their bunks.
>
> But you never hear her do a growl or whine,
>   For she's made of flint and roses, very odd,
> And I've got to cut my meaning rather fine,
>   Or I'd blubber, for I'm made of greens and sod:
> So p'r'aps we are in Hell for all that I can tell,
>   And lost and damn'd and served up hot to God.

Being lost and damned brings us to that section of Victorian society who might reasonably have supposed they were: the poor. By a 1579 Act of the Scottish Parliament, magistrates in burghs and justices of the peace in rural parishes had had conferred on them the right of assessment for poor relief, a right later transferred to heritors and kirk sessions. Very few parishes made use of these powers of compulsory assessment by the beginning of the nineteenth century, the Scots preferring to give relief through voluntary church contributions. Begging, by and large, was regarded as a suitable means of augmenting this tardy charity.

After twenty years' opposition to the forward-looking proposal that it should municipalize the city's water supplies, Glasgow Corporation Water Works Act finally got through Parliament in 1855, enabling the corporation, at a cost of a million pounds, to harness Loch Katrine and bring the water by pipeline to Milngavie reservoir, a supply later augmented by feed-ins from several other nearby mountainy lochs, notably Lochs Vennacher and Drunkie.

Thirty-four miles of tunnelling were completed, and a reservoir built at Mugdock all for £70,000. A million and a half pounds had been spent before the final link-up was complete, and the city was receiving 50 million gallons a day.

On 15th October 1859 the Queen and Prince Albert went by rail to Callander and then by coach to Loch Katrine. Although the day was wet and blowy, a large crowd turned out, making use of the cheap railway excursion fare offered. The guard of honour included detachments of the 42nd and 59th Highlanders. Lord Provost Stewart met the Queen, and aboard the *Roy Roy* they sailed to the mouth of the tunnel. 'Such a work is worthy of the enterprise of Glasgow,' said Her Majesty, turning the handle which caused the water to flow, 'and I trust it will be blessed with complete success.'

It was, and is: various extensions have kept Glasgow thoroughly on top of its water problem.

Various other Acts were passed in the sixties relating to nuisances, sanitary reform and the better organization of the police.

Most important of all, however, was the appointment of Glasgow's first Medical Officer of Health, Dr W.T. Gairdner, in 1862. The vital importance of hygiene and of preventative medicine finally began to be recognized during the seventies, though not until the Medical Officer of Health in the eighties, Dr J.B. Russell, revealed in frequent speeches that 25 per cent of Glasgow's families were living in single-roomed houses and more than half of these were also taking in lodgers, did the extent and degree of the squalor and human degradation prevalent in the city begin to be generally realized. Even then, some wealthy Glaswegians were none too keen to provide finance for the speeding-up of improved conditions.

The Glasgow Improvement Act of 1866 resulted in the

setting up of the Glasgow Improvement Trust, which, though empowered to levy a rate of 6d. in the pound, was inadequately financed. It cleared over 15,000 houses from the old heart of the city, aided also by the demolition work of the railway companies as they swathed their way through slum areas. It is not to under-estimate the social urgency of the problem the Trust had to face to say that the pressure put upon them by the railway company to abandon the old university, and their failure to provide new houses for those who were displaced by their demolitions, were both to prove disastrous. Had the university stayed where it was, additional buildings would inevitably have been added to the old, and the creation of a new future central problem area would thus have been avoided. Without new houses in which the displaced slum-dwellers could be accommodated, they simply flooded into areas like the Gorbals and Cowcaddens, which then in turn entered upon their decades of overcrowded decline.

Under a later Act a further six central acres were cleared. While tenements were now provided for the poor, the mixed land-uses of the rebuilt areas set in being other problems for the passing years to hatch.

The continuing failure of any authority adequately to provide for those thrown out of work and hard put to it to avoid destitution, bred in Glaswegians a dislike of rent originally based on sheer inability to pay. This dislike of rent has had some curious consequences. Just before the First World War, for instance, when overcrowding was still widespread, one house in ten was actually standing empty, lodgings being cheaper than a place of one's own. Out of this situation has arisen the belief that, regardless of the income of the tenant, housing should be a 'social service', a manifestly absurd proposition in our affluent society.

By 1909, the corporation had built more than 2,000 houses, just over a quarter of which were for poorer tenants. In his budget that year, Lloyd George introduced a 20 per cent tax on the increment value of all heritable property. This, on top of the unfavourable Scots rating system, put an end almost immediately to private enterprise building for the working class, or, indeed, any other class.

Along with the rest of Scotland, Glasgow was affected by

the Scottish Education Act of 1872, which set up the school board system in which was vested control of parish and burgh schools, the Scotch Education Department (as it was at first called) becoming the central authority responsible for the qualification of teachers, the approving of grants and the election of the members of the school boards.

Glasgow's first school board of fifteen members was voted into office the following year. It later became the practice in Glasgow for three members to be nominated each by the Church of Scotland, the Free Church and the Roman Catholic Church, three by Labour organizations while three members remained independent. That first school board decided that thirty new schools with accommodation for 22,000 pupils were needed immediately; so, borrowing over £1¼ million, it set in hand a modest building programme. Compulsory attendance was at last introduced for children between the ages of 5 and 13, the leaving age being raised to 14 in 1902. By 1892, education up to leaving age was, in general, free. It is interesting to note that it took England until 1899 to provide an equivalent to the Scotch Education Department, when the English Board of Education was formed. Scotland's continuing lead in Victorian times gave substance to the belief that her education was ahead of England's, a belief from which the substance has long since evaporated although the myth lives on.

In 1888, Glasgow children first presented themselves for the examinations of the Scottish Leaving Certificate. The department's inspectorate soon had under state control a more or less uniform curriculum, varied only by a few independent schools outside their authority. The most famous of these schools in the city were the Glasgow Academy, founded in 1846 and first located in Elmbank Street,[20] vacating its original building in favour of the High School for Boys (as the old grammar school, formerly in Rottenrow, George Street and after 1835, John Street, was now called) in 1878, when the academy moved to Kelvinbridge; Allan Glen's (1853), and Kelvinside Academy (1878).

The Co-operative and Trade Union movements also grew during these years. Both organizations could possibly be described as encouraging a process of self-education. There had been stirrings of early co-operatives among the Fenwick weavers in 1769, and at Govan, Tradeston, Lennoxtown and Kilmarnock around 1800. When Robert Owen returned from America, he threw much of his energy into trying to further acceptance of the idea of the Co-operative Movement. He met with many setbacks, and in the end much of the credit for persistently carrying on in spite of initial discouragement went to his disciple, Alexander Campbell, a Glaswegian. The movement received parliamentary sanction in 1852, through the Industrial and Provident Societies Act, although the right of co-operatives tc exemption from income tax, provided goods were sold only to members, came only with an amending Act of 1893. But the Glasgow Co-operative Society collapsed in 1864 as a result of overextending its branches, and it was not until 1871 that the Kinning Park and St George's Societies reasserted Glasgow's stake in the enterprise. In the meantime, the Scottish Co-operative Wholesale Society was formed in 1868, beginning business in Madeira Street. It then employed six people, had capital of £1,795 and had sales of just under £10,000 in its first year. In 1897 it was to build itself the imposing palace which had been unplaced in the City Chambers competition, designed by the firm of Bruce and Hay, on the south side of the river, as if to assert with a grandiose flourish its own success – a success reflected in its capital of more than £2½ million, its sales of over £4½ million and its staff of almost 4,800.

The smaller grocer always resented the advantages thus given to the Co-operative Movement, and middle-class housewives often refused to support it. To shop at 'the Co-op', was regarded as some kind of unthinkable betrayal by my own relatives when I was a child. But its social value has been immense, only now perhaps becoming less useful in an affluent society and against fierce competition from supermarkets some of which are owned by international operatives with enormously greater resources behind them.

It had been the enterprise of the weavers which had provided the impetus behind the first moves towards establishing the co-operatives. It was the miners who were principally behind the first practical steps towards the formation of Trade Unions. Since the trial and deportation of

the Edinburgh advocate Thomas Muir and other Friends of
the People in the 1790s, there had been substantial opposition
to any kind of unions, opposition strengthened by the
Combination Acts of 1799 and 1800. Alexander Campbell
became one of the leaders in the formation of Trades
Councils, which began to be set up in industrial centres after
1858. Campbell's friend Alexander MacDonald, a Lanarkshire miner who qualified at Glasgow university by
working at his studies in the winter and going down the pits
in the summer, and who had then become a teacher,
co-operated in helping to have carried through the Reform
Act of 1867 giving working men in towns the vote, and an
Act of 1871 which gave trade unions greater financial
security. Macdonald, having unsuccessfully contested the
Kilmarnock Burghs seat in 1868, entered Parliament in 1874
as the member for North Stafford – one of the first two
Labour members ever elected – and was instrumental in
having the Master and Servant Act, which discriminated
against the servant, superseded by the Employers and
Workmen Act, which put both on an equal footing and
recognized the right of collective bargaining. The Act
restricting strike action was also repealed.

In the late eighties, Keir Hardie (1856–1915) was associated
with John Burns and Tom Mann in a movement which
looked forward to the overthrow of the capitalist system by
1889, the anniversary of the French Revolution, Hardie, a
Glaswegian, was responsible for the formation of the
Scottish Miners' Federation before he stood unsuccessfully as
Labour candidate in a Lanarkshire by-election, having been
refused the Liberal nomination because some Liberal
supporters would not vote for a working man.

Because of Roman Catholic antipathy, and a tendency to
engage in internecine war, the pre-First World War Labour
Party never really got anywhere until 1909, by which time
the British Labour Party had tempted all the contending
Scottish Labourites into its centralized political fold. It is
interesting to note that Scottish Labour at first took over
several of the causes upheld by the Scottish Liberals,
including temperance, Home Rule, and shorter working
hours; and perhaps a sad reflection on the Scottish variety of
human fallibility that temperance was eventually abandoned,

because it was simply impossible to sustain, and that Home Rule for Scotland was ditched because by 1945 it had become inconvenient to Big Brother in England.

In 1914 three out of Scotland's forty MPs were Labour, Keir Hardie having been elected to an English seat in 1892.

That temperance cause which the Labourites espoused had its origins in a Maryhill movement of 1829, out of which grew the Glasgow and West of Scotland Temperance Society. Various bodies followed, notably the Scottish Temperance League in 1844, the Scottish Lodge and the Independent Order of Good Templars in 1869, and the Band of Hope Union the following year.

There was a real problem to fight, because drink shops were both the poor man's only apparent refuge from misery, and the certain means of increasing his destitution. Unfortunately, many of the earliest opponents of the misuse of drink nullified their efforts by failing to tackle the social miseries which drove the victims to the gin parlours. Nor was it helpful to make the drinking shops as uncomfortable as possible, since sordid surroundings merely encouraged increasing squalor.

Although a mild attempt at controlling drinking had been made with the Home-Drummond Act of 1828, the first effective control measure was the Forbes-Mackenzie Act of 1854, named after its sponsor, the Member for Peeblesshire. It set down the hours between which drink could be sold – from 8 a.m. to 11 p.m. – abolished the Sunday sale of drink and prohibited the sale of liquor within 6 miles of a tollhouse, the first blow to be struck against 'one for the road'. Later legislation followed, relating to such matters as the granting of licences by magistrates, the sale of drink to children under 14, the discretion of magistrates to order ten o'clock closing, and giving the police increased powers of supervision. Following a Royal Commission's report in 1899, an Act of 1903 set up licensing courts in burghs of 4,000 and over and in counties. It also increased the penalties for drunkenness. The Scottish Temperance Act of 1913 set up a system whereby the electors could vote for no change, no licence or the limitation of licences. While the majority has always voted for no change, the option system has led to the possibility of small intemperately temperate pressure-groups forcing the withdrawal of established licences through a well-organized campaign. This merely pushes the problem into someone else's bailiewick. In the case of the once dry burgh of Kirkintilloch, the local police had regularly to deal with home-coming drunks from neighbouring parishes.

Many of the old restrictions designed to curb nineteenth-century working-class drunkenness were carried over into the twentieth century and are quite out of line with the rest of Europe. Consequently, prior to reform in 1978, they adversely affected the tourist industry. It is sad to reflect that the churches opposed drink law reform as they have opposed many recent laws designed humanely to ease the position of such social unfortunates as homosexuals or the unhappily married. Truly, Calvin and Knox have much for which to answer!

The rate of alcoholism remains high in Glasgow (as, indeed, throughout Scotland), partly due to the Scots custom of absorbing 'pint and chaser' – in English parlance, sending a whisky down the gullet along with a pint of beer – but the despair of poverty need no longer be a cause of drunkenness. Other means and different agents to combat the contemporary misuse of alcohol are being found, since those well-meaning bodies which sought to grapple with the Victorian manifestations of the problem have either gone out of existence, or, as a result of their own extreme lack of tolerance, fallen into disrepute.

Public occasions, sad and gay, meant a good deal to the inhabitants of late Victorian and Edwardian Glasgow.

Not all of them were pleasant.

There were river tragedies, due to the overcrowding of the ferries crossing the Clyde. On 6th April 1861 the paddle-steamer *Lochgoil*, returning from Lochgoilhead with a full cargo of intoxicated Saturday excursionists, hove-to off Govan to allow some passengers to disembark on the Govan ferry, which came alongside. The drunken excursionists tumbled into the little ferry boat in such numbers that she was swamped. Half a dozen passengers were drowned.

Worse still was the sinking of the overcrowded ferry boat at the foot of Clyde Street at the end of November 1864, when the boat left the ferry-steps just as the *Inveraray Castle* was passing. The steamer's paddles were of the old-fashioned non-feathering type, which set up so considerable a wash that the ferry-boat capsized and some nineteen lives were lost (for some reason the exact number was never established). This accident led to restrictions on the number of passengers which these old row-boat ferries were allowed to carry, and to the placing of an order for the first steam ferry-boat with Hedderwick of Govan.

Then there was the murder of Jessie Macpherson, a servant to the Flemings in Sandyford Place, in July 1862. She had been visited by her friend Jessie McLaughlan on Saturday 4th July, and two days later was found dead in her bed by young Fleming, in the Fleming home. McLaughlan tried to maintain that she, Jessie Macpherson and old Fleming had been drinking together on the Saturday night, and that old Fleming committed the murder in a drunken passion. But the jury decided otherwise. Found guilty, McLaughlan was sentenced to be hanged, but reprieved.

The third Scottish banking disaster, the City of Glasgow[21] failure, took place in 1878. In this case not only had the directors made unsound advances of millions of pounds, but they had manipulated their books to conceal the true facts from the shareholders. The final deficit was over £5 million. As the bank was unlimited, most of the directors were ruined. Several were tried and imprisoned, but the effect on individuals who had lodged most of their savings with the bank, and on the business world generally – firm after firm failed for many weeks – was no less disastrous. Sellars' splendid new building, into which they had not yet moved, was never completed, became a warehouse and survived until 1959. As a result of the financial crash, the Scottish banks had to register under an Act of 1879 as limited liability companies, but further to help restore public confidence they commenced the practice of having their books audited by independent accountants.

The last public hanging in Glasgow, that of Dr Edward William Pritchard, took place in 1865. He was a fashionable, dapper Sauchiehall Street medico whom some thought little more than an elegant quack. He murdered his wife and his mother-in-law, the latter quickly because she had become suspicious about the lengthy illness of her daughter, who was in fact being given regular doses of antimony, a poison used in preserving bodies. The good doctor, prominent public lecturer and Freemason, was meanwhile having an affair with their Highland maid-servant. He was wearing a new pair of patent leather boots when he took his enforced departure from this life between the pillars of the old South Jail, facing David Hamilton's Nelson's Monument, on Glasgow Green. A huge crowd turned out to watch. Sermons were preached while pockets were picked. The doctor, whose career was to provide 'James Bridie' with the theme for his play *Doctor Angelus*, seems to have regarded these sordid proceedings with dignified contempt, and made a good end. He was hanged between the two central pillars of the Justiciary Court House, in the Saltmarket, part of the first correct Greek Doric Portico in Glasgow. The pillars were retained in J.H. Craigie's replacement buildings of 1913.

Glasgow readers must have been as shocked as those in the rest of Scotland when they learned about the Tay Bridge disaster. The bridge gave way while a train was crossing it during a stormy evening late in December 1880, its passengers being thrown into the waters below. Of more direct concern was the capsizing of the steamer *Daphne* while she was being launched from a Linthouse yard on 3rd July 1883; the 124 workers aboard her were drowned.

The following year a false fire alarm in the Star Music Hall, Partick, resulted in a stampede that killed fourteen people and injured twenty-four.

Queen Victoria's Jubilee provided the public with a happier interest, when, on 16th June 1887, in a city gaily decorated for the occasion, 1,000 poor people were entertained to dinner by the corporation, after a cathedral service; a Grand Review of regulars and volunteers was held on Glasgow Green, when the weather was fortunately kinder than it had been on the occasion of the famous 'Wet Review'; there was music in Kelvingrove, the Queen's and Alexandra Parks, a corporation banquet and at night a great ball in St Andrew's Halls. Her Majesty requested that a replica of the statue of Prince Albert which stood in George Square should be erected in Windsor Great Park.

Similar celebrations were held to celebrate the sixtieth year of her reign in 1897, and in addition there was 'a display of pyrotechnics' in the evening.

Allegorical figure on bridge over the Kelvin in Kelvingrove (1919)

Edwardian Glasgow's most talked-of murder was that of an old lady, Miss Gilchrist, who lived with her maid in West Princes Street. On 21st December 1908 her downstairs neighbour became suspicious that all was not well, and, on going to investigate, met the maid, Lambie, who had been out buying a paper. As she opened the door a man came out, greeted them and disappeared. Inside was the body of Miss Gilchrist, who had been murdered with considerable brutality. Papers were scattered about the floor, but her jewels were untouched, except possibly for a crescent brooch: 'possibly', because the testimony was Lambie's.

Because a dishonest character called Oscar Slater had been trying to sell a diamond ring pawn ticket, and had gone off to America on the *Lusitania*, the police formed the suspicion that he must have some connection with the crime. On very dubious identification by a passing message girl, one or two passers-by in the street and Lambie herself, Slater was tried, convicted and sentenced to death.

The sentence was changed by the Secretary of State to one of life imprisonment. Conan Doyle, the creator of Sherlock Holmes, pressed for a new trial. Edgar Wallace, the author of a stream of enormously popular detective novels, wrung from Lambie, by then married and in America, the admission that she might have mentioned the wrong name to the police, though she insisted that Slater had previously visited Miss Gilchrist's house.

Although Lambie refused to give further evidence when a new trial was eventually ordered, Slater got off on the technicality that the judge at the original trial had misdirected the jury by allowing the prosecution to blacken Slater's moral character. Slater, a far from attractive man, got less compensation than was his due; Conan Doyle felt that because of the work he had done he should share in Slater's £6,000; and no one in Glasgow believes that the mystery of Miss Gilchrist's death has yet been, or ever will be, solved.

The available opportunities for indulging private pleasures widened considerably.

By the eighties, most factory workers had Saturday afternoons free, although those who served in shops had to be behind their counters until ten o'clock at night on what consequently became the busiest shopping day of the week. Generally, leisure time increased.

Cricket had been played on Glasgow Green since the end of the eighteenth century, but although it has a surprisingly large following – as the BBC in Scotland discovered some years ago when they decided to devote less time to cricket results – it is not a game which flourishes naturally in a rainy climate.

Football is by far the most fundamental Glasgow game. Its three famous teams were all founded within a few years of each other: Queen's Park in 1867, Rangers in 1872, and Celtic in 1874. Unlike the other two, Queen's Park are no longer professionals; but in 1867 they brought Association Football to Scotland and helped to formulate modern playing conditions out of what had previously been little better than a rough and tumble scramble. Celtic (1874) and Rangers (1872) have had competing religious overtones since their foundation, with results frequently neither good for the reputation of football nor for Scotland. The Scottish Football Association was founded in 1873, and, through its Scottish Challenge Cup, helped the spread of the game.

Enormous crowds still turn up for Rangers–Celtic matches at Ibrox Stadium or Parkhead, or for the biennial international match with England. At one such international at Ibrox in 1902, the wooden platform collapsed killing twenty-three spectators and injuring more than 500. This disaster was exceeded by the even worse disaster of 2nd January 1971, when someone fell as the crowd was streaming down the steep steps of the eastern exit from Ibrox. In the resulting catastrophic human pile-up, sixty-six people died and more than 100 were injured.

Football has been the Glasgow man's absorbing passion now for nearly a century. Headlines which, were they not printed on the pink or green paper of the sports editions of the *Evening Times* or *Citizen*, would seem to portend international doom, stand above stories as eagerly read by those who have attended a match as by those unable to be present.

Interest in football seems to exist at different imaginative levels. To some, the game is a counterpoint of rhythmic motions, a kind of rudimentary ballet. To others its value is the usually harmless sublimatory release of tensions it provides through emotional identification with the 'hero' figure. Most fans probably just think it good fun, a game they like to watch and which can nearly always triumph over the Glasgow climate.

Rugby is played mostly by the pupils of Glasgow's fee-paying schools. Although it has a large following in the Borders, in Glasgow 'the general public takes comparatively little interest in it, and the support accorded it comes pretty much from the better class school element'.[22] In Scotland, unlike England, rugby is played only by amateurs.

Golf has continued to be a Scottish preoccupation since it was introduced from Holland in the fifteenth century, though it tends to be the recreation of the professional or businessman rather than the artisan. Bowls, an even more ancient game, has always had a strong Glasgow following among all social classes. Rowing and quoiting became popular in later Victorian times, as did cycling, after the development of Dumfriesshire-born Kirkpatrick Macmillan's invention of 1838,[23] and, in winter, curling.

Yacht-racing is now a popular pastime. In Victorian days it was the pastime of the rich. The annual Clyde Regatta was then the occasion for the big yachts to spread huge sails and race the various vintages of *Shamrock* built by Sir Thomas Lipton (1850–1931). He made his money from a chain of stores that cut out middlemen, brought produce direct from the 'Green Isle', and blended tea to suit the differing textures of water in the towns where his chain had branches, but never achieved his ambition to win back for Britain the Americas Cup.

Between 1884 and 1903 Glasgow used water-buses on the Clyde, the Cluthas, eventually twelve in number and covering the 3 miles between Victoria Bridge and Whiteinch Ferry. For most Glaswegians, the Clyde was still the pleasure-ground for the annual holiday. Clyde steamers grew more and more luxurious and even the competition of the railway companies for a time did not take the edge off the operating profitability of the surviving private owners. The most famous of the Clyde steamers, MacBrayne's *Columba*, built by J. and J. Thomson, made her first appearance on the river in 1878, and sailed every summer until 1936, most of her life paddling up and down the 'Royal Route' from the Broomielaw to Ardrishaig and back. Her sister ship the *Iona*, built in 1864, though less luxurious, achieved even greater longevity, surviving in service to the record age of 72. Laurence Lockhart, a nephew of John Gibson Lockhart, described the scenic and the cosmopolitan delights of a sail on the *Iona* from the Clyde to Oban in his novel *Fair to See* (1891):

What is there to do? What is there not to do? And see? First, if you have ever so little of an artist's eye or an artist's soul – that is to say, if you love nature at all – very surely you will find that love stirred and quickened within you all the live-long day – if you will only keep your eyes open – while threading with the *Iona* the wondrous labyrinth of her beautiful course. The mountain panorama which greets you as you start, noble though it may be, is but the noble promise of still better things....

The steamer is a varying stage, on which you can see going on, side by side, no end of little dramas; and as for the dramatis personae, who are they? or rather, who are they not? Honeymooning couples huddled together under umbrellas to screen them from the sun, and from the world's garish eye: inevitable reading parties from Oxford and Cambridge: indigestive blue-stockings, 'inverted' philosophers, saucey persons and leathery-looking lawyers; sportsmen *en route* for their shootings, yachting men for their yachts, gamekeepers, ghillies and figure footmen; bleary Germans and dyspeptic yankees calculating the exact number of cocked hats into which the Mississippi knocks the Clyde; jocund schoolboys, bread-and-butter misses, 'cock-lairds' and Cockneys; Highlanders and Mile-Enders; ladies and gentlemen – all sorts and conditions of men, natural and artificial, shamming and detective, bragging and counter-bragging, appreciative and depreciative, a *farrango*, a *pot-pourri, Olla Podrida*, a dainty dish to set before Democritus.

Other famous pre-war ships, which doubtless carried a similarly varied human cargo, and whose names were once summer music to Glaswegians' ears, included the Buchanan Steamers' *Isle of Arran* (1892); the Caledonian Steam Packet Company's *Duchess of Rothesay* (1895) and *Duchess of Fife* (1903); the Glasgow and South Western Railway's *Juno*

(1898), *Jupiter* (1896) and *Waverley* (1899); Captain Williamson's *Benmore* (1876) and *Kylemore* (1897); the 'dry' paddler *Ivanhoe* (1880) and the *Lord of the Isles* (1891), as well as the Williamson and Buchanan turbine steamers *King Edward* (1901) and *Queen Alexandra* (1912).

When the First World War broke out in 1914, forty steamers were plying between Glasgow, Gourock or Greenock and the Clyde Estuary, calling at piers or meeting ferries at eighty-five places. Alan J. S. Paterson has chronicled the late Victorian and Edwardian Clyde fleet in a book which he calls *The Golden Years of the Clyde Steamers* (1896–1914). Myself, I am no more a believer in years of gold or lead than in acts of black or white. But if one accepts such oversimplified conceits, then in a sense the late Victorian and Edwardian periods were also the Golden Years of Glasgow. It is doubtful if, in those summery August days of 1914, when an unheard-of game-massacring European nobleman was murdered in Sarajevo, many Glaswegians bothered much about the news when it first reached them. Yet the outcome of that far-away murder ended the 200-year-long era of Glasgow's success story. Nothing would ever be the same again.

Notes

1 The Bairds of Gartsherrie produced iron in vast quantity by pirating the hot blast system. From being poor farmers in the late eighteenth century, by 1855 they were among the richest industrialists in the world. They gave millions of pounds to Glasgow and the Baird Trust is still active to this day.
2 The Ayrshire collieries, however, kept up their traditional export trade to America, the West Indies and Ireland throughout the nineteenth century.
3 According to James MacKinnon in *The Social and Industrial History of Scotland* (1921), the credit should go to a Mr Newton.
4 Best remembered for such churches as Dowanhill (1865), Camphill (1875–78), Hyndland (1886); for the Sun Life Assurance Building in West George Street (1892) and many Helensburgh villas. During the depression which followed the financial collapse of the City of Glasgow Bank, Leiper, a shy bachelor, studied painting in Paris for some years, though he later returned to Glasgow and resumed his architectural practice.
5 A restoration by the Charles Robertson Partnership.
6 Then a student at the Art School when it was located at Ingram Street.

7 There is some evidence to suggest that Northpark Terrace, Hamilton Drive (1860) is Thomson's; a site plan and the fact that it was built for one of his clients.

8 Still a furniture shop, but now under different ownership.

9 Now divided into several shops.

10 The descendants of Burns's supercilious 'Bonnie Lass o' Ballochmyle'.

11 Removed from George Square to make way for an Information Kiosk, since demolished.

12 Pseudonym for James Bone, Archibald Hamilton Charteris and Muirhead Bone.

13 The date of this official visit was 22nd June. She later paid a private visit, as did her son, the Duke of Cambridge, and, amongst other royal personages the King of the Belgians, to say nothing of nearly 6 million non-royal personages.

14 Alfred Waterhouse, the competition assessor, turned down much finer designs by Honeyman and by Keppie and Mackintosh, for which no seeing Glaswegian will lightly forgive him!

15 Electricity had been introduced to Glasgow for domestic use in 1893.

16 I am not suggesting that pornography is a measure of sophistication; rather indicating the continuing restraints kept upon taste by Scottish Calvinism when such restraints no longer prevailed throughout London society.

17 One shilling is equivalent to five pence today, not allowing for inflation.

18 A characteristic of later Scottish painting, and of nearly all Scottish poetry, as if in defiance of our predominantly grey skies.

19 Seamills, as Airlie represents Fairlie.

20 Later the headquarters of Strathclyde Regional Council.

21 The City of Glasgow Bank was located in Virginia Street, on a site presently occupied by Marks and Spencer.

22 John K. McDowall, *The People's History of Glasgow* (1899).

23 But the Chevalier de Sivrae got in first with his wheeled 'hobby horse' of 1790, and Baron Karl Drais von Sauerbronn in 1810, with his 'Draisene'. Neither of them developed their invention commercially.

7

Two World Wars and Between

By the time war came in 1914 there was already a long tradition of voluntary military service in Glasgow. When the threat of Napoleon's invasion had seemed a reality, nine regiments of Glasgow volunteers were formed, including the Glasgow Light Horse (1796) and the Glasgow Volunteers (1803). Although they never had to fire a shot in anger, they were called out more than once upon rumours and alarms, and until Napoleon was finally defeated, slept with their muskets and their uniforms to hand.

During 1848, Europe's year of revolution, a volunteer cavalry force was formed. This became the Queen's Own Royal Glasgow Yeomanry.

After the Crimean War, menacing noises from the Paris of the Third French Empire resulted in renewed efforts being made to revive the volunteers, and in 1859, the Old Guard of Glasgow became the forerunners of the 1st, 2nd and 3rd Lanark Volunteers, the 1st recruiting from the West End, the 3rd from the South Side. The twenty-first birthday of the Volunteers was the occasion of Queen Victoria's 'Wet Review' on Glasgow Green, held in 1881 during torrential rain, which subsequently resulted in the deaths of some of the less robust of the 40,000 officers and men who had been on parade. This was also the year in which the voluntary forces were first grouped under territorial regimental designations, the 1st, 2nd, 3rd, 4th and 7th Lanarkshire Volunteers becoming The Cameronians (Scottish Rifles) and the 5th, 6th, 8th, 9th, and 10th forming the Highland Light Infantry. It was a Lieutenant W.A. Smith of the First Lanark Rifles, a volunteer later to become Sir William Smith, who in 1883 founded the Boys' Brigade. The BB, whose members until comparatively recently wore the original blue pill-box hats wrapped with a band of white, was organized on military lines and run in conjunction with a Sunday school, aimed at inculcating military-style discipline into working-class lads.

The Boer War produced eleven serving companies from Scotland. Many Glaswegians enrolled as regulars. In 1908, those who had volunteered became the core of the new Territorial Army. At the same time the Officers' Training Corps scheme, which was designed to produce what used to be called 'officer material' began to operate in public schools.[1]

Field Marshal Earl Roberts, whose equestrian statue still looks exultingly across Kelvingrove Park towards the university, addressed the students and others in May 1913, warning them of the need for a citizen army capable of engaging with the Germans at short notice should war come as a result of the German Kaiser's scarcely-concealed belligerence. But it was not easy for Lord Roberts to make his message carry conviction because, earlier in the year, Lloyd George had been thundering away about the folly of expenditure on armaments. While an audience in St Andrew's Halls attending the last of Lord Roberts' series of meetings passed a resolution which, had it been implemented, would have amounted to compulsory service in the Territorial Army, the war when it did come nevertheless took the British by surprise.

On the British side, there was a belief that Germany could not stand up for long against the combined forces of Britain, France and Russia. War, if it should come, would be a short-lived affair, over by Christmas, a belief it seems, also held by the Germans, though they, of course, envisaged winning it. Glasgow, like the rest of the United Kingdom, was quite unprepared for the long years of struggle and of fearful slaughter which were unleashed by the declaration of war on Germany by Britain, her Dominions and Empire, on 4th August 1914.

The exalted idealistic mood of the sensitive young men who went eagerly into the fight is enshrined in Rupert Brooke's well-known sonnet 'Now God be thanked who has matched us with this hour', and in less familiar lines by Lawrence Binyon, from his poem, 'The Fourth of August':

Now in thy splendour go before us,
Spirit of England, ardent-eyed,
Enkindle this dear earth that bore us,
In the hour of peril purified.

The cares we hugged drop out of vision,
Our hearts with deeper thoughts dilate.
We step from days of sour division
Into the grandeur of our fate.

The British Expeditionary Force of the regular army at first consisted of one cavalry division and four infantry divisions, later supplemented by a further two. Known as the Contemptible Little Army, it not only turned the first thrust of the German horde but secured the Channel ports, giving Britain time to arm.

Because the country was thought not to be ready to accept conscription, the first appeals were for volunteers to fill additional Territorial battalions. The Secretary of State for War, Lord Kitchener, appealed for 200,000 volunteers, using the famous finger-pointing poster. By 1915, Glasgow had contributed substantially more than its quota. The regiment most closely associated with the city was the Highland Light Infantry. Members of professions and trades formed their own fighting groups. Thus the 17th Battalion was largely recruited by the Chamber of Commerce and the 15th by the Corporation Tramway Department, spurred on by its manager, James Dalrymple, who used illuminated tramcars, banner posters round the Transport Department's offices in Bath Street and other startling publicity methods as part of a highly persuasive advertising campaign.

All in all, the H.L.I. had twenty-six battalions in action during the First World War. The Cameronians (Scottish Rifles), naturally also attracted Glaswegians. So, rather surprisingly, did the Cameron Highlanders, many Glasgow men responding to an appeal in the *Glasgow Herald* by the clan chief, Cameron of Lochiel, which had really been aimed at the men of the north-west.

The war had immediate effects on the wives and children of the private soldiers who responded to the call. The inadequate state of the national welfare arrangements resulted in numerous cases of hardship and privation, epitomized by a newspaper headline drawing attention to the plight of *The 12/6d. Woman*. The Prince of Wales immediately organized a National Relief Fund, to which Glasgow alone had subscribed nearly £240,000 within six months. It was the first of several such charities, a later one having the catch-phrase title of 'Jock's Box'. The extent of the need for such arrangements was made plain by Lord Provost Dunlop, who, in September 1915, announced that 100,000 women and children had already 'received relief'.

Amongst those who stayed at home, there was at first an attempt to carry on 'business as usual'. But the war's grip soon tightened. The German U-boat blockade began in February 1915, conscription was introduced in January 1916, and by early 1917 compulsory food rationing had replaced voluntary meatless days.

By 1916, the men who fought in the trenches knew the full horror of twentieth-century warfare. The bloodiest engagement was the Battle of the Somme, really a series of battles, fought between July 1916 and the end of the year. Huge hordes of men flung themselves against the entrenched positions of armed masses.

The histories of most of the battalions which fought in what used to be known as the Great War have been fully written up. The description which L.B. Oatts gives in his book *The Highland Light Infantry*, of what happened to some of the Glasgow men was more or less the common experience of all British regiments in France at that time.

The Glasgow Highlanders lost four hundred and twenty one all ranks at High Wood, but fought on until within six weeks their casualties had mounted to thirty-three officers and seven hundred and fifty men, which was just about all they had. They were reinforced by three hundred and fifty-five men drawn from other Scottish regiments, of whom some were young, some rather old, and some were just out of hospital. But they went on fighting, day after day, week after week, in conditions which the devil himself could scarcely improve in hell.... By the autumn, the battlefield had become such a sea of mud that men and animals were sometimes swallowed up in it; but there was still no let-up, although when the Battle of the Ancre had commenced in November, it had begun to snow.

Struggling through snow and sleet, the 16th and 17th H.L.I.

advanced together against the Redan Ridge at dawn – November eighteenth. The whole of the 17th and the right company of the 16th were decimated by machine guns and rifle-fire. But the survivors pressed on into the German Munich and Frankfurt trenches, overcame all resistance with the bayonet, and sent back fifty prisoners. Attacks on either side having failed, the remnants of the 16th H.L.I., about one hundred men under a sergeant major, then became isolated in the Frankfurt trench, which they held for eight days. At the end of it there were only fifteen left, who were then taken prisoner because they had become so weak from lack of food that they could no longer stand up.

After that, there were still two years of bloody battles to be footslogged through, the 15th and 16th H.L.I. being amongst those who faced up to Ludendorff's last desperate assault, which began on 21st March 1918.

Glasgow contributed to the other fighting services as well as to the army, although until comparatively recently the navy has remained very much an English service. More than thirty Clyde yards and engineering works turned out ships, many of which fell victim to German U-boat attacks and had to be replaced. A large repair programme was also carried through. The Mercantile Marine, who manned the Clyde-built ships, played the decisive part in defeating the German intention of cutting Britain off from the rest of the world.

Glasgow also specialized in the making of huge quantities of munitions, aeroplanes, uniforms and the other requirements of a nation at war.

There were, of course, sour overtones to be heard now and again. Some women who, for one reason or another, could not work, told vicious stories about the alleged excesses and extravagances of their earning sisters. Some fighting at the front accused those at home of profiteering. A Glasgow Academical, D.S. MacCall, neatly capped a speech by the Minister of Munitions in 1915, who, referring to the strategy at the western fronts, had declared: 'We must keep on striking, striking, striking ...', with four topical lines titled 'The Miners' Response'.

We do: the present desperate stage
Of fighting brings us luck;

And in the higher war we wage
(For higher wage) *We struck.*

Women came into the factories, and in long tartan skirts took over from the men as conductresses on the trams, making Glasgow the first city to employ women in this role. The war, indeed, hastened the emancipation of women, the vote being given to them in February 1919.

In September 1918, more than four Christmases after the war had started, Bulgaria asked for a truce. Although there was general realization that an armistice was probably in the offing, the suddenness with which it came surprised many people.

On the morning of 11th November a poster appeared in the *Glasgow Herald* office window emblazoned with a Union Jack and carrying one word – VICTORY!

A special edition of the paper was soon on sale in the streets. The chimes of the university gave the news to the West End. Classes ceased immediately. Hooters sounded in factories, sirens on ships. Flags and tricolours miraculously appeared from drawers and cupboards. Factory workers laid down their tools. A great crowd gathered in the streets, and the Lord Provost pronounced the civic joy from the back of a lorry in George Square.

'The greatest day of rejoicing Glasgow has ever known,' was how the *Glasgow Herald* summed it all up, telling us that: 'In the absence of military bands, a huge effort was made to import a melodic note to the jubilations by solo cornet and melodeon players and by solitary pipers. Now and again an unexpected bugle note was added, and the happy discord was increased by the clanging of the impatient warning bell of the tramway cars as they made their way through the surging crowd.'

That day there was a victory flight over the city, and in the evening the students organized a torchlight procession.

Banquets and celebrations were held during the weeks that followed. Field Marshal Sir Douglas Haig, as he then was, received the Freedom of the City in May 1919, and the Prince of Wales was given the same honour in March 1921 when he declared: 'Glasgow's achievements in the war stir one indeed.'

Glasgow had high hopes that its pre-war prosperity would

continue through the days of peace. But by nightfall on 12th
November the city was shrouded in a cold yellow fog, which
was to prove symbolic of what was to come.

The end of the war had certainly taught the fighting men
the meaning of disillusion. What had there been of 'grandeur'
about the fate met by nearly three and a half million of
Britain's young men on foreign fields? The mightiest human
struggle the world had ever seen may have begun in a mood
matched by Brooke's poetic heroics. It certainly ended with
the realistic bitterness of Siegfried Sassoon's attacks on
incompetent leadership, and the bitter pity of Wilfred
Owen's poem 'Futility':

> Are limbs so dear achieved,
> Full-nerved – still warm – too hard to stir?
> Was it for this the clay grew tall?

Even the imperialist's darling Rudyard Kipling celebrated
the finish of 'the war to end wars' with an aphorism,
'Common Form':

> If any question why we died,
> Tell them because our fathers lied.

With the return home of the ex-servicemen, it was not to
be long before 'sour division' opened up again.

Early in the nineteenth century, Glasgow had gained a
reputation for political militancy, mainly because of its
Chartist riots. This reputation was further increased as a
result of wartime labour troubles, chiefly in the munitions
industry where the necessary dilution of skilled workers with
unskilled labour caused resentment. This was not helped by
the inevitable deterioration in housing conditions, bad
enough in 1914 but worse after four years during which no
resources could be spared to build new homes.

Even during the war, in 1915, strikes and violence,
stimulated by the Clyde Workers' Committee, had resulted
in a visit to Glasgow by the Prime Minister, Lloyd George.
However, the Welshman's verbal wizardry failed to work its
accustomed magic upon the Clydesiders, and there was
nothing left for the Government but to resort to strong-arm
tactics. The militants were imprisoned in Edinburgh, among
them the communist schoolteacher John MacLean (who has

surely inspired more good poets to produce bad verse than any other Scot).

There was an ugly scene in George Square on the last day of January, 1919, when a crowd of strikers gathered outside the City Chambers to be told by the Lord Provost that two Glasgow men in high office, the Prime Minister, Bonar Law, and the Minister of Labour, Sir Robert Horne, had refused to intervene. A clash with the police ensued, and among those arrested was Emmanuel Shinwell. The day was dubbed by the press 'Black Friday'.

Three years later, Glasgow attracted more permanent political attention when a group of Independent Labour Party men known as The Clydesiders got themselves elected to Parliament. In 1914, Glasgow had only one Labour MP in the House of Commons. By 1922, after the apparent settling of the Irish question had freed Catholic voters from the need to support the Liberal Irish Homerulers, ten out of the fifteen Glasgow seats were captured by ILP members, along with a further five elsewhere in Scotland. Nine seats went to trade-union-nominated Labour MPs.

Long-haired 'Jimmy' Maxton, belligerent 'Manny' Shinwell and Thomas Johnstone, literary hater of *Our Noble Families*, amongst others, made the Clydeside presence audible in the House, sometimes beyond the breaking point of its traditional tolerance. One ILP man, John Wheatley, reached the Cabinet as Minister of Health in 1924. Though they were at war with conventional Labour MPs like Ramsay Macdonald, most of them eventually outgrew their extreme Marxist convictions. Johnstone became an outstandingly able and patriotic Secretary of State for Scotland under Churchill, and later the leader of many Scottish enterprises, including the North of Scotland Hydro-Electric Board. Lord Shinwell, as he became, was a Minister in Attlee's post-Second World War Government. David Kirkwood eventually accepted a peerage. Not all the others managed to preserve, as did James Maxton, a personal charm which mellowed with the years to make him eventually one of the best-loved members in the House.

Post-war Glasgow's dissatisfaction with men and affairs also played a part in the founding of the Scottish National Party. The position of Secretary for Scotland was abolished after 1745. Scottish matters were then dealt with by a series of 'managers' who controlled Scottish patronage, the most famous of them being Henry Dundas, Viscount Melville, 'the uncrowned ruler of Scotland', as Lord Cockburn dubbed him. Early in the 1880s nationalist feeling pressed Gladstone and the Government towards the eventual reinstatement of a Scottish administrative head, resulting in the creation of the Scottish Office in 1885. A Scottish Home Rule group was set up in 1886, and within a decade there was strong Liberal support at Westminster for a Scottish Parliament; support, in fact, that culminated in 1913 in the passage through the House with a majority of 145 of the second reading of a Home Rule Bill, which might have brought practical results but for the outbreak of the war with its overriding supra-national concerns. By 1923, the Liberal Party had been fragmented, the Scots backing the emergent Labour Party. A Glasgow Labour MP, George Buchanan, put forward a Home Rule Bill in 1926, which failed, as did the 1928 bill of the Reverend James Barr. In 1928 the Scottish National Party was launched with the support of Robert Bontine Cunninghame Graham, the writer and traveller who had a home, Ardoch, on the north bank of the Clyde; R.G. Muirhead, whose family tanning business was at Bridge of Weir, in Renfrewshire; the Duke of Montrose, whose seat of Buchanan Castle (now a ruin) at Drymen, was less than 20 miles from Glasgow; novelist Compton Mackenzie and poet C.M. Grieve ('Hugh MacDiarmid'). Though the Scottish National Party scored no political successes in the between-the-war years, indirectly they helped to stimulate a fairly widespread revival of Scottish consciousness, to say nothing of that literary revival titled, somewhat grandiosely by the Frenchman, Professor Denis Saurat, 'The Scottish Renaissance'.

These were real grounds for the dissatisfaction of which the temporary success of the Independent Labour Party and the arrival on the scene of the Scottish National Party were political reflections. After a vigorous short-lived spurt, all the traditional Scottish industries based in and around Glasgow went into decline.

The textile industry, with the exception of carpet-making, was so squeezed by both Lancashire and foreign competition that it virtually went out of existence within a decade, taking with it the last of the 'job' weavers who worked to special order in the East End of Glasgow.

The coal industry, faced again with the pre-war lessening of demand from the iron industry, continued to decline and had little success in meeting competition in foreign markets during the twenties. It was, indeed, the coal-owners belief that reduced wages could alone remedy a situation producing huge losses that spearheaded the General Strike of 1926.

The proposal upon which the miners and the employers failed to reach agreement was that there should be either a reduction in miners' wages or an increase in their working time in an effort to achieve profitability. For example, a hewer's wages were to come down from £3 18s. per week to £2 5s. 10d., or his hours to go up from seven to eight a day. On 1st May 1926 the *Glasgow Herald* commented grimly on the news of the breakdown of negotiations, declaring: 'The country now finds itself plunged into an industrial struggle the end of which it is exceedingly difficult to tell.' The Trades Union Congress called for a sympathetic strike. The government asked King George V to declare a national emergency. Unwisely, the Trades Union Congress responded by declaring general strike action from midnight on 3rd May, and thus found itself in a direct constitutional clash with the Government.

In the hours between, the politicians were busy with their speeches. Lloyd George said: 'There is one thing I dislike about the situation more than anything. There is a great similarity in it as to the methods that led to the great war – desultory and dilatory diplomatic exchanges, leisurely negotiations, never touching the real issues, and then the parties hurling ultimatums at each other.' George Lansbury thought it unfair that the miners should be asked to take less money or work an hour a day longer prior to discussions on the reorganization of their industry. J.H. Thomas, with remarkable originality of phrase, declared: 'The outlook is indeed black.' And Emmanuel Shinwell seemed to hint at the remoter realms of metaphysics and theology by reminding his hearers that the miners were standing out for a weekly wage of 50s., and asking: 'Can a man be a Christian on such a wage? He might think he was, but it was very difficult.'

For the first time, though probably not for the last, the Trade Union Movement overestimated its strength and underestimated the point at which the wider public will not put up with arrogant, bullying, sectional interests. The National Citizens' Union appealed for patriots to help man essential public services. The Roll of Voluntary Workers asked people to sign on at St Andrew's Halls. Sign on they did, and, for the six days the general strike lasted, they drove tramcars, moved supplies and kept life going. The *Glasgow Herald, The Bulletin*, the *Daily Record*, the *Glasgow Evening News*, the *Evening Times* and the *Citizen* all combined to produce a slim sheet called *Emergency News*.

The TUC soon realized that it had made a bad miscalculation and could not possibly win the struggle, although the return to work was gradual, and long delayed in the case of the miners.

'A victory for common sense,' said Stanley Baldwin. 'It had been once more demonstrated,' said the *Glasgow Herald*, itself now resolved to employ only non-union labour, 'that the people of Britain will not accept the dictation of any section, and that the community has within itself resources, vitality and adaptability equal to the overcoming of any emergency.' The unions' 'big battalions', it added, were 'neither so reliable nor so important a section of the community as they had imagined.' The following year the Government passed the Trades Disputes Act, prohibiting sympathetic strikes, an Act which, had it not been repealed by the Labour government of 1945, might have allowed the United Kingdom to compete against other trading nations after the Second World War with less 'wild-cat' disruption and loss of production arising out of industrial disputation than, in fact, was to prove possible.

The day after the return to peaceful normality, Messrs Paisley's advertised on the front page of the *Herald*, 'summer living suits for chauffeurs in blue, brown, claret, green or grey' for £7, with a matching cap at 12s. 6d. A Rolls-Royce to go with the suit and cap could be had for a little over £1,900 pounds, while a humbler car for you to drive yourself could be yours for a little over £200 – a Bean, perhaps, or a more dashing Voisin. A packet of ten Players cigarettes to smoke while you drove, or were driven, to the Palais de Danse – of which there were nearly fifty in the city during the twenties, all offering new dances like the Charleston, the

Foxtrot and the Black Bottom – cost 6d.

Something of the violence which bad social conditions and outworn religious rivalries engender was reflected in the gang warfare which troubled Glasgow's conscience through much of the twenties. It had reached a climax when Percy Sillitoe, later knighted, came from Sheffield as Chief Constable and proceeded to break up those bands of mindless hatchet-wielding, bicycle-chain-slashing thugs. There was also an alarming number of prosecutions among the city magistrates for fraud, five in all being sent to prison – giving rise to a music-hall joke about a wee man who arrived with his horse outside a pub and asked a pompous passerby to 'mind' it for him.' 'My man, d'ye no ken who I am?' the pompous one asked – 'No, sir.' – 'I'm a Glasgow magistrate' – Pause while the wee fellow digested the information, and thought for a moment. 'Och it's aa' richt. I'm only gaen in for a quick yin, an' ye'll no get faur wi' the beast in that time.'

During the thirties, some increased home demand for coal and export agreements concluded with the Scandinavian countries, Canada and Ireland helped to absorb production for a few years. But confidence in the coal industry was gone, and in the Lanarkshire coalfields alone the labour force fell by 50 per cent between 1914 and 1932.

The iron industry was also in trouble. There was a drastic decline in the production of Scottish pig iron, while the decline of locally produced ore and the closure of the Glengarnock works in 1926 – the only works in Scotland producing the kind of basic Bessemer they required – induced Stewart and Lloyds to move to Corby in order to be nearer their English source of supply. There then followed amalgamations among the steel makers, until by 1936 the Steel Company of Scotland and the Lanarkshire Steel Company were both under the control of Colvilles. Thereafter, Colvilles went in for improvements and for modernization. Although these changes had not resulted in Scotland possessing a fully-integrated steel works by 1939, at least they prepared the way for such a step in the post-Second World War years.

Shipbuilding in some respects fared worst of all. After a brief post-war boom caused by the need to replace war-lost tonnage, and a further brief boom brought about by the hold-up of orders due to the General Strike, the Depression set in. The rusty hull of John Brown and Company's order 'Number 534', later to become the Cunard liner *Queen Mary*, towered in its uncompleted state above Clydebank, a symbol of the stagnation which had overcome not only the industry but the whole of the business world. Government help towards finishing '534' in 1933 made John Brown's yard a busy place until the launch the following year; but not even a 'scrap-and-build' recommendation from the Government did much to help the Upper Clyde yards.

There were a number of reasons for the severe decline in shipbuilding orders. Foreign buyers were no longer ordering from the Clyde, many countries which were formerly customers having established shipbuilding industries of their own. Even British shipowners were finding it cheaper to build in foreign yards. Indeed, but for increased naval construction as the thirties wore on and the building of the *Queen Elizabeth*, launched in 1938, the social disaster which occurred would have been even worse than it was.

The fact is that the Slump of the early thirties was virtually worldwide. Tramp steamers for which there were no cargoes lay idle and rusting at anchor in the Gareloch and the Holy Loch. Unemployment in the United Kingdom was nearly 3 million by the end of 1931, and by the following year approximately 30 per cent of the working population of Scotland, most of them in or around Glasgow, were unemployed. Dole queues and straggling processions of hunger marchers became familiar sights, and posed in my young mind, as I set out in my parents' car on a weekend afternoon drive to the country, the problem of the haves and the have-nots, an antithesis which social measures have very considerably ameliorated throughout the United Kingdom, but to which there is fundamentally no ultimate solution under any known system of Government, since no amount of egalitarian adjustment can counter the handiwork of non-egalitarian Nature.

But the twenties and thirties in Glasgow were by no means all gloom. The British Broadcasting Corporation set up its first studios at 141 Bath Street in 1922, moving the following year to 202 Bath Street. After a brief period when its headquarters were at 5 Queen Street, Edinburgh, it returned to Broadcasting House, Glasgow, developing around the former Queen Margaret College.

In the days when the programme came out of Bath Street, there was for me the memorable experience of listening in the parlour of our Ashton Terrace home to the 'aunts' and 'uncles' of 'Children's Hour', pricking the crystal with the cat's whisker to get a clearer sound through the headphones. I made my own first appearance before the microphone as a broadcaster singing 'Linden Lea' in my piping, unbroken treble voice. Later, there was the extraordinary fascination of Christmas Eve 1929, when my father brought home a 'wireless' which gave forth its own sound – Christmas carols, comedians, a Mozart symphony and of course the well-loved 'aunts' and 'uncles' in a new round aural dimension. Not even the introduction of television, for all its greater cleverness, ever managed to reproduce for me such a glimpse of boundlessly enriching possibilities as did the first sounds out of that self-amplifying radio set.

In these early days, and for several decades thereafter, the BBC accepted the duty, incorporated by implication in its charter, of fostering the Scottish languages and the nation's culture. But in spite of that remarkable series of broadcasts the *Foundations of Scottish Music* – the voluminous research material for which was accidentally turned over to the paper-salvagers by an over-zealous clerkess during the Second World War – the Scots plays and the dialect verse-readings, the smoothing out of our native Scots sound from our ears and our tongues was inevitably accelerated by the mere invention of broadcasting. The process was further hastened through the cinemas when 'the talkies' reached Glasgow in 1929.

The first cinema to instal the new invention was the 'Coliseum', on 7th January showing *The Singing Fool*. Even in the days of the silent films, when the plushier cinemas had instrumental groups and the cheaper ones made do with vamping pianists, 'the filums' became the Glasgow rage, and new stucco film-palaces went up in every suburb, and multiplied in the centre of the town. One of them, Green's Playhouse, was, until the removal of a gallery in the sixties deprived it of that distinction, the largest cinema in Europe.

Theatres did well too. The Alhambra alternated variety with drama, as did the Kings. Opera companies went to the Royal, where the lushest pantomimes in town were to be seen. There was an enormous vogue for 'light' plays, purveyed throughout well-attended 'seasons' for many years by the Brandon Thomas Players and later by the Wilson Barrett Company.

The Scottish National Players, a company of talented amateurs seeking to encourage native drama, drew into their circle the playwright Dr Osborne Mavor, first in the guise of 'Mary Henderson' then later as 'James Bridie'. They usually played in the Royalty, later the Lyric Theatre. It became the custom in our family to go to a 'musical' on Hogmanay, and while I must admit that I found those long ago performances of musical comedies like *No, No, Nanette*, *The Desert Song* and *The New Moon* neither very musical nor particularly comic, the sense of red-plush occasion was certainly something to savour.

Variety was so popular between the wars that it sustained the Pavilion and a new enlarged Empire Theatre built on Sauchiehall Street opposite the Lyric, the one now replaced by shops and offices, the other by an Electricity Board's headquarters.

Some old favourites among Glasgow's periodicals disappeared in the twenties. The *Scots Pictorial* merged with *The Bulletin*, and the *Baille*, which had long delighted Glaswegians with its pithy comment and pungent cartoons, ceased publication. The *Scottish Daily Express* joined the dailies, and the *Scottish Field* became a national monthly, much read in Glasgow though then produced in Perth.

Between the wars the physical scene underwent major changes. In 1918, a Royal Commission on Housing was set up. It found that more than 45 per cent of the people of Scotland were living in overcrowded conditions, by which was meant more than two people to a room. The majority of the members of the commission came down heavily against the private builder, declaring that 'most of the troubles which we have been investigating are due to the failure of private enterprise to provide the necessary houses sufficient in quantity and quality'.

This was not wholly a fair judgement. Not only were Glaswegians reluctant to pay as much in rent for a house as their English counterparts, making it very difficult for a private builder to operate at the profit level without which he could not for long have remained in business, but the Rent Restrictions Act effectively discouraged builders from putting up houses for renting. On top of all this, there was the peculiar Scottish rating system, whereby part of the rates were at the time paid by the owners, who, prior to 1914, had been able to recover rate increases from their occupiers in the form of increased rents. As a result of all this, tenements which, had they been properly maintained, might have had a long lease of useful life, fell into disrepair, a process of decline accelerated by renewed overcrowding brought about by the bad times of the twenties and thirties. Some older 'spec' tenements, of course, had been equipped, so to say, with built-in obsolescence, and must thus have been unacceptable in terms of human dignity even when they were new.

A controversial pamphlet, *Cancer of Empire*, reporting upon Glasgow's housing conditions, was published in 1924. Its author, William Bolitho, described his visit to a tenement 'backland' single-end, or one-room home.

> On each landing opens the water-closet, which the municipality installed thirty years ago. This is clean – the municipal inspectors are vigilant; but on an average twenty-five persons share its use. In some houses this number is nearer fifty. On the other side of the tiny landing opens a long, impenetrably black gulf; the central corridor of five homes. We feel our way, knock at a door and enter, calling out 'Sanitary'. A small room, one side of which is taken up by the Scots fireplace, like an enclosed iron altar, with two hobs on which the teapot is everlastingly on the boil. The floor is worn wood, there are irregular square inches of frayed oilcloth. An enormous drabbled woman, who is dressed in the same dish clothes which do not show the dirt so plainly, however, as her face, explains the arrangements....
> She has five children.... There is the bed, set into a niche, deep, evil-smelling, strewed with heaps of the same material as her dress.... Bed, hearth and chair: humanity's minimum.... Under the window is the 'jaw-box', the boarded greasy sink, with polished brass syphon tap.... On the mantel-piece are two china dogs ...

The conclusion reached by the majority of the Royal Commission was that responsibility for rehousing such unfortunate families as these should rest with the local

authority. So Glasgow Corporation began to build houses
for letting – 'council houses', as they were called – for the
most part semi-detached cottage-type dwellings each with its
own garden. All round Glasgow 'estates' of these grey-harled
brick houses sprang up. The rents were low, the subsidies
being found, in effect, by the property-owning rate-payers
and by the tax-payer at large. Although there was, and is, a
huge waiting-list for a council house in Glasgow, a
millionaire was as eligible a tenant as a motor-mechanic.
Scots folk have always objected to means tests, the method of
income assessment employed to calculate entitlement to the
dole during the Slump. By 1939 about 20 per cent of
Glasgow's population was living in subsidized council
houses, regardless of family income and therefore of the
genuine social need for subsidy. By 1939 Glasgow had
extended its boundaries to take in such districts as
Knightswood and Cardonald.

All these new areas were designed to relieve pressure on
the overcrowded slum area of a city which by then had the
highest population density-rate in Europe.

Public buildings went up too, but in nothing like the rich
profusion of the high Victorian period. The Glasgow head
office of the Bank of Scotland, 110-12 St Vincent Street,
originally the head office of the Union Bank, was the work of
James Miller (1860–1947). In spite of its simpler Greek detail,
it is very much the kind of imposing large-scale building
which Victorian and Edwardian architects had been putting
up for banks all over Britain – 'temples of Mammon', some
humbug or other called them. Much more original, though
naturally still reflecting the idiom of a previous age, is 200 St
Vincent Street, Sir John Burnet's last design, built in 1929.

Churches of the inter-war period usually also held fast to
elements of traditionalism, whether as is shown by the
severely modified Gothicism of James Taylor Thomson's St
John's Renfield Church, Beaconsfield Road, built in 1931, or
in Sir Robert Lorimer's St Margaret's Church, Knightswood, with its Baltic-looking saddleback tower.

But there were signs that the uneasy architectural
compromising of the thirties would soon give place to
something new.

The Cosmo Cinema,[2] which opened in 1939 to specialize

in showing Continental films, was a dignified brick building with some glazed ceramic 'faience' showing Scandinavian influence. T. Harold Hughes's and D.S.R. Waugh's reading room for Glasgow University, dating from the same year, and circular in design, excited much comment when it first went up and still manages to maintain its distinctive dignity in the company of massive post-1939 war structures.

An apt flamboyance rather than dignity is the keynote of the most ambitious and forward-looking addition to the Glasgow scene during the between-the-war years, Sir E. Owen William's Scottish Daily Express and Evening Citizen building, now the offices of the *Glasgow Herald*, its black glass facings and long lines of windows looming effectively against its western neighbour, St David's 'Ramshorn' Kirk.

In a way, perhaps the most exciting buildings that Glasgow had the chance of experiencing between the wars were the best of what went up in Bellahouston Park for the Empire Exhibition (Scotland) 1938. The scene was dominated by Thomas S. Tait's 300-feet-high tower, rising up from a hill in the centre of the park. The two Scottish Pavilions and the acoustically splendid concert hall raised visions of an exciting environmental future which the Second World War dampered in more senses than one; for Tait's Tower, intended to be a permanent memorial to the exhibition, had to be hurriedly dismantled when it was realized that it was giving navigational assistance to German airmen.

My own memories of the 1938 exhibition are of the exceptionally wet and windy weather (which, although it forced a claim on the guarantors, did not prevent the turnstiles clicking up a total of 13½ million visitors); of the appearance of Queen Mary, powdery and frail-looking as an Oscar Wilde heroine, driving through cheering crowds whose acclaim she acknowledged with a small wave of the hand and ever so slight inclination of the head; and the shimmering cascades of floodlit water which flowed down the central liquid 'staircase'.

There were other vigorous manifestations of contemporary trends in the Glasgow of the thirties. Erik Chisholm (1904–65) in 1930 founded his Active Society, and through it and the concerts which succeeded it between 1930 and 1937 brought to Glasgow some of the then leading *avant garde* composers including Bartok, Casella and Hindemith, as well as the romantic Medtner and the native Francis George Scott.

They usually performed in the Berkeley Hall, mostly to tiny audiences. Chisholm was more successful in attracting wider support for his pioneering productions mounted by the Glasgow Grand Opera Society. With this entirely amateur body, Chisholm managed to stage the first performance in English of Mozart's *Idomeneo*, Berlioz's *The Trojans* (with Guy MacCrone, author of *Wax Fruit*, in the role of Aeneas in 1935), and a Scottish opera by W.B. Moonie, *The Weird of Colbar*. It was not as successful as its predecessor, *Jeanie Deans*, by Greenock-born Hamish MacCunn (1868–1916), which has several times been revived. MacCunn's freshly youthful overture *Land of the Mountain and the Flood* firmly holds its place in the repertoire and has been recorded on Compact Disc by the Scottish National Orchestra. The Tuesday concerts, where one's presence in evening dress was expected at least in the more expensive seats, were deliberately 'highbrow'. Looking back now on the supposed 'difficulties' of Bartok, Sibelius and the others who featured on these programmes,[3] it seems strange that their music should have come to seem almost a refuge of familiarity from the serial and electronic probings of so much of the 'difficult' music by the younger composers today. Many of them seem to have achieved successfully a kind of non-masterpiece neo-eighteenth-century cosmopolitanism which makes the export or import of their product pointless, more or less the same being available from native pens or synthesizers in every European country.

Scotland has never produced a great composer, but it can claim one outstanding composer of songs. 'Hugh MacDiarmid's' English teacher at Langholm, Francis George Scott (1880–1958), having graduated as Bachelor of Music at Durham University, spent the last twenty-five years of his working life as lecturer in music at Jordanhill Training College for Teachers. He wrote many of his finest settings of the poems of Burns, MacDiarmid and others at his Glasgow home, 44 Munro Road. Scott had no Scottish art-song tradition to build upon, so he set about creating his own. Lacking practical experience with an orchestra, his larger orchestral works seem less assured of their survival than the forty or so of his best songs, at least half-a-dozen of them as forward-looking as anything of their kind being written in the mid-twenties. Such songs as 'Milkwort and Bog-cotton', 'The Old Fisherman', 'The Tryst' and many others are assuredly made of the stuff of survival. Certainly I have always considered Francis George Scott a great song-writer of the second order, evoking deeper responses than Warlock or Quilter or Gurney. His time will yet come.

William Montgomerie, an east-coast man, has a little poem of the thirties, 'Glasgow Street', which goes:

> Out of this ugliness may come,
> Some day, so beautiful a flower,
>   That men will wonder at that hour,
>   Remembering smoke and flowerless slums,
> And ask – glimpsing the agony
> Of the slaves who wrestle to be free –
> 'But why were all the poets dumb?'

The question is rhetorical, but nevertheless there was a practical answer. Glasgow did not have very many poets during the twenties and thirties. Indeed, apart from William Jeffrey, who wrote his cool classical verses between daily bouts of journalizing, there were none of any consequence. But 'Hugh MacDiarmid', though a Borderer, knew enough about Glasgow to be anything but dumb.

> The houses are Glasgow not the people – these
> Are simply the food the houses live and grow on
> Endlessly, drawing from their vulgarity
> And pettiness and darkness of spirit
> – Gorgonising the mindless generations,
> Turning them all into filthy property
> Apt as the Karaunas by diabolic arts
> To produce darkness and obscure the light of day.
> To see or hear a clock in Glasgow's horrible,
> Like seeing a dead man's watch, still going though he's dead.
> Everything is dead except stupidity here.

Like most of MacDiarmid's polemic, while containing a basis of truth the detail was inaccurate and unfair. Joe Corrie (born 1894), a miner-turned-playwright, whose one-acters were for long the staple diet of amateur drama companies in Scotland was neither 'dead' nor stupid when he wrote *A' Jock Tamson's Bairns* and *The Auld Blue Cup*. Nor, in still lighter vein, was W.D. Cocker whose 'The Deluge' reflected a faint glimpse of that ironic blend of the serious and the absurd frequently reflected in MacDiarmid's own early poems in Scots.

The most frequently read novel about Glasgow between the wars was *The Shipbuilders* by George Blake (1894–1961) which, like James Barke's *Major Operation* published in 1936, the year after Blake's book appeared, deals with the devastating effect on middle-class husbands of the breakdown of their marriages. Read in their day, too, were Dot Allan's *Hunger March* and *Charity Begins at Home*, both set in Glasgow.

John Buchan, the first Baron Tweedsmuir, could hardly be claimed as a Glasgow novelist, although he arrived in Glasgow as a boy, lived in the villa suburb of Pollokshields, and was educated at Hutcheson's Grammar School and Glasgow University. At Oxford he formed those connections which were later to help him combine the roles of man-of-letters and political figure, leading him eventually to the Governor Generalship of Canada, in which country he died in 1940. The references to Glasgow in his autobiography *Memory Hold the Door* are nowhere nearly as sympathetic as the uses made of the city's background in the novels of Anna Buchan, his sister, who wrote under the pseudonym 'O. Douglas'.

The Glasgow novelist who had the widest reputation in the thirties was Dr A.J. Cronin. His *Hatters Castle* deals with the Turkey-red dyeing industry established in the Vale of Leven by the Stirling family. *The Green Years* has also a Clydeside setting. The mythical Dr Finlay of television case-book fame was originally Cronin's creation, though Cronin cannot be held responsible for the melodramatic puerilities on which this over-prolonged return to the Tannochbrae of the twenties expired after a run of nearly a decade.

Of the same generation as Cronin was Dr Osborne Mavor, who, as 'James Bridie', produced a series of divertingly discursive plays which pleased both London and Scotland,

and have held their place in the repertoire: *A Sleeping Clergyman, Tobias and the Angel, Mr Bolfry, The Anatomist, Daphne Laureola* and many others. His own autobiography, *One Way of Living* (1939), gives a racy account of a Glasgow-based life in the twenties and thirties.

Edinburgh rather than Glasgow has provided the background to most of our more distinguished twentieth-century painters; but J.D. Fergusson (1874–1961) whose best work was done in early life abroad and whose associations were with the French post-Impressionists, lived the latter part of his life in Glasgow. A fine collection of his work has been presented to the University of Stirling.

By far the most varied and generous single gift of works of art came to Glasgow through the munificence of Sir William Burrell, a Glasgow shipowner who left a collection worth, by the standards of 1970, somewhere in the region of £4 million, along with a sum of money to build a gallery in which to house it. Unfortunately, there was a delay of more than a quarter of a century in beginning work on the gallery, partly because the money was never adequate for the purpose for which it was intended, and partly because Sir William, making his will in the days before internal atmosphere-control was as sophisticated as it is now, originally insisted that his art treasures should be housed more than 17 miles beyond the centre of the city. However, the generous gift of Pollok House and its spacious grounds by Mrs Maxwell Macdonald to the National Trust for Scotland and Glasgow Corporation, enabled a site to be chosen in the park of Pollok. An architectural competition limited to United Kingdom architects was organized. It was won by Barry Gasson. The completed gallery is one of the most forward-looking in design yet to be built, both in its setting and for its varied purpose. It is clearly one of the outstanding buildings of the last quarter of Glasgow's twentieth century, and an attraction of European significance.

While the business use of the motor-car developed between the wars, pleasure motoring also increased in popularity, though not yet to the detriment of the traditional Glasgow pleasure, 'doon the watter' sailing. In the 1939 summer season there were still twenty-seven steamers in the Clyde fleet, although the last of the independents, the

amalgamated Williamson-Buchanan Line, had sold out to the London Midland and Scottish Railway's subsidiary, the Caledonian Steam Packet Company, in 1935. Their turbine steamers *King Edward* and *Queen Mary II* – the numeral a courtesy gesture towards the younger but larger Cunarder of the same royal name – appearing thereafter in the yellow-and-black topped funnel of the LMS, while the *Queen Alexandra*, with a third funnel added, and re-named the *Saint Columba*, wore the red-and-black colours of MacBrayne and took over from the veteran *Columba* on the Ardrishaig run. The *King George V* also went to MacBrayne to undertake the Staffa and Iona summer sail from Oban.

The departure of the *Columba* was the beginning of the end of the great days of Clyde pleasure cruising. Some years later a senior MacBrayne executive who happened to be sitting next to me at a dinner, told me that during her last few seasons, the frailties of age lay so heavily upon the old ship that whenever he and his colleagues thought about her they felt slightly apprehensive.

During these last few seasons she was the ship which carried me off every summer to our holiday home at Innellan, on the Cowal Coast. In a book of mine, *The Lowlands of Scotland: Glasgow and the North*, first published in 1953, and, with suitable revision, in print for more than thirty years, I set down my recollections of one of these 'doon the watter' trips, which have now almost ceased to be a possibility after an unbroken run of more than 150 years. Since this is avowedly a personal portrait of my native city, and the traditional sail 'doon the watter' was for me a keenly anticipated annual pleasure, it seems appropriate to quote it here.

We were to set out, I think, on the first day of July; mother and father, nurse, four children, dog, cat and goldfish. Although we could depend on being able to purchase rather more than could the Reids, nevertheless, a great deal of luggage had to be taken. The packing was done systematically during the last days of June. I do not think I slept much on the night before the day of our departure.

It began early. We got up at five in the morning, and had breakfast half an hour later. For some reason, that breakfast

Pollok House (1747-52) by William Adam and completed by John Adam. The terraces and pavilions by Sir Rowand Anderson

had a special quality of its own. Its ingredients were those of many another breakfast eaten since – porridge, bread and butter, and a boiled egg – but I can still remember the extra flavour those comestibles seemed to acquire that morning. (No doubt it was in a similar mood of anticipation that the poet Southey generously praised the excellence of Scottish breakfasts while staying at Old Meldrum.)

After breakfast, we children were expected to keep out of the way of our elders, for a horse-drawn lorry arrived outside the house at six o'clock to cart the luggage down to the quay. I was given the job of guarding the cat while the luggage was being grunted and manoeuvred round the bends of the staircase. The cat, a venerable beast who lived to be 18 and would then be about 12, had the idea that if he managed to escape while the front door stood open to let the carters move freely in and out, he would not have to undergo his annual holiday ordeal of transportation by basket; hence the need for one of the family to stand guard.

At last the luggage had rumbled away, the cat had been safely basketed, and it was time to prepare ourselves for the arrival of the taxi. That taxi-drive itself was something of a novelty. Usually, I went to children's parties in a cab: a musty affair, upholstered in faded green, and driven by a red-nosed mufflered coachman, whose characteristic smell was almost as strong as that of the horse that pulled the contraption.

Ordinary mortals who go about their affairs during the hours of daylight would do well to take an occasional ride through an industrial city at half past six in the morning, if only to remind themselves how large a section of the community has to do 'day labour, light denied' in order to keep essential public services running. The new sun shone out from a clean sky this July morning, glistening the roof-tops of the tenements, and lighting up even the drabbest side-streets with the promise of a fair day.

The *Columba* lay on the south side of the river, her two red-and-black funnels setting off nobly her huge, gilded paddle-boxes. The moment you climbed up her gangway, your nostrils were assailed by a peculiar aroma that was all her own. After some years, I discovered that it was a mixture of heated engine oil, good galley cooking and well-scrubbed cleanliness, to which, down the river, the scudding tang of salty spray was added. But at that time, analysis did not matter. The smell was wholly entrancing.

We were to establish ourselves in the cabin, or the 'saloon' as it was more grandly called. The 'saloon' consisted of a number of seated bays lined with dark-red velvet plush, and richly draped with similar hangings. It gave an impression of well-established opulence and time-saturated sea-going. All went well at first. I carried the cat's basket down the companionway, and the cat remained obligingly silent. But at the entrance to the 'saloon', a liveried steward looked at me and my burden with an unmistakable air of hostility.

'What's in that basket?' he demanded.

'Provisions,' I answered, with a happier promptitude than I have displayed on many a more important occasion since. He grunted and let us past. We chose an empty bay, and comfortably dispersed our bits and pieces.

Those final moments of waiting seemed the most interminable of all. Above our heads, busy feet tapped out their walking patterns on the deck. In the orange glow of the engine-room, the great gleaming monsters hissed and sizzled quietly to themselves, as if anticipating the moment when the flicker of a dial and the loosening of a lever would send them plunging backward and forward in all their pride of power.

Seven o'clock! Five minutes past! And then the mishanter occurred. A long, thin stream of clear liquid suddenly raced down the floor. Its place of origin was unmistakably the basket at my feet.

In a moment the steward was at my side.

'Your provisions seem to be leaking, sir,' he observed acidly. (That 'sir', to one of my tender years, seemed an additional humiliation.) 'You'd better take them on deck.'

I was delighted. I certainly had no desire to spend my first voyage in the feminine confines of the cabin. Now, someone would *have* to stay on deck to see that the cat was not shipped prematurely ashore.

Up there, things were happening. The captain, an impressive and recognizably Highland figure even beneath the disguising weight of his gold braid, was pacing his bridge, which straddled the ship from one paddle-box to the other between the two funnels. (It has always seemed strange to me that, until about 1920, it apparently never occurred to the designers of paddle-steamers that the funnel was a fairly major obstacle in the way of the helmsman's vision.) The captain took one final look at his watch; then he pulled the clanging brass levers at his side. The paddles began to thresh the water, nosing the ship's bow out towards the centre of the river; with a couple of dirty splashes, the ropes were tossed into the water, to be retrieved fussily by puffing steam capstans at bow and stern; and then the long, lean hull, shuddering a little at first, began to slide slowly forward.

Past close miles of shipyards, resounding with the racket of the riveters welding together the rusty hulks of the ships that would sail tomorrow's seas; past docks, full of towering ocean-going liners, and queer-looking tramp ships with foreign characters scrawled across their sterns; past grumphed-up, dirty old dredgers, squatting in the middle of the river, digging away the mud that forever strives to slip back into its ancient bed; past low-built hoppers carrying the mud far down the Firth to be dumped in the deeps around Ailsa Craig; past the chain-drawn car ferries of Renfrew and Erskine; past Bowling, with its stone-pencil monument to Henry Bell, and its huge oil port and depot cut back into the hills; past Greenock and Gourock, and over the broad Firth to Dunoon and Innellan.

My generation grew up under the certainty of a developing war threat that neither my immersion in literature nor a determination to become a violinist could shut out from my awareness for long. After the Munich affair of 1938 I joined a searchlight battery of the Territorial Army in order to put in the necessary service to enable me to apply for a commission in my father's old regiment, The Cameronians (Scottish Rifles).

Glasgow's Territorial Battalions began to double themselves between Munich and the invasion of Poland. I went to my first camp in the early summer of 1939 with the 7th Cameronians at Dunfermline. Summoned by telephone from a summer lawn, I crossed the Clyde on the paddle steamer *Duchess of Fife* from Innellan to Gourock, to join the 9th Cameronians on 2nd September, our headquarters down a lane opposite Langside Public Hall.

On the morning of 3 September, on which the Second World War was declared, we started piling sandbags against the battalion office's windows, Glasgow heard its first air-raid warning – a false alarm as things turned out. At sea it was a Glasgow ship, the Anchor-Donaldson liner *Athenia*, newly out of the Clyde on her way to Canada with evacuees, that was to be the first British casualty of the war at sea. Thus in a sense, the war which one hoped by some miracle might yet not happen but knew in one's heart could not be avoided, struck one of its first blows at Glasgow children.

There was considerable bitterness among Clydeside industrialists just before and during the early months of the Second World War because of a belief that an unfair proportion of government contracts since Chamberlain plucked the sting out of the Munich nettle had gone to the South. C.A. Oakley who, during the war, was to become Scottish Controller of the Ministry of Aircraft Production and later Scottish Controller of the Board of Trade, and therefore has authority behind his opinions, has gone on record as saying: 'An impression does remain that the English firms who doubled or trebled their capacity in the 1938–40 period – taking their opportunity of doing so at the taxpayers' expense – were willing to put their younger executives in charge of their new plant, and that the West of Scotland firms, who would not make any major extension to their factories, or open new ones, denied to their youngest executives comparable chances'.

Unlike its predecessor 'the war to end wars', the war of 1939, so long expected, affected everyone from the start. This time there were no public heroics. The mood was one of sober resignation mingled with a curious amalgam of disgust, guilt and, inevitably, a fear of the unknown perhaps best caught by the self-exiled W.H. Auden:

> I sit in one of the dives
> On Fifty-Second Street.
> Uncertain and afraid
> As clever hopes expire
> Of a low dishonest decade....

The decade was low and dishonest because most of us chose to shut our minds to the terrible things which were happening to the Jews in Germany and to the Ethiopians in

Africa; dishonest because most of us kidded ourselves into believing that without commitment on our part, something would somehow happen which would let us off the hook, the bad turn suddenly good and our islanded lives be no longer threatened or disturbed.

Long before it could be the time for voyaging back, when 'the lost traveller, with sun bleached hair/Dazed on the gangway' could 'come home again'[4] from distant battlefields, six long years were to be lived through. This time at least, no one thought it would 'all be over by Christmas', in spite of stories about friends holidaying in Germany in 1938 whose 'Baby Austins' had fashionable collisions with German tanks, which turned out to be made of papier mâché.

Gas masks were a universal issue, and were supposed to be carried everywhere. Dave Willis, then one of the most popular of the long line of 'Scottish Coamics', delighted Glasgow audiences with a song that went:

> In my wee gas mask
> I'm working out a plan,
> 'Though all the kids imagine
> That I'm just a bogey man.
> The girls all smile
> And bring their friends to see
> The nicest-looking warden
> In the A.R.P.
>
> Whenever there's a raid on,
> Listen for my cry
> An aeroplane, an aeroplane
> Away up a-ky
> Then I'll run helter-skelter
> But don't run after me
> You'll no get in my shelter
> 'Cause it's far too wee.

Children and old people were tearfully evacuated from Glasgow and Edinburgh to safer country places. Many of them drifted back again after about six months, when it began to look as if the urban dangers might not be as serious as had been supposed.

Other townies remained 'exiles' in the country almost for

the duration. The novelist Robin Jenkins has dealt amusingly yet profoundly with the difficulties which the introduction of city children and their often difficult parents into rural families sometimes produce in *Guests of War* (1956).

Air-raid shelters were built, those at the bottom of our gardens being dubbed Anderson shelters, named after Sir John Anderson, the Home Secretary in 1938. The entrances to tenement closes were faced with baffle-walls. Barrage balloons floated above the city.

Clothes rationing froze fashions. A scheme for food rationing had been prepared well in advance, but although delicacies, especially fruit, were often in limited supply, there was always plenty to eat. Restaurants were limited to a maximum charge of 5s. per head, and it was astonishing how much continued to be offered for that sum throughout the war. Some food myths were created, like the supposed efficacy of carrots for increasing sharpness of vision at night in the severely blacked-out streets. (By a curious coincidence, Woolton Pie, another war-time speciality also commended by the Minister of Food, Lord Woolton, contained carrots as a major ingredient.) Glasgow swallowed the carrot-myth along with the lave [the rest].

There were shortages from time to time, particularly during the middle years of the war. Cigarettes were difficult to come by, and so was paper. The paper shortage sometimes made it difficult to meet the full demand for them. It also forced some limitation on the number of books which could be published. Many of those that appeared used a poor-quality paper, which was often a dirty grey when new and speedily yellowed in the post-war years. Books, though produced under licence number, were nevertheless in steady demand, as was entertainment of all sorts.

Driving at night, with masked headlights showing only little rectangles of light, was an unpleasant experience. Petrol was only available for essential purposes, though it was surprising how apparently unessential some essential purposes managed to seem. Even among the services in training, restrictions on transport were severe.

Public transport presented problems too. Glasgow's tramway service operated at a reduced level. Long-distance travellers found themselves faced with conscience-troubling posters asking: 'Is Your Journey Really Necessary?' To most people the need to struggle for a place in an overcrowded train only arose once a year at holiday time. Thousands of Glasgow men and women in the Forces no doubt still have memories of long journeys to and from brief home leaves overcrowded in compartments or crushed in corridors.

Many of the Clyde steamers sailed out beyond the arms of the Firth to become mine-sweepers. An anti-submarine steel-net boom which stretched across the Clyde from the Cloch to Dunoon divided the estuary in two, Dunoon and the Holy Loch being served from Gourock, Rothesay and the Kyles of Bute piers from Wemyss Bay.

It is right and fitting to lay emphasis on the civilian population when considering Glasgow's 1939 war, since this was the first war affecting the United Kingdom in which those out of uniform were liable to be as dangerously involved as the soldiers at the front – a good prospect for the future of peace, I remember reflecting when air-raids started to take their toll of civilians on both sides. Scotland had to bear only a small share of the brunt of the air war launched against these islands by the Germans. Most of that share, however, was directed against Glasgow and the Clyde.

There was a minor daylight raid on 19th July 1940. The first night raid came on 18th September, when bombs dropped on George Square but missed the major buildings, Queen Street Station and the tunnel which leads into it. It did, however, remove the building at the east end of Royal Exchange Square, the site on which Glasgow Corporation Planning Department was later erected in an early post-war undistinguished style[5]. Another bomb set fire to the cruiser *Sussex* at Yorkhill, causing the evacuation of the nearby Royal Hospital for Sick Children because of a danger that her magazine might blow up.

The most serious attacks on Clydeside were made in 1941, when Clydebank and Greenock took the full weight. In the three days, or rather nights, between 13th and 15th March, 1,083 people were killed and over 1,600 injured, mostly in Clydebank, where only seven houses remained entirely undamaged. As a result, this town with a population of 55,000 had to evacuate its fifty thousand or so survivors. Many of these folk were involved in vital production work, and their spirit in quickly overcoming the need to travel substantial distances to and from work was wholly admirable.

Between 5th and 6th May the raids against Greenock killed 341 people and injured 312. Whisky stores and sugar refineries were a major hazard in the fires which broke out. Worse still could have been the dangers which would have followed if the Admiralty oil storage tanks at Bowling, containing more than 12 million gallons, had been hit by any of the hundred or so bombs which the Germans tried to land on the site. 'Greek' Thomson's splendid Queen's Park St George's Church was unfortunately totally destroyed by fire in the last raid on Glasgow, on the night of 23rd March 1943.

Glasgow had thirteen raids in all, and had dropped on it 183 high explosive bombs, 37 parachute mines, 3 oil bombs and thousands of incendiaries. By comparison with what Bristol or Coventry endured, this was slight punishment. But the Secretary of State for Scotland was later to describe the Clydeside raids as being 'as severe as any other areas of Britain'.

Towards the end of 1943, the course of the war turned. Because of this, and because German technology was consequently prevented from improving the range of its V-I 'flying bombs' and its V-2 rockets, Glasgow was spared the renewed ordeal which London and other English cities and towns had to face from rocketry long after the offensive power of the Luftwaffe against the civilian population had been broken by 'the Few' in the Battle of Britain. Amongst the Spitfires which swept the Germans out of the skies was the City of Glasgow Fighter Squadron (602). Many other Glasgow men served in the air force, either in the Glasgow squadrons formed subsequently, or as individuals on Atlantic duties, protective and offensive, in the Far East and above Normandy beaches in the summer of retribution, 1944.

The loss of life among service personnel in the Second World War was mercifully much less severe than in its predecessor, there being less actual fighting. As the added names on war memorials show, only about a third of the total of those killed between 1914 and 1918 fell between 1939 and 1946.

Conscription was introduced from the start of the 1939

war, and once again the Territorial battalions of both the Highland Light Infantry and the Cameronians (Scottish Rifles) included many Glasgow men, enrolled or conscripted. It is probable that about 150,000 Glaswegians in all served in the armed forces. To many of these men and women, the war took them for the first time away from their native place. While travelling under war-time conditions must certainly have broadened their minds it sometimes also induced understandable nostalgia, distance lending a focusing enchantment to the remembered view, an experience I reflected in a poem now included in my *Collected Poems* and in *The Oxford Book of Scottish Verse*, 'The Exiled Heart'.

Two purple pigeons circle a London square
as darkness blurs and smudges the shadowless light
of a winter evening. I pause on the pavement and stare
at the restless flutter of wings as they gather flight
like rustling silk, and move out to meet the night.

And my restless thoughts migrate to a Northern city –
fat pigeons stalking the dirty, cobbled quays,
where a sluggish river carries the cold self-pity
of those for whom life has never flowed with ease,
from a granite bridge to the grey Atlantic seas:

the bristling, rough-haired texture of Scottish manners;
the jostled clatter of airless shopping streets
where lumbering tramcars squeal as they turn sharp corners;
the boosy smell from lounging pubs that cheats
the penniless drunkard's thirst with its stale deceits:

where my heart first jigged to the harsh and steady sorrow
of those for whom mostly the world is seldom glad;
who are dogged by the flat-heeled, footpad steps of to-morrow;
for whom hope is a dangerous drug, an expensive fad
of the cushioned rich, or the young and lovesick mad:

where chattering women in tea-rooms, swaddled with furs,
pass knife-edged gossip like cakes, and another's skirt
is unstitched with sharp words, and delicate, ladylike slurs
are slashed on the not-quite-nice or the over-smart,
till their cigarette smoke is a lazy, prickled hurt.

I remember Glasgow, where sordid and trivial breed
from the same indifferent father; his children side

with the mother whose sour breasts taught them first to feed
on her hot, caressing hates that sear and divide
or swell the itched, distorting bladder of pride.

Yet my casual smile is the tossed-down beggar's penny
the goaded heart throws out in vain to procure
the comfortable forgetfulness of the many
who lie in content's soft arms, and are safe and sure
in the fabled Grecian wanderers' lotus-lure:

who forget the sullen glare of the wet, grey skies,
and the lashing Northern wind that flicks the skin
where hum-drum poverty's dull and listless eyes
are pressed to the window, hearing the friendly din
of the party, watching the lights and the laughter within.

But oh! I cannot forget! So I wait, and wonder:
how long will the thinly-dividing window hold?
How long will the dancing drown the terrible anger
of those, the unwanted, who peddle their grief in the cold,
wrapped in their own despair's thick and unkindly fold?

Yet evil is no pattern of places
varied, like terraces from town to town.
A city's charms and individual graces
are but the sculptor's bleak and basic stone,
the photographic face without a frown.

The wound is in this bewildered generation,
unfriended, lost within the Freudian wood,
its compass-point no longer veneration
of that lost God who rewarded the simple and good,
vivid and real, now, only in childhood.

For we, the children of this uncertain age,
breathing its huge disasters and sad airs,
have seen that our warm, humanitarian rage
is impotent to soothe war's animal fears,
and cannot quell the lonely exile's tears.

So the heart, like a wounded seabird, hungers home
to muffled memories on fainter-beating wings
which once soared over history's clouded foam;
to that first shore where each new hero flings
his careful stone that fades in slow, concentric rings.

One other more prosaic confession of nostalgia, I must record. On a Sunday afternoon in 1942, walking in Lowestoft, I suddenly recognized the unmistakable lines of the Clyde steamer *Duchess of Rothesay*. There she was, lying in the harbour camouflaged in the grey paint of a minesweeper. I felt as if I had suddenly come unexpectedly upon an old familiar friend with whom I had shared happier days!

Glasgow's most important functions between 1939 and 1946, were probably as a sheltered port and as 'the arsenal of the Empire'. During the war years more than 300 merchant ships were built in Clyde yards. The total tonnage of 1,634,216 included HMS *Howe*, the aircraft carriers *Indefatigable* and *Implacable*, the battleship *Vanguard* and a huge quantity of smaller ships, including submarines, corvettes, escort vessels and landing craft. More than 25,000 repair jobs were also rushed through, some of them major undertakings, like the putting together of a ship blown into two sections by a mine.

The Clyde also became the chief port in the United Kingdom, handling about 80 per cent of our incoming merchant shipping. Some of the ships that arrived berthed at a new specially built port in the Gareloch; others were unloaded at anchor in the lochs of the Clyde, a fleet of little ships and barges ferrying their cargoes to the nearest railhead. Fleets of fighting ships, British, Canadian and American, assembled in the Clyde. So did the Norway convoy of May 1940 and others, including convoys to Malta and to North Africa. Many of the D-day landing rehearsals were carried out on the Clyde, and the famous Mulberry Harbours, without which the Normandy landing could not have been sustained, were organized in the Gareloch. More than a hundred Scottish firms were involved in making piers and other parts of this remarkable enterprise, all within a fixed delivery schedule.

The Clyde's great liners *Queen Mary* and *Queen Elizabeth* steamed 950,000 miles between them, carrying 1¼ million soldiers, the speed of their camouflaged hulls fortunately making them a difficult target for German U-boats.

Enormous quantities of ammunition and equipment were manufactured in and around Glasgow. Even the Kelvin Hall was turned into a factory where barrage balloons and inflatable rubber dinghies were produced.

Womenfolk spent their energies generously in running service canteens for visiting soldiers, sailors and airmen. It is said that about 90 per cent of American troops spending leave in the United Kingdom came to Glasgow. A tile showing a Free Dutch Army soldier, and presented to Glasgow women who had organized wartime club facilities, stood by a fireplace in my parents' home long after a generation had grown up to whom the war was merely part of history.

There were local excitements ranging from the surprising arrival of Hitler's deputy Rudolf Hess, who baled out of an ME 110 over Eaglesham on the night of 10th May 1941, to the dreadful explosion of a French destroyer, the *Maille Breze*, at Greenock on 30th April 1940, killing most of her crew and causing severe damage to the town.

Although an end to the war had so often seemed so impossibly far away during these long six years, when it came at last, on 9th May 1945; Glasgow celebrated V.E. (Victory in Europe) Day with energetic gaiety. According to the *Glasgow Herald* report:

> People of all ages, conditions and sizes who had been thronging the city streets as if waiting for nightfall made George Square their resort when night settled down.
>
> Long before the lights had sprung up to shed beauty and carnival gaiety upon the Square, over which towered the mass of the Municipal buildings, the junketing had begun. Dancing had gone on intermittently among the young, the leadership of which seemed to fall upon high-spirited liberty men from the Navy.
>
> They danced jigs and eightsomes in front of the City Chambers, performed sweeping wonders with the palais glide, and wound in long serpentine columns, singing and laughing in happy eddies, round the staider islands of civilian sightseers.

The 1945 election returned a Labour government with a majority of 200, a result which to our European Allies seemed to smack of ingratitude to Churchill, the man whose determination had at one stage seemed almost all that stood between Hitler and the achievement of his territorial ambitions for the Third Reich. Just as the mood of realistic determination in which the 1939 war had begun differed from the feeling of exalted crusade which accompanied the outbreak of the 1914 war, so the mood of 1945 differed from that of 1918. With fighting less continuous and the expectation of survival among members of the armed forces much greater than the life expectancy of a week which faced the average second lieutenant on his way to the trenches in 1916, there was more time for thinking. Soldiers given compulsory instruction in current affairs were actively encouraged to plan the brave new world which every generation feels so certain it can build out of the failures of the past.

Yet Glasgow played virtually no part in the political shift that brought the Attlee Government into power, only one seat – Kelvingrove, which Walter Elliott lost by a small majority to the Labour candidate J.L. Williams – changing party allegiance. Glasgow was represented in the 1945 House of Commons by five Conservatives, seven Labourites and two I.L.P. members.

One result of the introduction of the newly-created Welfare State was that progress towards improvements in the social services were plain for all to see. Perhaps because of this, in the immediate post-war years, strikes were few and comparatively small. It was not, of course, V.E. Day that finally marked the end of the conflict, but V.J. Day, 15th August 1945, when Japan capitulated after the dropping of two atomic bombs, which undoubtedly saved the lives of thousands of Allied soldiers, sailors and airmen. The severe cost to the civilian population of the nation which elected to enter the war with the aggression of Pearl Harbour has always seemed to me to have been, on balance, entirely justified.

Notes

1 In Scotland, public schools are, in fact, private schools!
2 Now the Glasgow Film Centre.
3 I retain a precise visual image of Hindemith, a stockily bespectacled profile, playing his own viola concerto, *Der Schwanendreher*, with stolid Germanic efficacy, before a St Andrew's Halls Tuesday audience.
4 'The Armistice' by John Lehmann.
5 Now an office block, the Planning Department now being located in an extension to the City Chambers.

8

Renewal and Renaissance

In the post-war years, the news which dominated the thoughts of Glaswegians was inevitably mostly international: the Berlin blockade; political fermentation in the Middle East (before and after the setting up of the state of Israel); the Russian acquisition of the atomic bomb; the war in Korea; Kennedy's successful defusing of the Cuba missile crisis; space exploration and the first American man on the moon; the long war in Vietnam and the resulting American humiliation; the murders of John F. Kennedy, Robert Kennedy and Martin Luther King; the Yom Kippur war and the ensuing economic crisis in the Western world; the sectarian troubles in Ireland and in the Lebanon; Fascist white oppression in South Africa; and, of course, Britain's eventual entry into Europe.

Inevitably, too, there were problems at home. Food rationing dragged on until July 1954, and in 1947 there was a power shortage aggravated by one of the century's severest winters.

The most urgent problem Glasgow had to face was housing. No houses had been built during the war, so the pre-war problem of overcrowded slums was by now compounded with the demands and needs of a rising generation. 'Pre-fabs', quickly erected little bungalows originally intended to last for ten years, went up on vacant sites all over the city. By 1970, seventy-eight pre-fabs were still occupied in Glasgow and it was to be another decade before the last of them came down.

Mandatory planning was introduced for the first time with the Planning Act of 1947. A survey of Glasgow's permanent housing stock was carried out and over 100,000 dwellings –

251

nearly one third of all the city's homes – were found to be at, or beyond, the end of their structural lives. In human terms this meant that at least 100,000 families were living in houses where the fabric was damp or crumbling and where there was neither hot water nor acceptable internal sanitation. This, too, in spite of the fact that between 1919 and 1939, the Corporation of Glasgow had built more than 50,000 council houses for letting.

These conditions were emphasized in the *Clyde Valley Regional Plan*, produced by Sir Patrick Abercromby and Robert (later Sir Robert) Matthew in 1946. With 700,000 people squeezed into an area of three square miles, at an average density of 400 persons to the acre – in some locations the figure was as high as 700 to the acre – Abercromby and Matthew reckoned that 500,000 people would have to move out of the area to allow redevelopment at very much lower densities.[1]

Twenty-nine zones in Glasgow were therefore designated Comprehensive Development Areas, among them Gorbals,[2] Anderston, Townhead, Bridgeton and Gallowgate; areas lying around the city centre and with tenements about 120 years old; areas, too, in which mixed uses had evolved in the nineteenth century, partly because of the earlier need for workers to live within walking distance of factories, partly because of chance.

Between the wars the concept of the 'garden suburb' caught people's imagination. Most of the council houses that went up in suburbs like Knightswood, Mosspark and Carntyne had their own front and back doors leading into their own gardens. One of the problems of the pre-1939 garden suburb development was that a lot of land was needed to accommodate a relatively small number of people. There were approximately fifty people in fourteen dwellings per acre in the garden suburb housing estates. Clearly, in the face of the massive problem of post-war inner city deterioration other solutions had to be found.

Since only half of the overcrowded proportion of the population could be rehoused in the inner city, two courses of action were embarked upon: the construction of new towns – East Kilbride, Scotland's first new town, laid out as a garden city, was designed in 1947; Cumbernauld, concentrated in

Sauchiehall Street, begun early in the nineteenth century

linked, village-like localities, in 1956; Glenrothes in 1948; the linear town of Irvine, attached to the old town of that name, in 1966; Erskine in 1970 – and, as a quicker expedient, the decanting of some families elsewhere in Scotland through overspill agreements with towns as far apart as Dumfries, Haddington and Wick. Housing estates were built in small towns under the powers given by the 1957 Housing and Town Development (Scotland) Act. Partly because these towns naturally looked for additional industries to provide employment for their immigrants and partly because in some cases the climate and the way of life was very different in the overspill towns to that to which urban Glaswegians had been accustomed, the overspill solution was not an unqualified success.

For its part, Glasgow's first post-war building effort resulted in the creation of such huge peripheral housing estates as Drumchapel and Easterhouse, made up of modern tenement-style dwellings and each the size of a town like Perth, yet initially built without communal facilities. It was not long before social unrest became endemic in them.

In the late fifties, as these schemes were nearing completion, Glasgow turned its attention to the redevelopment of the inner city. A fresh review of the problem, approved by the Secretary of State for Scotland in 1964, proposed the demolition of 103,289 houses in the twenty-nine Comprehensive Redevelopment Areas. Of the 300,000 people to be displaced, less than half could be rehoused in the city. Even so, the densities to be accepted were higher than those proposed by Abercromby and Matthew. This was achieved by the construction of high-rise blocks of flats.

Once again, as with Drumchapel and Easterhouse, mistakes were made. The great architect Corbusier originally proposed higher-rise living as one element in a balanced development scheme. In Glasgow, tower after tower was put up, so to say, out of the Corbusier context, to house families with children, the middle-aged and the old, all of them dependent for tolerable access to their homes on vandal-proof lifts. The result was again something of a social disaster, neatly summed up by a popular street ballad of the time:

Ye canny thraw a piece frae a twenty storey flat,
Twenty thoosand hungry weans will testify to that.

With hindsight, it is easy to be critical of Glasgow
Corporation for sanctioning these mistakes, but the need for
housing the young and re-housing those living in inhuman
squalor was urgent and pressing. While possibly the policy of
bulldozing absolutely everything in the Comprehensive
Redevelopment Areas was unnecessarily extreme, the great
majority of what was thus destroyed was probably in no
condition to lend itself to restoration and conservation.

By the late 1960s, Glasgow was in the final stages of
clearing away the worst of its slums. The Housing (Scotland)
Act of 1969 now encouraged a policy of redevelopment and
environmental improvement. In 1970, The Scottish Civic
Trust (of which I was then director), with the financial
support of Glasgow Corporation, launched 'Facelift Glasgow', a three year voluntary campaign to encourage
stone-cleaning and the processing of back-court tenement
improvement schemes in the private sector, among many
other smaller-scale local clean-up activities. The local
authority also commissioned Lord Esher to undertake a
study, *Conservation in Glasgow: A Preliminary Report* (1971),
in which this distinguished Englishman made it plain that, in
his view, the city possessed the finest heritage of Victorian
buildings in these islands; a view which I found was
enthusiastically endorsed by Sir John Betjeman when I
conducted him around the city. Since then, and perhaps as a
result of the Esher Report, the centre of the city was
designated an Outstanding Conservation Area, a status
conferring protection on all the buildings within the area
boundaries. Many have been fully and splendidly restored;
others, on the insistence of the local authority, have been
reconstructed behind their distinguished façades, notably
Burnet's Stock Exchange building, the Western Club and the
Royal Bank of Scotland, all in Buchanan Street (as is the
highly successfuly restoration and conversion of the old
Princes Square into the complex of up-market shops and
restaurants that is now the attractive Princes Arcade).
Successful, too, is the restoration of the Ca d'Oro building in
Jamaica Street and Treron's in Sauchiehall Street, both

Stock Exchange Building

Jon Magnusson 1988

Glasgow Stock Exchange (1894) by Sir John James Burnet

destroyed internally by fire. Stone-cleaning, using techniques much improved from the early often damaging grinding process has spread throughout the city. The sooty-grey look of Glasgow has somehow disappeared. Once again, the city is a honey-coloured place with contrasting warmly glowing reds, punctuated by the glass-fronted office structures of the late twentieth century and, alas, some, mostly fifties and sixties pre-fabricated structures that one might call Lego-like were it not an insult to that charming Danish toy which, unlike the offending buildings, can be taken down at night and put back into the box!

Much of the rehabilitation of the older tenements in the city and its Victorian and Edwardian suburbs has been undertaken by community-based housing associations, with governmental financial support through the Housing Corporation.

After the re-organization of local government in 1975, Glasgow Corporation was replaced by Glasgow District Council, though happily the new body still preserved the title of Lord Provost for its first citizen. The wider overlord tier was Strathclyde Regional Council, with responsibilities in an area reaching from Oban, in the north, to the Mull of Kintyre, in the south.

In 1976, Strathclyde Regional Council persuaded the government to abandon the development of yet another new town at Stonehaven, fifteen miles or so south-east of Glasgow, on the grounds that it made more sense to capitalize on the existing infrastructure. The newly established Scottish Development Agency, as part of its remit, took a close interest in urban renewal plans.

The Glasgow Eastern Area Renewal project, commonly abbreviated to GEAR, was set up in 1976, covering an area of 4,000 acres noted for its more or less unrelieved air of appalling depression and evidence of urban decay, much of it in areas of council housing built forty years before. A decade after GEAR began work, more than 4,000 houses had been rehabilitated, mostly by housing associations. Some 2,000 new houses had been built by the Scottish Special Housing Association, and over half that number again put up by private developers, attracted to the area as a result of the new positive approach and obvious success of the GEAR project's impact on the districts of Calton, Bridgeton, Camlachie, Parkhead, Dalmarnock, Shettleston, Tollcross, Sandyhills and in the Cambusland Investment Park, an industrial estate on the site of a former steel foundry.

The former Beardmore's Parkhead Forge provides an outstanding example of renewal. It was once a major source of employment in the area, before the collapse of the west of Scotland's old nineteenth-century heavy industries. Where once the forges steamed, sizzled and glowed, an extensive new shopping centre now stands.

Compared with the scale of the problems still to be tackled, what has been achieved perhaps seems little enough; yet it has transformed the attitudes of the people living in these areas, where unemployment is often over 21 per cent and, in some cases, 50 per cent of economically active males are without a job. In measuring the progress Glasgow has made in renewing its East End, it should also be remembered that almost one third of the city's population exists at, or below, supplementary benefit level and that over two thirds of council tenants receive supplementary benefit. As Glasgow approaches the last decade of the twentieth century, with the British political balance – not, of course, supported by the Scots, whose overwhelming vote throughout the eighties was against London-controlled Thatcherite policies, of advantage to the rich but not to poorer people – the danger is that cut after cut in public housing expenditure may frustrate Glasgow district's urgent need to rehabilitate and reinvigorate such areas as Drumchapel and Easterhouse, making by now essential tasks such as replacing the high-rise lifts difficult, if not impossible. Glasgow, which has achieved so much towards renaissance and regeneration, could yet be faced with renewed and more widespread problems of social and economic disruption than it has hitherto had to contend with.

The average visitor to Glasgow is perhaps unlikely to find himself wandering about in what might be called the city's problem areas, although the average Glaswegian, and certainly any serious writer about the city, has a positive duty to inspect them. Outstanding as these East End environmental improvements undoubtedly are, it is the good things that have happened in other spheres of Glasgow activity that have really won for the city its newly enhanced reputation.

I have already mentioned conservation in the Outstanding Conservation Area of the inner city, but there are many other Glasgow Conservation Areas, including that encompassing the West End, which also enjoy Outstanding status. In all, there are 800 listed buildings in Glasgow. New uses have had to be found for many of them, including the handsome warehouses in the Merchant City and elsewhere. Many of these huge buildings have been successfully converted into flats of high quality, and are much sought after. Indeed, there are signs that this type of conversion may also prove the solution to the future of many of the old warehouses in the Broomielaw district, near the river.

Perhaps the most far-reaching change to come over the city in the post-war years has been the collapse of the heavy industries on which so much employment once depended, and the growth of high technological industry, tourism and the service industries.

Glaswegians had an emotional attachment to those heavy industries, which in the previous century made Glasgow the workshop of the world, providing a dependent Empire with its ships, locomotives and factory machinery; an attachment that has hampered acceptance of the inevitable. One after another the great shipbuilding yards on the Clyde, including those with famous names like John Brown's and Fairfields, found themselves without orders and were forced to close. John Brown's yard, like the former Lithgow yard at Port Glasgow, now both under foreign ownership, still maintains a precarious toe-hold on the river that once clanged or flashed with the riveters or welders along its winding length, as the ships that were to sail tomorrow's seas were fashioned. Oil-rig construction has become the object of much present-day craft skill, though the former Yarrow's yard still specializes in warships. Nationalized as part of British Shipbuilders and then sold off again piecemeal, the outlook for those few yards that survive in a competitive world would not appear to be good. Even the much-vaunted steel strip-mill at Ravenscraig, established in the fifties, seems likely to go the same way as the car-making plant at Linwood, set up in 1961 amidst a flurry of high expectations.

Today, the move towards internationalism seems inevitable. Most of the supermarkets where, in the fifties and sixties, we learned to do our American-style shopping, are now owned multinationally. There are very few independent firms of any size still left under Scottish control. The inventive self-made Scot who pitted himself against world competition and won, is unfortunately a creature of the past. Increasingly, Glasgow, like the rest of Scotland, has to rely on foreign initiative and investment, with all the dangers of sudden withdrawal from peripheral areas that this involves in times of recession. A substantial number of Scots still emigrate every year, while increasing numbers of English people arrive to fill Scottish jobs. The language problem, however, makes the free exchange of labour among the member countries of the European Community little more than a theoretical possibility.

Increasingly, Scotland has become in all but name simply the most northerly province of Britain. Edinburgh, the centre of Westminster-controlled government, the headquarters of the declining national Church, Scots Law and a northern power in the British banking, finance and insurance world, has for meanness of funding allowed its great Festival of Music and Drama to decline in international significance. At the same time, Glasgow has advanced its reputation to the point where it was awarded, over Edinburgh's claims, the status of European City of Culture for 1990. For too long Glasgow's 'Red Clydeside' tradition stuck in Europe's mass-memory, jolted awake from time to time by the tiny minority of ludicrously be-tartaned fans descending on London and other European capitals in support of Glasgow football teams and behaving with destructive mindlessness; unfortunately a code of misbehaviour now emulated by some of their English counterparts.

Images and myths of a more literal sort have become a major part of life in Glasgow, as elsewhere in the Western world. Television came into Glasgow homes with the death of George VI in 1952, followed by the coronation of Queen Elizabeth the following year. Both these events, of course, were transmitted from London. The first studio drama production from Scotland was transmitted on 20 January 1954, from the BBC's premises at 5 Queen Street, Edinburgh; a performance of Cedric Thorpe Davie's admirable realization of Burns's dramatic cantata *The Jolly Beggars*, sung by the Saltire Singers and which I had the unique honour of introducing.

The stream of information, entertainment and trivia brought by television to people in their own armchairs soon had its effect on the traditional media of communication. It quickly drove out of existence two newspapers: in 1957 Glasgow's most civilized evening paper, the *Evening News*, once edited by the novelist Neil Munro and the popular pictorial tabloid the *Bulletin* in 1960. Within the next decade it also brought about the closure of more than forty cinemas, including most of those in the city suburbs. A few survived for a time, purveying the heady delights of bingo, but many of these have subsequently had to put up their shutters in the face of the drawing power of the ubiquitous 'telly'. True, during the early eighties the fortunes of some large cinemas in the city centre were revived when their auditoria were subdivided into three or more smaller cinemas offering different programmes and, in some cases, employing various techniques to ensure a surrounding realism from the screen.

Theatres also soon began to disappear: the Queens in 1952, the Royalty (latterly called the Lyric) in 1953, the old Metropole in 1961, the huge Empire in 1962 and the Alhambra in 1969. The Empress at St George's Cross had a brief reincarnation, renamed the Metropole; but with the virtual disappearance of the Cross itself as a result of road development, the Metropole also soon failed. In 1957, the Royal, in Hope Street, became the studios of Scottish Television, but with the opening of adjacent purpose-built studios for the television company, the Royal is the one phoenix to have risen from Glasgow's theatrical ashes, becoming in 1975 the home of Scottish Opera. The Edwardian King's Theatre, at Charing Cross, is now municipally owned, staging London pre-runs and amateur productions. The Pavilion, in Renfield Street, mounts the occasional popular Scots play, variety shows and a long-running Scots pantomime during the Christmas season. The Mitchell Theatre, in the new Mitchell Library complex, provides a small theatre for amateur groups. Experimental theatre has a home in the Tron Theatre, converted out of the old Tron Church.

Across the river, the Citizens Theatre, housed in the old

Princess Theatre in the Gorbals, became the home of Scottish drama under the aegis of James Bridie (O.H. Mavor). Bridie, in collaboration with Guy MacCrone, the novelist, and others, set up his Glasgow company in the Athenaeum Theatre, which was part of the complex housing the former Royal Scottish Academy of Music and Drama in Buchanan Street. The Glasgow Citizens has long since changed course completely and is now the centre of avant-garde productions and Brechtian reinterpretations, sometimes spectacularly successful, sometimes not.

In 1950, the part-time Scottish Orchestra transformed itself into the full-time Scottish National Orchestra, at first under various conductors of foreign origin but from 1959, and for twenty-five years thereafter, under the baton of Sir Alexander Gibson. He raised it from being a passable local band into a recording orchestra of European standing, a status that has been upheld by Sir Alexander's successors. After a brief stay in the now demolished Black Cat cinema, the orchestra's home became the City Hall, in the merchant city, before moving to the new Concert Hall, at the top of Buchanan Street.

So far as music is concerned, Scotland has distinguished itself more obviously in the executive department than in the creative. The song-writer Francis George Scott, a Border man from Hawick, spent the last forty years of his life in Glasgow and died there. Of the next generation of Scottish composers the only one who is a native Glaswegian, and whose music is performed beyond the confines of his native country, is Thomas Wilson.

To Sir Alexander Gibson, Robin Orr (then Gardiner Professor of Music at Glasgow University), Ian Rodger, Ainslie Millar and others, goes the credit for bringing into being Scottish Opera, which now has its headquarters and rehearsal rooms in the former Engineers' Institute in Elmbank Street and its performing home in the Theatre Royal. Scotland's first professional opera company has staged the major operas of Gluck, Mozart, Rossini, Verdi, Wagner, Strauss and Britten, and achieved remarkable successes by European standards. Its performance of Wagner's *Ring* – in the Kings Theatre, before the company moved into its permanent home – was an outstanding event

The Tron Kirk, now the Tron Theatre
(steeple c. 1595 and 1635; building, 1794) by John Adam

in Glasgow musical life, as was its *Mastersingers*. Another memorable production was Berlioz's *The Trojans*, with Dame Janet Baker as Dido, given in English in a single evening and without the usual cuts. Several operas have been commissioned from Scottish composers, Thea Musgrave's *Mary, Queen of Scots* (1977) being the most noteworthy.

During the eighties, in common with many companies elsewhere, Scottish Opera succumbed to the cult of 'producer's opera'; an aberration whereby the setting of an opera may be wrenched out of the musical time-context of the score and transported backwards, or more usually forwards, to a different period, frequently further distorted to be made to carry a non-existent political meaning undreamt-of by its creators. One thinks, for example, of a notorious production of *Don Giovanni*, where the main stage properties were a coffin and a WC, and the endless visual diversions rained so thick and fast on the audience's attention that it was almost impossible to be aware of Mozart's music. 'Producer's opera', like the bowdlerization and rewriting of Shakespeare's text in the eighteenth century, is a cult that will undoubtedly pass; the sooner the better. Young tigers' teeth should be content to sharpen their egomania on plays of the mood and the moment, and not on the murdering of masterpieces.

Scottish ballet, brought into being on a permanent basis in 1969, has also won for itself considerable acclamation; though competition internationally is, if anything, even stiffer in the world of ballet than that of opera.

The performing arts must necessarily depend for their development upon steady support from the local authority and, through the Scottish Arts Council, from central government. The Arts cannot, and never have been able to, exist without patronage, unless admission prices are to be allowed to soar beyond the means of ordinary people. The Arts, of course, are not unique in this respect. Schools, libraries and even council housing all come into a similar category. The trend throughout the eighties has increasingly been for government to seek to off-load social responsibility on to industrial or commercial patrons. Up to a point this is perhaps a good thing: but only up to a point. Private sector patrons are probably unlikely to want to support the new or experimental; and, in any case, there is clearly a limit to the burden which they can be expected to bear, using their shareholders' money. Continuity, especially where opera is concerned, is essential in the interests of long-term forward planning. Interestingly enough, a report relating to the Arts in Glasgow appeared in July 1988, demonstrating clearly that not only did the Arts bring in money to the city, but were responsible for creating and supporting a goodly number of jobs.

Unfortunately, post-war architecture went through a bad patch. Leaving aside the proliferation of the already-mentioned 'Lego buildings', where cheapness seems to have been all, and the high-rise tower blocks and other examples of the 'new brutalism', now happily discredited, a few buildings have gone up which might possibly qualify for listing and preservation in the twenty-first century. Some might choose the Ladywell Housing Scheme of Honeyman, Jack and Robertson, which went up in 1964 on the site of the former Duke Street prison for women. Others might favour the London architect William Whitfield's existing University Library and Art Gallery, its complex of closely related towers a massed relief in the context of the many single high-rise towers now punctuating the city skyscape; or Derek Stephenson and Partners', Heron House (1970), designed to blend with 'Greek' Thomson's St Vincent Street Church; or the Scottish Amicable Building of King, Moir & Ellison (1976), which catches the eye yet does not too greatly discomfit Salmon's art nouveau 'Hatrack' building next door; or Jack Coia's St Charles Roman Catholic Church in Kelvinside Gardens, which has an exposed concrete frame with infilled panels of rustic-facing bricks, a free-standing tower and, inside, a delicate vaulted concrete ceiling and sculptor Benno Schotz's 'Stations of the Cross'; or J.R.M. Kennedy and Partners' student housing and pub, Strathclyde University (1984); or perhaps the National Bank of Pakistan, in Sauchiehall Street, by Elder and Cannon (1981). The one building, however, that would undoubtedly get almost everyone's vote is the Burrell Gallery, in the grounds of Pollok House, so well designed to show to advantage the varied art collection it houses and fitting so cleverly into the landscape it actually adorns. It is the work of Barry Gasson, who won the commission by competition, and was completed in 1983.

New ideas on the ideal surroundings for effective schooling have resulted in the carrying through of an extensive rebuilding programme. In bygone days, urban schools were frequently crammed into the odd corner with little playing space. Today, regulations demand that a two-stream primary school must have four and a half acres, while a secondary school for a thousand children must have fourteen acres, seven for the school and seven for playing fields.

Glasgow has received a number of architectural awards in recent years. In 1988, it received a Europa Nostra Diploma of Merit for the redevelopment of the Merchant City and the Maryhill/Woodlands areas, a special award made in connection with the Council of Europe's Year of the Environment, 1987/88. In 1988, it also received a Europa Nostra Silver Medal for the outstanding regeneration of its Merchant City, based on housing. Glasgow has also received a number of Civic Trust Awards. Some of these have gone to educational buildings, including Glasgow University's Institute of Virology (1963) and the College of Nautical Studies (1969).

A.J. Jury's splendid restoration of the City Hall and Bazaar – the Bazaar the work of Doctor Cleland, *circa* 1817, the 1840 hall designed by George Murray – and the sensitive restoration by Derek Sugden (of Ove Arup and Partners) of C.J. Phipps's Theatre Royal (1895), are both highly satisfactory achievements. The transformation of the former Fishmarket, in the Bridgegate – through which the spire of the original Merchants' House points skywards – into a Covent Garden-style centre by the Assist Architectural Practice (1982) is also an outstanding contribution to the city's environment, though the fact that it is a little away from the main shopping area may militate against commercial success for a time, until it gets better known.[3] The nearby enormous glassy shopping centre on the site of the former St Enoch's Station may eventually bring more customers.

One of Glasgow's most important buildings is Charles Wilson's Trinity Free Church College, crowning the Park Area's Conservation Area. It ceased to function as a teaching establishment in 1973. After two decades, during which various proposals for its re-use were put forward, but came to nothing, it was converted to luxury flats by James Cunning, Young and Partners in 1987/88, ensuring that the dramatic grouping of its campanile and twin towers with that of the famous Park Church – now only a spire attached to modern offices – remains to enliven the city's skyscape.

Drama, of course, is not confined to the theatre or to skyscapes, and post-Second World War Glasgow has had its share of the real-life variety. At the lowest level, there were its sensational murders: for instance, the Pollokshields murder of 1946, when a man shot a clerkess and an office boy at Pollokshields East railway station. It took the police ten months to find the murderer at Carlisle, during which period there was a deal of apprehension in the city's South Side. In due course Charles Brown, a twenty-year-old railway fireman, was tried and sentenced to death. It came out that he had a fondness for gangster films – he had seen one such film, *Scarface*, five times – and at parties was fond of pretending to be a gangster. While totally opposed to the pietistic censorship which some individuals, supported by the government, seek to impose upon television, the endless diet of criminal violence now transferred from the cinema to the television screen and proliferated nightly in millions of homes, does seem to me a dubious infliction which may very well prove to have long-term harmful social effects. Nevertheless, censorship would have effects much more harmful.

Another admirer of gangsters and gangster films, Peter Manuel, described by a senior police officer who had to do with the investigation of his crimes as 'one of the worst and most horrible murderers ever to cross the scene of criminal history in Scotland, if not in Great Britain', was responsible, in all probability, for nine murders in the Glasgow district between 1956 and his execution in 1958. He was charged with murdering a seventeen-year-old girl, Anne Kneilands (he reduced her head 'more or less to pulp', according to one report); with several cases of breaking-in and stealing; with the murder of a Mrs Watt, whose husband was for some time in custody, one of Manuel's specialities being the planting of blame on others; with the murder of Watt's daughter; the

murder of Isabelle Cooke, aged seventeen; the murder of
Peter Smart, his wife and eleven-year-old son, all shot at
close range while asleep, and the theft of a motor-car. He was
also strongly suspected of having murdered a taxi-driver in
Northumberland, but was not charged with this offence.
Manuel, who had produced a confession when the police
arrested his father on minor charges, sacked his own counsel
during his trial and then, in the words of the Judge, Lord
Cameron, conducted his own defence 'with a skill that is
quite remarkable'. On Lord Cameron's direction, Manuel
was acquitted of the Kneilands murder because of lack of
corroborative evidence, but found guilty of all the other
major charges and hanged.

Manuel, the sex-maniac who stripped his young victims to
their lower clothing without actually sexually assaulting
them (although he first came to the notice of the police as a
suspected rapist as well as a housebreaker); the man who
wanted to be thought a high-time crook in the eyes of
Glasgow's criminal fraternity; whose whole sense of values
was so deranged that his indignation at being accused of
shooting an eleven-year-old sleeping boy reflected his belief
that it would have been in order had the victim been a man;
Manuel, who was found sane and fit to plead, serves to
remind us, in an age where sympathy often now seems to be
more readily extended to the murderer than his victim and
relatives, that, once again, in Lord Cameron's wise words,
'badness need not necessarily mean madness'.

Now that the death penalty has been abolished, the public
has to some extent lost interest in its murderers. An increase
in crimes of violence is, however, a feature of late
twentieth-century Glasgow life. There is an unhealthy aspect
to the publicity now afforded men guilty of cruelly violent
crimes but who have taken up sculpture or painting while
serving a life sentence. Apart from the fact that the efforts of
prison artists are frequently over-praised because of their
unusual situation, such men can find themselves quite
profitably 'romanticized', as in the case of *The Hard Man*
(1977) by the playwright Tom McGrath, and the 'lifer'
Jimmy Boyle. Seeing these things, I always find myself
wondering about their silenced victims and their surviving
relations.

The worst tragedy, if numbers be the token of measurement, to sadden post-war Glasgow was the Ibrox disaster. On Saturday 2 January 1971, at Ibrox Stadium, the home of Rangers Football team, sixty-three people died as a result of being crushed or covered by the bodies of others on Stair Thirteen after the game. The accident was caused by somebody falling at a time when those on the stairway were packed closely together, and were being pushed downwards by those above and behind. Needless to say, extensive improvements were carried out afterwards to ensure that such an accident should never occur again.

In Glasgow, as elsewhere, the Festival of Britain was celebrated in 1951 with, among other things, an exhibition of industrial power, held in the Kelvin Hall. The Kelvin Hall was replaced as the city's main exhibition centre in 1985, with the opening of the undistinguished-looking, accoustically poor, though undoubtedly useful, Scottish Exhibition Centre at Finnieston. One of the arguments for putting up a glorified gigantic tin shed was that over the next two or three decades the needs of exhibitors will undoubtedly have changed. Be that as it may, the Kelvin Hall now houses Glasgow's Museum of Transport.

The Glasgow Garden Festival, covering a pan-shaped area on the South bank of the Clyde but including the Exhibition Centre and its carparks (linked by Alastair Wallace's attractive Bell's Bridge) was an outstanding success. Unlike its immediate predecessor in 1938, with its large pavilions, the main attraction in 1988 was the gardens themselves, radiating out from a circular central space and a fretwork town centre with shops. After a summery May and June, however, the weather of 1988 repeated the rain-lashed pattern of fifty years ago, providing a July and August among the wettest of the century.

When originally writing this book (which first appeared in 1972) I recorded the Glasgow tendency 'to think of the Arts as a luxury benefiting only a privileged "middle-class" few. Money spent on their housing and support, the argument runs, would be better spent in helping accommodate the homeless.' Such arguments, I went on, 'are fallacious, both on practical and on theoretical counts. The needs and aspirations of society have to be considered as a whole if a general state of well-being is to prevail.'

Kingston Bridge, carrying the inner city motorway over the Clyde at Broomielaw

After instancing primitive man's 'fundamental need for the kind of satisfaction to be deprived from Art by drawing and scratching on the damp walls of his caves', I quoted John Davidson, the Greenock poet, who declared that all that ultimately mattered was 'a satisfied imagination'. Imaginations, he maintained, were satisfied at different levels. A raising of the level at which satisfaction can be obtained represents an advance in the values of a sophisticated civilization. Glasgow, I then suggested, needed more such influences, not fewer.

Glasgow's annual 'Mayfest' may be more of a people's affair than Edinburgh's International Festival of Music and Drama. The Glasgow event is perhaps aimed rather more at winning converts to the Arts than presenting the best of whatever can be hired in the cultural market-places of the world. Festivals, at whatever level, come and go; but in the Scottish National Orchestra, Scottish Opera, Scottish Ballet, the Citizens' Theatre, the Burrell Collection and the expansive magnificence of the city's older art collection housed in the Kelvingrove Gallery, Glasgow's art provision has become an integral part of day-to-day life, not some brief display of imported wares that vanish when the tents are folded up and put away for another year.

Music and poetry are not for everyone, any more than are dog-racing or tiddlywinks. Tastes differ; satisfactions become absorbed at varying imaginative levels. Much of Glasgow's imaginative satisfaction nowadays inevitably derives from television. For various reasons, partly economic and partly related to the smallness of the Scottish population, neither the BBC in Scotland nor Scottish Television can claim to have done much to help raise the level of satisfaction of their viewers over the years. In spite of some outstanding presentations, like the production by the late Pharic MacLaren of Lewis Grassic Gibbon's *Sunset Song* and George Mackay Brown's *Three Orkney Tales*, little enough originating in Scotland stays long in the memory. Glasgow's long-defunct magazine of the Arts, *Counterpoint*, the first edition of which resulted in the creation in front of the viewers of Benno Schotz's magnificent head of the poet Hugh MacDiarmid, which now stands in Broadcasting House, Queen Margaret Drive, also falls within this category. The 'Taggart' detective series, at a different level, perhaps accurately epitomized the face of Glasgow toughness, which is also reflected in much recent Glasgow fiction; and there were those on both sides of the border who found the 'Tutti Frutti' series irresistibly funny.

Radio Scotland, founded in 1978, is reputed to attract a higher regular audience listening than any English region, yet its content is often trivial and parochial. In recent years Radio Clyde has profitably provided a diet of 'pop' and what is sometimes described as 'easy listening'. Its audience figures show that there is a large Glasgow audience for its product.

What will happen to even the present limited broadcasting standards in Scotland once purely market-orientated stations and satellite broadcasting have made their broad-fronted onslaughts upon our eyes and ears is anyone's guess.

There is nothing wrong with satisfying the mass imagination at its lowest level, provided material is constantly offered which could raise the satisfaction level a little. There is something inherently disturbing in the opposing viewpoint, as pungently expressed by Lee Loevinger, of the American Federal Communications Commission; a viewpoint also widely held in our own country. TV, he declared, 'is a golden goose that lays scrambled eggs.[4] It is futile, and probably fatal, to beat it for not laying caviar. Anyway, more people like scrambled eggs than caviar. TV should be recognized for what it is, the literature of the illiterate, the culture of the low-brows, the wealth of the poor, the privilege of the under-privileged, the exclusive club of the excluded masses.' Mr Loevinger is really rationalizing the American practice of swamping the air with a choice of commercially sponsored triviality, levelling all standards down to the lowest common denominator while securing to the operator the maximum profit from the minimum expenditure. The so-called 'excluded masses' are not so dumb as they are sometimes supposed to be, as is shown when a carefully staged choice is made easily and attractively available to them.

Fortunately, literature still survives amidst the morass of television double-think and smoothy-talk. During the 1939 war, and immediately after it, William Maclellan published from an address in Hope Street the work of what Eric Linklater called the 'Second Wind' generation of writers of the 'Scottish Renaissance'. The banner was always a wide one, held over such diverse writers as Sydney Goodsir Smith, Douglas Young, Ruthven Todd and George Bruce among the poets, and Edward Gaitens, Fred Urquhart and Robin Jenkins among the story-tellers. Myself apart, none of the group were actually native Glaswegians; but it was from Glasgow, through Maclellan's anthologies, *Poetry Scotland* and *Scottish Art and Letters*, and in the club-rooms of the Scottish Arts Group in Blythswood Square and those of the Saltire Society in Wellington Street, that much of the creative excitement then being generated was communicated to the public.

Almost all the poets who appeared under Maclellan's aegis are to be found today represented in the standard Scottish anthologies, while the work of such painters of the period as Donald Bain, Andrew Taylor Elder, Isobel Babianska, Millie Frood, William Crosbie and Marie de Banzie, was thought of sufficient importance for the Scottish Arts Council to mount and circulate an exhibition of it in 1979.

Post-Scottish Renaissance Glasgow poets like Edwin Morgan and Tom Buchan are wide in their range and usually strongly radical in their leanings – in Buchan's case leanings apt to pull him towards disruptive violence of imagery. He sees Scotland, with some justice, as the 'crèche of the soul', the 'land of the millionaire draper, whisky vomit and the Hillman Imp',[5] the 'nirvana of the Keelie imagination'. Morgan's sympathies are altogether kindlier. He has the advantage of an energetic sense of humour, typified by his poem dealing with a hygiene problem that often causes owners of Glasgow buildings expense and those who line up in street bus queues some annoyance, 'The Starlings in George Square':

The City Chambers are hopping mad.
Councillors with rubber plugs in their ears!
Secretaries closing windows!
Window-cleaners want protection and danger money.
The Lord Provost can't hear herself think, man.
What's that?
Lord Provost can't hear herself think.

At the General Post Office
The clerks write Three Pounds Starling in the savings-books.
Each telephone booth is like an aviary,
I tried to send a parcel to County Kerry but –
The cables to Cairo got fankled, sir,
What's that?
I said the cables to Cairo got fankled ...[6]

Earlier in this book, I included my poem, expressing nostalgia for the Glasgow I left behind to go to the war in 1939. It might perhaps be appropriate to include also the poem setting out my reactions to the kind of weekend futility

from which the City, in common with many others, seems
unable to shake itself free: 'Glasgow Nocturne'.

Materialized from the flaked stones of buildings
dank with neglect and poverty, the pack,
thick-shouldered, slunk through rows of offices
squirting anonymous walls with their own lack

of self-identity. 'Tongs ya bass, Fleet,
Fuck the Pope' spurted like blood; a smear
protesting to the passing daylight folk
the prowled-up edge of menace, the spoor of fear

that many waters cannot quench, or wash
clean from what hands, what eyes, from what hurt hearts?
O Lord! the preacher posed at the park gates,
what must we do to be whole in all our parts?

Late on Saturday night, when shop fronts doused
their furniture, contraceptives, clothes and shoes,
violence sneaked out in banded courage,
bored with hopelessness that has nothing to lose.

A side-street shadow eyed two lovers together;
he, lured from the loyalties of the gang
by a waif who wore her sex like a cheap trinket;
she, touched to her woman's needs by his strong

tenderness. On the way from their first dance,
the taste of not enough fumbled their search
of hands and lips endeared in a derelict close.
Over the flarepath of their love, a lurch

thrust from the shadow, circling their twined bodies.
It left them clung before its narrowing threat,
till she shrieked. They peeled her from her lover,
a crumpled sob of a doll dropped in the street,

while he received his lesson; ribs and jaw
broken, kidneys and testicles ruptured, a slit
where the knife licked his groin. Before he died
in the ambulance, she'd vanished. Shops lit

up their furniture, contraceptives, clothes and shoes
again. Next morning, there was a darker stain
than 'Tongs ya bass' and 'Fleet' on the edge of the kerb;
but it disappeared in the afternoon rain.

Younger poets include that master of comic stairhead
Glasgow, Tom Leonard, and Liz Lochhead, probably more
important as a playwright than a poet. Poets from other airts
who have resided so long in Glasgow as to have become
almost adopted Glaswegians are Alexander Scott and Stewart
Conn.

Novelists are usually more numerous than poets. Since the
war, several local novels have attracted the interest of
Glaswegians. Such Glasgow-based stories have included
Nancy Brysson Morrison's *The Winnowing Years* (1949),
Robin Jenkins's *Happy for the Child* (1953)[7] and Archie
Hinds's *The Dear Green Place* (1966), added to which might
be listed Cliff Hanley's *Dancing in the Streets* (1958), an
autobiographical account of a Glasgow up-bringing. Literary
agents state categorically that novels with a Glasgow setting
are not easily marketable to publishers. Yet a surprising
number of Glasgow writers concerned with topics other than
sexual athletics do seem somehow to break through this
formidable barrier, even if none of them – not even William
McIlvaney's much praised *Docherty* (1975) (not actually set in
Glasgow) or his detective story *Laidlaw* (1977) – has yet
turned out to be the late twentieth-century's Great Scottish
Novel so diligently sought by newspaper reviewers.

Other post-war Glasgow fiction[8] of merit includes:
George Friel's *Mr Alfred M.A.* (1972), the saga of a seedy
schoolmaster who is the Archie Rice of the Scottish
educational world; Iain Crichton Smith's *Goodbye, Mr
Dixon* (1974), strong in its 'feel' for an identifiable but
unnamed Glasgow; Alan Spence's story-sequence *The
Colours They Are Fine* (1977); 'Arthur Young's' study of a
young hospital doctor's dilemma, *The Surgeon's Knot* (1982);
McIlvaney's *The Papers of Tony Veitch* (1983), a sequel to his
Laidlaw, set in the Glasgow underworld, but, as in his
previous novel, with dialect too often suggesting the clever
author rather than his dumber characters; Jim Taylor's

Wasters (1983), a series of tales depicting the impact of recession on contemporary Glasgow life; and James Kelman's *The Bus Conductor Hines* (1984), the sometimes more than ordinary thoughts of an ordinary man. There is also the brilliantly written, if rather oddly constructed, *Lanark* (1981) by Alastair Gray.

Glasgow's reading habits have changed over a generation. Those brightly shelved, tuppence-a-night lending libraries, to be found during the late forties in every suburb, well stocked with romantic and other novels, have been driven out of business by the paperback revolution. But the statistical evidence from the Glasgow District Library department seems to suggest that year by year, more and more people are reading books, though perhaps fewer of these books are works of fiction; a decline which would undoubtedly have pleased the mind of that fastidious Glasgow benefactor, Mr Stirling.

A much-thumbed non-fictional work in city libraries is the Glasgow volume of the *Third Statistical Account* (1958). It deals with many aspects of the city's way of life, though it is decidedly weak in its coverage of Glasgow's culture and sub-cultures. One of the book's most interesting sections is that in which the sociologist J. A. Mack describes the various disorders which produce 'socially incompetent families', Glasgow possessing a large minority of these. In such families, he tells us, the children

for a variety of reasons, are the victims of physical or moral or emotional neglect or of all three combined ... The organisation of many households is very loose indeed. the (official) inhabitants of a house are not clearly known from day to day. Temporary changes as a result of quarrels, reorientation of affections or simply convenience of sleeping arrangements are very common. In such households where there are children, there is, strictly speaking, no parental control. The parents may change partners, and one or other move out temporarily. Even without this type of instability, the large and ranging numbers of adults of different generations with different standards of behaviour, all taking turn, so to speak, in disciplining or indulging the children, makes it impossible for the children to be brought up to any pattern of behaviour consistent with the wider society. These children may be normal as individuals ... But it is to be suspected that they provide a high proportion of these persistent young criminals whose criminality has nothing psychologically abnormal about it.

Then there are the unfortunate children who live 'from drinking-session to drinking-session'. Edward Gaitens's *Dance of the Apprentices* (1948) depicts one such family, the Macdonnels, in the inter-war years. Idealized politics are discussed against 'a background of seductive triviality' the 'dispiriting background of the Gorbals'.

When Jimmy, the sailor son, comes home from a voyage and gets engaged to a 'good-living' girl, he promises to give up drink, a promise which horrifies father Macdonnel, who had been anticipating the usual drunken party on Jimmy's return until his sailor's pay was exhausted. But three hours later, brother Eddy, who had been inspired by Jimmy's unexpected conversion, looks out into the street to see Jimmy (wearing his Aunt Kate's hat) and their father staggering arm-in-arm, as large bottles of whisky waggle from the pockets of the two men. Behind them, laughing like witches, comes Mrs Macdonnel and Aunt Kate with the sailor's hat on, followed by six of Jimmy's pals who are carrying between them three large crates of bottled beer.

In the orgy that followed, Eddy decides that 'human behaviour' has passed his understanding. 'He was thinking of Jeannie Lindsay and wishing he might find her standing at her close mouth in South Wellington Street. But it was very late. He hurried round the corner in a queer emotional tangle of sexual shame and desire, his romantic thoughts of Jeannie mingled with the shameful memory of his mother dressing up in men's clothes and Bridget Delaney pulling up her skirts to the hips to show her bare legs to the men.'

Pre-war Glasgow was dominated by its trams. Transport in the city has been revolutionized since 1946. The construction of much of the inner ring road, sweeping round the north and west sides of the city and crossing the Clyde over the Kingston Bridge, not only removed traffic from the city centre – enabling pedestrianization to be implemented in Sauchiehall Street, Buchanan Street and Argyle Street – but

A84
S.E.C.

Greenock M8
Kilmarnock & Glasgow Airport

M8

7

provided easy access to the M8 motorway, serving central Scotland and linking with the M74 route to the south. It is now theoretically possible to drive from Greenock or Glasgow to London or Plymouth without once having to stop at traffic lights. The Clyde tunnel, which opened in 1963, eased cross-river traffic to the west of the city.

The Greater Glasgow Transportation Study appeared in 1968, and recommended a co-ordinated road and public transport system. Accordingly, the old low-level railway through the city was reconstructed and electrified, with new or rebuilt stations at Partick, Finnieston, Central Low Level, Argyle Street, Bridgeton, Dalmarnock and Rutherglen, thus giving quick access to the pedestrianized heart of Glasgow's shopping centre. The Cathcart circle has been electrified, as have the lines down both the north and south banks of the Clyde and the west coastal rail link with London. A major bus depot has been located at Anderston and another at the top of Buchanan Street.

Inevitably, the tramcar had to go, its road-centred absence of manoeuvrability an increasing hazard in busy streets. An historic procession of Glasgow's trams from past decades wound its way through the streets for the last time on 4 September, 1962. So affectionately did some of those who turned out feel towards the trams – the old coloured trams (blue for Kirklee to Rutherglen, green for Dennistoun to Knightswood, yellow for Clarkston to Hyndland, white for Mosspark to the University, and so on) and the still older open-ended cars, single deckers and the dignified 'Coronation' models, once the pride and boast of Glaswegians – that they actually wept unashamedly.

In 1974, the former LNER paddle steamer *Waverley*, built in 1946 and now the last sea-going paddler in service in the world, was handed over to the Waverley Steam Navigation Company by the then chairman of the Scottish Transport Group, Sir Patrick Thomas, for the sum of one pound. After extensive refitting she has since operated under private management on the Clyde for many seasons. She also makes profitable annual forays out of English and Welsh piers

Glasgow's inner city ring road: approaching the Kingston Bridge from the North

before the Clyde season begins. Service routes across the Firth are now operated by car ferries. I have yet to meet the man who can develop an affection for a car ferry.

The Clyde estuary, traditionally Glasgow's playground and one of the most beautiful waterways in the world, was subjected to unnecessarily damaging intrusions during the sixties and seventies. An electricity power station at Inverkip has a chimney of huge proportions that dominates the landscape for miles around. Reputedly it has not operated at full capacity since it was completed, except for a brief period during the miners' strike of 1980. Urged by the daemon subconsciously whispering that heavy industry must be preserved at all costs, a policy doomed to inescapable failure, an ore terminal and general port has been constructed at Hunterston. If, as seems intended, the strip mill at Ravenscraig ultimately closes, the terminal will lose its point and purpose. A yard for the construction of oil-rigs, erected at the mouth of the River Ardyne, almost opposite the entrance to the beautiful Kyles of Bute, built only one rig and was then dismantled, although neither was the scarred landscape fully restored nor the promised water marina constructed.

Economic prosperity is obviously the essential basis of modern urban life. Development to serve such prosperity must be located and accepted somewhere. But industry cannot forever be allowed to go on issuing short-term threatening ultimatums to job-anxious planning authorities, or to public inquiries, of the order 'either we go just there, where we want, or else we'll transfer our expansion abroad'. If the industrialization of further sections of areas of outstanding natural beauty in close proximity to Glasgow is really inevitable in Scotland's economic interests,[9] then it may be necessary for the government of the day to accept as a public charge an element of social capital cost. This could mean, for instance, that an oil company with its terminal on the estuary would have to agree to situate a refinery inland in the interests of amenity, the government meeting the social cost element should the inland site be more expensive to set up than the coastal site. If governments and the electorate are not willing to accept a measure of social control of this sort, including the financial implications, then strategic planning may be reduced to little more than a kind of academic game, its reasoned decisions constantly overthrown by commercial or political expediency.

In Glasgow, as elsewhere, there are increasing signs that the citizens want to make known their own views on decisions that may drastically affect their future way of life and that of their children. Groups like the New Glasgow Society, much concerned with public participation in Glasgow's planning process, have sprung up, covering the interests of the city as a whole, sometimes acting perhaps with rather more energy and less discretion than has pleased officialdom. More localized societies have come together at Maryhill, Springburn, Govan, the West End and elsewhere. Thus in Glasgow at any rate, the common accusation that Civic Societies are 'middle-class' is simply untrue. Most of these amateur bodies look for support and encouragement to The Scottish Civic Trust, a charitable organization that has existed since 1967, when its headquarters were set up in Glasgow and which organized 'Facelift Glasgow'.

Any portrait of Glasgow ought to end with something about Glasgow people; yet it is impossible to write meaningful generalities about a race which, out of one end of the genetical chance-machine, has produced perhaps the worst possible ethnical mixture of rowdy Irish and dour Scot; a runted, stunted, violent minority of low intelligent quotient; the 'boys' or 'lads' who start fights at football matches, daub bus-shelters and buildings with aerosol paint sprays, slash the seats of railway-carriages, scatter litter and broken glass about, and generally indulge in the sort of mindless behaviour that leaps into television features and shouts from newspaper headlines, unjustly smearing the reputation of the whole city in the eyes of the world beyond.

Even in the days when thuggery was less prevalent, and more easily dealt with than it seems to be now, Glasgow was sensitive in its appreciation of those who enhanced its fair name. A Glasgow shoe manufacturer, A.P. Somerville, inventor of the square-toed shoe that let Glasgow men stand closer to the bar, bequeathed a large sum of money to the city so that a St Mungo prize could be awarded every three years to whoever was deemed to have done the most for Glasgow's reputation in the period under review. Winners have included the popular wartime labour Lord Provost, Sir Patrick Dollan; the man who, as curator of the Art Galleries, did much to make Glasgow picture-conscious, Dr T.J. Honeyman; the founder-chairwoman of the Glasgow Treelovers Society, Dr MacKenzie Anderson; a late distinguished minister of Glasgow Cathedral and Moderator of the General Assembly of the Church of Scotland, the Reverend Dr Neville Davidson; the conductor for twenty-five years of the Scottish National Orchestra, Sir Alexander Gibson; Glasgow Corporation's best-known Director of Parks, Arthur Oldham; and that doughty upholder of everything Glaswegian, the journalist Jack House.

The majority of Glaswegians are 'couthy' and kindly, easy-going and tolerant, perhaps not ultra-sophisticated by the standards of London, Paris or New York, but catching up fast: still marginally, if loosely, more attached to the Church than their English counterparts, and perhaps a little less willing to go fully along with the so-called permissiveness of society, at any rate in public. Glaswegians are the consumers of more cakes and sweeter lemonade than anyone else in the United Kingdom. By modern standards, they are still moderately industrious, although today they sometimes lack comprehensively involved indigenous leadership: many of the citizens who in bygone days would have played a dominant part in the policy-making of the city's organizations no longer living in the city but commuting from Helensburgh, Killearn or perhaps even that 'other place', Edinburgh. By the early years of the twenty-first century, the increasing cost of oil-based energy may make commuting a costly business, and bring about a residential return to the city of those best able to provide it with cultural and environmental leadership.

Whatever else happens, I doubt very much if Glasgow humour will change. Its flavour today is much the same as it was half a century ago.

During the First World War, an English officer rode past a Bantam H.L.I. lance-corporal marching some twenty sturdy German prisoners down a country lane.

'You all right there, Lance-Corporal?' the officer asked.

'Fine, sir,' the Bantam answered. The officer remained unconvinced.

'Sure you can manage all these men on your own?' he inquired.

'D'ye ken whit's in my hand, sir?' the Bantam asked, opening his palm. The officer found himself peering down at a common type of hand grenade.

'Why yes, of course. A Mills bomb.'

'Ay, sir, but whit they ken and I ken but you dinna is that the pin's oot.'

Forty years later, a middle-class father had been persuaded to take his football-daft son to the annual ritualistic Rangers versus Celtic match.

Those who have never attended a football match along with perhaps 30,000 others may not have had cause to appreciate that the sheer press of numbers makes the provision of normal sanitary arrangements impossible.

To this particular father's dismayed astonishment, a little Glaswegian beside him suddenly stopped shouting, unbuttoned his fly and relieved himself. The father, a little startled, instinctively stepped back.

'Whit's the matter wi' you, heh?' came the indignant query. 'Shoes leakin', or somethin'?'

That, ultimately, is Glasgow: utterly realistic and down to earth.

I was born in Glasgow. I believe in it. I like its still under-appreciated marvellous buildings and its cheerfully average people; its balanced attitude to life and its occasional flights of imaginative achievement; its more or less temperate climate and its neighbourly hills and lochs. When, at different periods of my life, I have had to live away from it, sooner or later, I have become overwhelmed by a compelling nostalgia. Though Glasgow and its ways have often infuriated me – and sometimes still do – back I have always come, bound by invisible ties to the city of my birth.

The loquacious but humourless St Paul is neither an author whose works lie by my bedside nor one of my favourite men: but I have often found myself silently quoting his proud answer to the Roman Tribune, before whom he was defending himself: 'I am a citizen of no mean city.'

By that, in the end, I stand.

Notes

1 For the statistical details behind Glasgow's regeneration I am much indebted to James H. Rae's 1986 essay, 'Regenerating the City – the Glasgow Experience from *The Catylist*,' Summer, 1986.

2 Made notorious by Alexander McArthur's novel, *No Mean City* (1935), Sir Arthur Bliss's ballet, *Miracle in the Gorbals* (1946) and Robert MacLeish's play, *The Gorbal's Story* (1946).

3 In 1988, alas, it became commercially unviable and closed its doors. A new use for the restored building will be found.

4 This was written before the salmonella egg scare revealed that the poultry industry fed hens with a product containing the remains of their predecessors, thus turning hens into unwitting cannibals and resulting, understandably, in a decline in the consumption of eggs.

5 The small car produced at the ill-fated Linwood factory, near Paisley.

6 From 'The Second Life' (1968).

7 Jenkins, now resident in Dunoon, has since become the most distinguished Scottish novelist living.

8 Chronicled in *The Glasgow Novel* (2nd Edition 1986) by Moira Burgess.

9 The Glasgow tenement consists of three or four storeys or levels. Each landing, or level, has usually the front doors of two flats. Entrance to these homes is through a close or passage leading to the common stair.

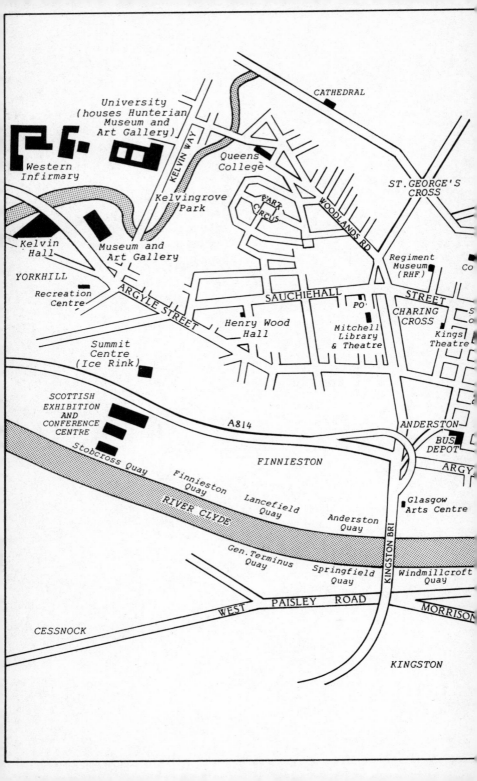

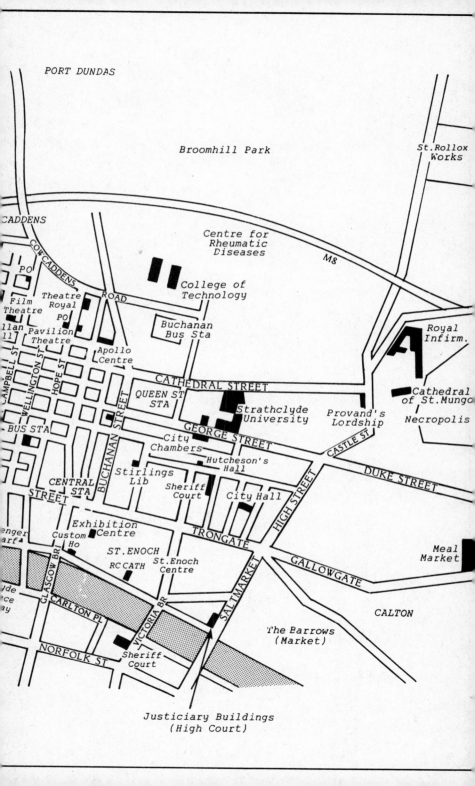

Index

Index